AMERICAN

REALISM

EDWARD LUCIE-SMITH

AMERICAN REALISM

For Marti Koplin, and in memory of Allen Koplin

Half-title page: John F. Peto, *Market Basket, Hat and Umbrella*, after 1890. Milwaukee Art Museum, Layton Art Collection.

Title-page: William Merritt Chase, *Near the Beach, Shinnecock*, c. 1895. The Toledo Museum of Art, Toledo, Ohio. Gift of Arthur J. Secor.

First published in the United Kingdom in 1994 by Thames & Hudson Ltd, 181A High Holborn, London WC1V 7QX

www.thamesandhudson.com

First paperback edition 2002

British Library Cataloguing-in-Publication Data A catalogue record for this book is available from the British Library ISBN 0-500-28356-7

Printed and bound in Singapore by C.S. Graphics

CONTENTS

The real subject is what an individual has known and felt about things encountered in a world of real people and actual doings.

THOMAS HART BENTON

I think of the painted picture as an embodiment of the very problem that we face with the notion 'reality'.

MARK TANSEY

Dᴇғɪɴɪᴛɪᴏɴѕ ᴏғ the word 'realism', when this is applied to art, have always
given trouble, though one would never guess this from the confident
stance of the *Oxford English Dictionary*:

> Close resemblance to what is real, fidelity of representation, rendering of the
> precise details of the thing or scene.

The more closely one examines this attempt to supply boundaries for the word,
the more these boundaries seem to shift and dissolve. Illustrative citations
offered by the *OED* itself tend, perhaps involuntarily, to undermine aspects of
the definition offered. Two are especially relevant because they demonstrate
the shift in the meaning of the word which has taken place since the rise of
Modernism. The first comes from D. L. Morgan's *Psychology for Teachers*,
published in 1894 – that is, just on the far side of the great Modernist divide:

> Realism ... involves the introduction of such details as shall assimilate the
> representation of actual fact, and the incorporation of the results of
> generalisation in individual persons or concrete things.

The second comes from a more recent and much better-known book, *Art and
Society*, by the defender of the Modern Movement, Herbert Read, published in
1937:

> My underlying contention [is] that there is an inherent contradiction between
> art and vulgarism (or, to confine ourselves to aesthetic terms, between art and
> realism).

The former quotation carries the subliminal message that realism in art reflects
the way in which 'everybody' sees the world. This notion is reinforced by
definitions which the *OED* itself offers for 'real' and 'realistic'. 'Real', it says,
means 'having an objective existence, actually existing as a thing'. 'Realistic'
means 'representing things as they actually are'. Nevertheless, all of this is
undermined by Herbert Read, who in effect tells his audience bluntly that
realistic representations cannot be art at all.

It seems to me that we tend to approach the idea of realism in art in two
different, frequently self-contradictory ways, and that this lies at the root of
the difficulty in finding an agreed definition for the word. I would like to
propose that under a single umbrella there are to be found two separate
versions of what is real. For convenience, these can be labelled 'conceptual
realism' and 'perceptual realism'. In its purest, most undiluted form,
conceptual realism, which seems to be much the older of the two, can be
defined as a kind of inventory of what the observer believes to be in front of
him at a given moment. This inventory, and the way in which it is presented,
are both to a large extent governed by experience, not only of things seen in the
past, but of habitual ways of seeing them. An extreme example is ancient
Egyptian tomb-painting. In this, the human figure is presented in what seems
to twentieth-century viewers a strangely distorted way. The head is shown in
profile, but the eye is drawn as if the figure were looking at us full-face; the
shoulders and torso are presented frontally, but the legs are once again drawn
in profile, usually in a striding position, so that one leg does not conceal the
existence of the other. There is every reason to believe that for the ancient

1 **Thomas Eakins** *The Gross Clinic* 1875
Patterned after Old Master models, notably Rembrandt's
two great *Anatomy Lessons*, *The Gross Clinic* nevertheless
has 'the force and immediacy of a work of nature' (Lloyd
Goodrich). Eakins departs from established narrative
conventions by creating a composition that is not easy to
decipher at first glance. The patient, being operated on for
the removal of a piece of dead bone in his thigh, is almost
hidden. The one sentimentally dramatic touch is the presence
of his mother, to the left, who covers her face with her hand.
Eakins's contemporaries found the painting brutal and
objected particularly to the blood on Dr Gross's hand and
scalpel, and on the hand and cuffs of his assistant, Dr Barton.

Egyptians themselves these paintings were perfectly realistic, a satisfactory representation of what they saw.

If this example seems unduly remote, let me choose another. In the English sporting paintings of the eighteenth and early nineteenth centuries, horses are most frequently, though not invariably, shown in profile. When they race, they are always depicted in a 'flying gallop' position (which is also used for rapidly moving animals in Palaeolithic art). It took the work of photographic pioneers, such as Eadweard Muybridge (1830–1904), using stop-motion techniques, to prove that this inherited, universally accepted perception of the way in which a galloping horse moved was entirely incorrect. The horse never in fact had all four legs extended at the same time, no matter how fast it was moving. Our notion of realism often has more to do with what we think we are going to see than with what is in front of our eyes; and the point is strengthened by an ironic detail. The sporting paintings just described were not commissioned for primarily aesthetic reasons, but as literal and truthful records of particularly successful and valued equine specimens.

2 **Currier after Severin** *Peytona and Fashion in their great match for $20,000* 1845
This sporting print, showing a match between two thoroughbreds, puts the horses in the 'spread' galloping position, generally considered correct until Muybridge's photographs (Ill. 3) were published.

3 **Eadweard Muybridge** *Racehorse* 1884–85
Sequential photographs of this type proved that previous ideas about the way horses moved at speed had been erroneous.

Images of this type found a minor place in the American artistic canon, in some of the horse prints produced by the incredibly prolific firm of Currier & Ives. Horses, however, play only a comparatively small part in a vast output of lithographs, most of which illustrate not merely aspects of nineteenth-century American life but the universal tendency for such illustrations to become piece-by-piece inventories, which are in their own way like the conceptual assemblages of ancient Egyptian painting: that is, each item exists for its own sake, independently, rather than cohering with the others present. The impulse to reduce images to signs, always present in this type of popular print, can most easily be measured when the print itself, as occasionally happens, derives from some more sophisticated image. The famous Currier & Ives lithograph *The Life of a Hunter – A Tight Fix*, published in 1861, derives from a painting

by Arthur Fitzwilliam Tait (1819–1905), an English-born artist who arrived in America at the age of thirty. It is a melodramatic composition showing a hunter at the mercy of a wounded bear. It is fascinating to see how the print subtly alters the original. The most conspicuous change is in the attitude of the hunter himself. In the original painting he sprawls haplessly in the snow; in the print he is given the attitude of a Greek warrior in combat – a stylized indication of his determination to resist. This is obviously something that the lithographer felt was not spelt out in the source. Realism is always readily qualified by the artist's *conception* of what is happening, as distinct from his *perception* of it.

A more sophisticated variant of this conceptual impulse can be found in much of the social realist art produced in America in the 1930s. Art of this type is essentially theatrical, following a tradition inherited from such eighteenth-century painters as William Hogarth and Jean-Baptiste Greuze. It spells out its didactic intentions by means of a careful selection of physical types (actors), objects (props) and surroundings (sets). Like a theatrical performance, it is more focused and more intense than life. In strictly realistic terms, this characteristic intensification often defeats its object. By assembling so many relentlessly meaningful things in one place, the artwork loses the random quality we instinctively associate with 'real life'.

Much social realist art departs even further from the norm which many spectators carry in their heads as a measure of what they think of as reality. For example, in paintings by Ben Shahn, and also in those of William Gropper and Jack Levine, appearances are routinely subjected to processes of visual rhetoric – in other words, they are caricatured – in support of a particular cause. Such paintings are 'real', in the fullest sense, only to those who are in complete agreement with the case the artist is pleading. Nevertheless, critics and art-historians continue to attach to them the conventional label 'realist'.

Perceptual realism is, in theory at least, entirely concerned with the business of sight: with the business of seeing things without preconceptions, as innocently as possible. In its most extreme guise, perceptual realism becomes a

ABOVE LEFT
4 Arthur Fitzwilliam Tait
A Tight Fix 1856
A dramatic composition showing frontier life, painted by an English-born artist settled in New York.

ABOVE RIGHT
5 Currier & Ives after Arthur Fitzwilliam Tait
The Life of a Hunter – A Tight Fix 1861
The composition, presumed to be after Tait's second version of the painting (now lost), but which may have been the lithographer's own variant, has been 'improved' and is more stylized and thus easier to read. Here the hunter, rather than sprawling as in Tait's original, is in the pose of a classical Greek warrior. The probable source is the 'Strangford Shield' in the British Museum, London – a Roman copy of the shield carried by Phidias's Athena Parthenos in Athens.

record, not of objects, but of the way in which light falls upon and reveals objects, or is obstructed or interrupted by the presence of objects – which may include figures – within an environment. Attempts at realism of this kind made their appearance in European art at least as early as the seventeenth century. Vermeer's celebrated *View of Delft* is a generally accepted example. It is now agreed that for this, and indeed for the majority of his other pictures, Vermeer probably made use of a *camera obscura*, a device which is the ancestor of the modern camera, but without the power to fix an image onto a film or plate.

During most of the period surveyed in this book, perceptual realism has been greatly affected by our experience of photography; and photographic images of all kinds, from the humblest to the most ambitious, have become important signifiers in our culture – so much so that we tend to reject images which show no trace of photographic influence as being not fully realistic.

Nevertheless, as has increasingly come to be realized, the camera is a deceptive guide to and recorder of the nature of visual reality. It is not merely that what appears on film, or in a print made from that film, can be manipulated *post hoc*. It is also that the lens has its own way of seeing, which is not necessarily that of the human eye. As all photographers know, the camera is monocular, and looks fixedly at objects rather than scanning them (as a pair of human eyes does). In addition, different focal lengths of lens, set at different apertures, produce different results. A 'long' lens, for example, which brings objects closer to the camera, produces violent compression of foreground and background.

Even before perception becomes contaminated by ideation, it is therefore affected by purely mechanical quirks. We are vulnerable to the effect of these quirks, because we trust the camera (which can fix fleeting images for prolonged contemplation) more than we can trust our own eyes (which are incapable of doing so). We continue to give this trust even though the supposed neutrality of the photograph is a long-exploded myth.

In an important sense, therefore, perceptual realism can be defined as no more than another concept, one among many. Yet the notion of the perceptual as a separate realm, independent of the supposed realities we generate within ourselves and impose on the external world, does have value. It acts as a reminder that this external world exists, and that at many moments it actively rejects the stereotypes we try to impose on it. The evidence offered by Muybridge's photographs is an instance of the way in which some unexpected event can crack the carapace of accepted visual convention, and reveal the presence of an alternative.

What we take to be visual norms have been further challenged – but from a wholly different direction – during the course of the twentieth century, by the stylistic plurality of Modernism: not only by the pull towards complete abstraction, which strengthens at certain moments and then diminishes again, but by the fact that the Modernist artist is expected to establish originality. This originality, itself very difficult to define, has more and more tended to displace technical skill as the criterion of talent. The artist's merit is evaluated, not on the basis of skill in producing an image of the world as most people see it – or think they see it – but on the recognizability of his or her personal handwriting, and the presence or absence of a unique vision of the world which, even when figuration is still present, may carry it to the very limits of recognizability. This, essentially, is what Herbert Read was trying to say when he equated realism with 'vulgarism'. By vulgarism he meant the lowest common denominator of visual perception, which, he believed, the true Modernist should always attempt to avoid.

The cumulative effect of this long-sustained challenge, supported by so many major artists, has been to push realism out of the central position in Western art which it enjoyed enjoyed from the Renaissance onwards. If one reads Vasari's *Lives of the Artists*, for example, one immediately sees that he made two assumptions which seem totally alien to the way we now think and speak about art. For him, the progress of art was like the progress of science. Each succeeding generation of artists was able to build on the achievements of its predecessor, instead of being forced, as now, to start from a *tabula rasa*, completely anew. In addition, this progression was for Vasari largely a matter of mastering specific skills, which would permit what seemed to him a yet more accurate representation of aspects of the visible world. This is why he laid so much emphasis on topics such as perspective, human anatomy and chiaroscuro.

Paradoxically, because it has been pushed out of this central position, in our own day the word 'realism' has had its meaning greatly extended, and at the same time blurred. That is, there are paintings which seem at least moderately realist in a Modernist context (the Bay Area Figuration of the 1960s and 1970s is a case in point) but which would not have seemed so in the pre-Modernist context.

In fact, twentieth-century realism is even more difficult to define than realism in general because the way in which we perceive it, and evaluate its presence or absence, is governed by the instinctive relativism of our own critical attitudes – based in turn upon our knowledge that our visual culture has no single point of focus. A critical attitude of this kind is obviously in conformity with the new approaches to art which have been suggested by Structuralism. These see artistic activity not as an absolute but as an elaborate and ever-shifting interplay between content, means of expression and context. Realism (like feminism, which has made brilliant creative use of structuralist thinking, not least in the new feminist art criticism) is essentially what we perceive it to be in the circumstances of the time. As an absolute value or quality it is now, just as perhaps it always has been, unattainable.

In taking American realism as my subject, I am obviously making the assumption that there is a close connection between the realist impulse and the development of art in the United States. It is a link rooted in the whole social and political tradition which has formed the American nation. What does that tradition consist of? Here I must risk some broad generalizations. First, the nation was from its beginnings essentially democratic, a society regulated by consent. There were of course occasions when the consensus broke down: one precipitated the American Revolution, the other the Civil War. Second, modern America is the product of successive waves of immigration. In the seventeenth, eighteenth, nineteenth and early twentieth centuries the people who came there from Europe had a particular interest in leaving rigid hierarchies and social structures behind them. Their culture, in addition to being democratic, was anti-elitist (which is something slightly different). There is no specifically aristocratic tradition in American art, no sense that the professional artist labours chiefly for a leisured and privileged class, shut away from the rest of society. Thirdly – and this is once again largely a product of the fact that Americans are a nation of immigrants, making new lives for themselves through the labour of their own hands – American attitudes were for a long time strongly pragmatic, in cultural matters as well as in purely practical ones.

American realism, as an artistic phenomenon, can be connected with the philosophical approach advocated by John Dewey (1859–1952). Dewey's belief was that common sense was much more than an elusive chimera – that it remained 'a useful and usable name for a body of facts'. In art, this approach leads both artist and spectator towards the kind of work which presents the world as 'everyone' would see it. Dictionary definitions set aside, this is still the way in which many people, especially those who are not art specialists, would describe the realist impulse in painting and sculpture. Taken in these terms, realist art seems particularly apt as an expression of a national culture which, from the start, put equal emphasis on equality and practicality.

The definition of American realism as a specific phenomenon in the history of art can, however, be greatly narrowed by turning away from these social and philosophical considerations and looking at a much more specific issue: the role of photography. Photography was not an American invention, but it has played a more prominent role in American visual culture than in that of Europe, where it originated.

Once again, there are a number of reasons. One is the fact that, while Americans are undoubtedly inheritors of the European Old Master tradition, this inheritance is more remote than it is for artists working in Europe itself. The first painters working in the United States were primitive limners. The earliest artists who, in terms of professional skills, needed to fear no comparison with European contemporaries were John Singleton Copley (1738–1815) and Benjamin West (1738–1820), and it was no accident that both eventually chose to pursue their careers in England. The America of that time could offer them neither the necessary patronage nor the direct experience of earlier works of art which an ambitious artist needed.

The photograph, when it became available, proved ideally suited to the American situation. In a consciously egalitarian society, it democratized portraiture, which had hitherto been the preserve of the well-to-do. At the same time it proved to be the ideal medium for documenting the appearance of America itself, then still not fully explored. It was the photographs made in 1861 by Carleton E. Watkins (1825–1916) that first attracted Albert Bierstadt to the Yosemite Valley, which was to inspire some of his most spectacular landscape paintings, 'safe haven for the wilderness myth that lay at the heart of America's definition of itself'.[1]

From Bierstadt's time onwards, American painting has had a peculiarly intimate relationship with the camera, which has manifested itself in the work of generation after generation of artists. For the record, let me cite some of the best known examples here. Leading the file is Thomas Eakins, arguably America's greatest artist of the pre-Modern epoch. As is well known, Eakins was fascinated by photography and made photographic studies of humans and animals in motion which in some respects surpass those of Muybridge. It is evident that he used photographs as preparatory studies for paintings and watercolours, in one or two instances copying them literally. It is also evident that the way in which he treats the fall of light in his most ambitious paintings – in full-length portraits for example – is heavily influenced by his experience of the way in which the camera would record the same subject matter.

William Harnett, the brilliant *trompe-l'oeil* painter whose work has often been loosely described as photographic, was, it has recently been surmised, influenced by the still-life compositions of the Alsatian photographer Adolphe Braun (1811–77), which he probably saw while he was living and working in Europe.

American art of the twentieth century has conducted a long and complex dialogue with the camera. At the beginning of the century, the Pictorialist photographers were attempting to rival effects which they found in traditional painting and drawing. At the same time, however, the artists of the Ashcan School, the majority of whom began their careers as illustrators, making sketches of news events for newspapers not as yet equipped to print photographs, were making informal compositions influenced by the new snapshot cameras.

Their successors, the Precisionists, were often skilled photographers in their own right. Some of the best-known of Charles Sheeler's compositions, among them the famous *Rolling Power*, are based directly on his own photographs. Georgia O'Keeffe, closely allied to the Precisionist group, was influenced by the work of her husband Alfred Stieglitz (1864–1946), one of America's most celebrated photographers. Her close-up images of flowers, which are among her most typical products, clearly owe much to photographic exemplars.

An interest in photography was one of the things which Magic Realism took over from Precisionism. There is a long series of photographs made in the 1940s by two leading members of the group, Paul Cadmus and Jared French, together with the latter's wife Margaret, on the beaches at Fire Island and Provincetown, and also in the artists' New York studios. The images bear a close relationship to their paintings. A selection of them has recently been brought together in the book, *Collaboration*, which calls attention to a hitherto neglected aspect of Magic Realism.[2]

The dependence of both Pop Art and its successor Photorealism on photographic imagery is so obvious that it does not need to be stressed. Nor does the rise to 'high art' prominence, in the 1980s and 1990s, of American artists who use photography not simply as source material but as their primary means of expression. The names of Robert Mapplethorpe, Cindy Sherman and, recently, Jeff Koons come to mind. In fact, the continuity and importance of its relationship to photography is one of the things which most clearly divide American Modernism from its European counterparts.

Despite this, all realism in American art came under serious challenge from the mid-1940s onwards. The reason was the triumph of Abstract Expressionism. One of the things which gave this new style its impetus was

America's changed position in the world. Abstract art came to be perceived as symbolic of the new cultural, as well as political, hegemony exercised by the United States. Under the patronage of leading museums, most of all the Museum of Modern Art in New York, and in alliance with official agencies such as the Office of the Co-Ordination of Inter-American Affairs, Abstract Expressionism became a weapon in the Cold War. As Max Kozloff was later to note in an important essay published in the magazine *Artforum*, a direct parallel was drawn between the idea that America was now the 'sole trustee of the avant-garde "spirit", and the US government's notion of itself as the sole guarantor of capitalist liberty'.[3]

Not surprisingly, realism was increasingly forced to the margin during the 1940s and 1950s, and has not been fully rehabilitated today. Other reasons for its fall from grace included the feeling that abstraction allowed the expression of intenser feelings of individuality, and thus raised art itself to a higher plane. In the minds of the leading American critics of the mid-century – men such as the brilliantly eloquent Clement Greenberg – realism was indeed an act of 'vulgarism', just as Herbert Read had implied in the sentence already quoted from *Art and Society*.

Artists who clung to realism did, however, derive some paradoxical advantages from their exiled situation, if they were shrewd enough to see what these were. What they did became transgressive; and the twentieth-century avant-garde has, from its beginnings, found energy in transgression. In other words, it became possible, perhaps for the first time in several centuries, and certainly for the first time in the whole history of American art, to employ realism for purposes of shock. The Pop artists in particular had the same effect on the settled hierarchies of Abstract Expressionism that the young Annibale Carracci and the young Michelangelo da Caravaggio had on the desiccated world of late Mannerism in Italy. Reading some of the early, vociferously indignant reactions to Pop, I hear an echo of Professor S. J. Freedberg's comment on Annibale's 1583 altarpiece showing the *Crucifixion with Saints*, now in S. Maria della Carità in Bologna: 'Never before this within the sixteenth century had an image been created with so minimal an intrusion of the processes of idealization, with such avoidance of the means of rhetoric, or *with so blunt a confrontation with the simple truth*.'[4] The italics are my own.

Pop, however, arrived at a moment when the world of contemporary art was becoming increasingly plural, when the whole dialectic of styles, with each new stylistic impulse both answering and replacing its immediate predecessor, had begun to break down. From the 1960s, realistic representation was just one option among the many that were available to artists. This led to increasing confusion, among American critics and artists, about what realism really was. In an artistic universe where so much art continued to be in the broad sense abstract, it was easy to see anything which was figurative (especially if it involved the representation of the human figure) as being more or less realistic. The context – this is a phenomenon I have already noted – made things seem realist which would not have been accepted as such at any earlier epoch.

This confusion was noted by artists themselves, and among some at least it had an unexpected result. They seemed to reject Modernism as a whole. What now attracted their concentrated attention was the work of certain pre-

Modernists. In other words, they made a sort of return to aspects of the Old Master tradition. Why should this be the case? It seems particularly strange because, as I have pointed out, American art is, thanks to the historical circumstances prevailing when the nation was built, somewhat distanced from this tradition.

I think three reasons can be given. One depends directly on the historical circumstance mentioned above. Despite the current magnificence of American museums, Old Master painting is, even in the contemporary American context, essentially exotic. Attraction to the exotic is a persistent element in Modernist art. So too is the spirit of transgression, which I have already alluded to as an integral component in Modernism. Going back to Old Master models may not *épater la bourgeoisie*, but it is extremely well calculated to irritate and throw off balance the American intelligentsia, brought up to regard Modernism as a profound and irreversible change equipped with a whole panoply of unchallengeable moral values.

The third reason – and this is perhaps more surprising – is the fascination with craft skills which is inbred in American society, thanks to its pioneering origins. A Modernism which increasingly devalued such skills (as was the case, for example, with the Conceptual Art movement prominent in the American art world during the late 1960s and 1970s) gave no satisfaction to those artists who were oriented towards the craft aspect of what they did. In true Modernist fashion, they therefore rebelled against what they saw as a form of intellectual tyranny. Interestingly enough, the models to which they turned were of very particular kinds. On the one hand they looked at Caravaggio's methods of intensifying the viewer's experience of the thing seen, through skilful manipulation of effects of light. On the other they looked at the academicism of Jacques-Louis David. What was the attraction of the latter? Perhaps twofold: first, it was this academicism against which the first generation of the Modern Movement had specifically rebelled; second, the methods taught in David's studio placed an emphasis on internal construction – from the skeleton of a figure to its flesh and muscles and finally to the epidermis – which was the contrary of the wilfully neutral vision of photo-based art.

Yet, inevitably, this return to parts of the pre-Modern tradition was often combined, often voluntarily but sometimes involuntarily, with ideas taken from American Modernism itself. The Modernist ethos could be challenged, but the Modern Movement itself could not be abolished. For instance, both Philip Pearlstein and Neil Welliver – leading realists of a kind opposed to dependence on the photograph – are emphatic that their way of composing a picture, of organizing a surface, is tightly linked to things learned from contemporary American abstraction.

The American realism of the present moment thus seems to represent yet another incarnation of impulses which have been working their way out during the whole history of American art. These impulses include the need to come to terms with and define the nature of the American environment – intellectual as well as purely physical – but also to mark the separation from Europe, and to catch the essence of a particular emotional tone. The subject of American realist art is not merely the experience of the everyday, but the whole business of setting this within a specifically American context.

6 **George Caleb Bingham** *Fur Traders Descending the Missouri* 1845
An evocation of the 'half-civilized, half-savage' life of the frontiersman,
originally entitled *French Trader and Half-Breed Son*.

CHAPTER 1

From the American Revolution to the Civil War

FROM ITS beginnings, American painting was motivated by the desire to represent reality. All other impulses were stripped away by the unique conditions imposed by a pioneer society. The earliest typically American paintings were illustrated maps. There followed primitive portraits and equally primitive representations of landscape. Vivid but technically unskilled, the portraits provide an accumulation of characteristic features from which the sitter could be 'read', rather as one reads a personal description in a letter. The landscapes seem to go further than this. In representations of farms and homesteads, what motivates them is the desire to claim ownership of the soil, and to record the changes imposed upon it by the hand of man.

The first fully professional painter in the United States – Benjamin West, as yet hardly formed as an artist, had left America in 1760 – was John Singleton Copley (1738–1815). Largely self-taught, Copley became a portraitist of considerable accomplishment, able to compete with European artists on their own terms. The early *Boy with a Squirrel* (1765) offers striking proof of his powers of observation. When it was sent to England for exhibition, it was admired for its brilliant rendition of detail, but also criticized for 'coldness' and 'overminuteness' – accusations which were to follow much American realism thereafter. Sir Joshua Reynolds said that it was 'a wonderful picture to be sent by a Young Man who was never out of New England, and had only some bad copies to study'.[1]

Accomplished as he was, however, Copley lacked self-confidence. His aim was to improve himself by absorbing the European grand manner at first hand. In 1774–75 he made a tour of Europe, in order to study the work of the Old Masters, and then he settled permanently in England. His style changed and lost its initial modest precision. Yet Copley did not entirely abandon his old self. In addition to painting portraits, he now made some interesting attempts at history painting. The most original of these is the earliest, the famous *Brook Watson and the Shark* (1778), which uses the established grand manner in an entirely original way, as a vehicle for vivid reportage. The painting anticipates work done by Jacques-Louis David during the Revolutionary and Napoleonic periods, which also attempts to unite the notion of the sublime with events which were happening in the present day. It is realist to the extent that it illustrates a contemporary event – an incident in Havana harbour – in a vivid and immediate fashion.

As his career makes plain, Copley did not in fact think of himself as a generically American painter. This feeling came later; and when it came it first rooted itself, quite naturally, in landscape painting. As Barbara Novak has said, 'America's search for some sense of the past in the raw new world focused on an idea of landscape that was at once strongly nationalist and moralist.'[2]

The career of Thomas Cole (1801–48) goes to show that the products of this search for an American identity were not, at least to begin with, stylistically homogenous. Sometimes they were entirely fantastic, as in *The Titan's Goblet* (1833); sometimes they represented an effort to marry a sensibility based on Claude Lorrain and the European ideal landscape to the recalcitrant facts of American nature. Cole's masterpiece, *The Oxbow (The Connecticut River from Northampton)* (1836), is an example of this.

7 **John Singleton Copley** *Boy with a Squirrel* 1765
Painted in Boston when Copley was only twenty-five, this was sent to England for exhibition, where it was seen and warmly praised by Sir Joshua Reynolds.

8 **John Singleton Copley** *Brook Watson and the Shark* 1778
This later painting by Copley adapts neo-classical conventions to a dramatic real-life event.

9 **Thomas Cole** *The Titan's Goblet* 1833
A romantic fantasy with no connection to
observed reality.

10 **Thomas Cole** *The Oxbow*
(The Connecticut River near Northampton) 1836
Here Cole tries to marry a sensibility still based on the
idealizing classical landscapes of Claude Lorrain with
the intransigence of American nature.

11 **Fitz Hugh Lane** *Brace's Rock, Eastern Point, Gloucester* 1863
In her pioneering study, *Nature and Culture*, Barbara Novak stresses the link between American landscape paintings of this type and the Emersonian Transcendentalist concern that spirit animates matter.

12 **Frederic Edwin Church** *Rainy Season in the Tropics* 1866
A visionary South American landscape which nevertheless roots itself firmly in observed scientific fact.

Cole's work, which retains an essentially European accent (he did not emigrate to the United States until the age of eighteen), has come to seem less firmly rooted in American soil than that of Luminist painters such as Fitz Hugh Lane (1804–65). Now regarded as the greatest of all American marine painters, Lane was in his own time an artist of purely local importance, who found patrons in and around his local Gloucester in Massachusetts, but who made little impact on the American public at large. Today, the magical tranquillity of his work has made him into an American icon.

Modern analysts have detected several layers of influence in Lane's art – including a faint residue of ideas from European masters such as Claude, or Joseph Vernet; plus a continuing subterranean link with the primitive artists who were the first American landscape painters. Additionally, much of Lane's best work, and that of American landscape painters in general, at least up to around 1875, bears a strong affinity with the transcendentalism of Ralph Waldo Emerson – with, for example, the view that 'The feat of imagination is in showing the convertibility of every thing into every other thing. Facts which had never before left their stark common sense suddenly figure as Eleusinian mysteries.'[3]

Describing one of Lane's paintings, *Brace's Rock, Eastern Point, Gloucester* (1863), Novak summarizes this whole tradition:

> In the painting, all the natural actualities of the scene have been manipulated into a more abstract planar order, from which the painting derives much of its power, a power intensified by the hard focus on details, such as the water ripples, that are normally soft. As with Copley much earlier, we become aware of a curious animation in the inanimate. And, again, this animation is not obviously anthropomorphic, as were the trees of the late eighteenth-century picturesque painters, but rather reveals that awareness of spirit in matter which so concerned Emersonian Transcendentalism.[4]

Like Cole, Lane concerned himself with the scenery of the eastern United States – the original area of settlement. There were other artists who went much further afield in search of subjects; of these, the most celebrated in their own time were Frederic Edwin Church (1826–1900) and Albert Bierstadt (1830–1903).

Church travelled widely, not only within the United States but in South America (Colombia and Ecuador), gathering material for his spectacular panoramic landscapes. Because of their immense sweep, these have sometimes been likened to those of J. M. W. Turner, but their mechanisms are really very different from Turner's. Even the most improbable of Church's compositions, such as *Rainy Season in the Tropics* (1866), with its symmetrical double rainbow spanning the canvas, have a firm foundation in observed scientific fact; and there is no sense that these facts have been subjectively transmuted.

Church's landscapes were enormously popular, both because they satisfied curiosity about places still not fully known and because they seemed to confirm the optimistic theology of the time. In them, love of God and respect for science were combined. A contemporary English critic remarked that Church was 'a painter of what might be termed phenomenal nature, scenes which awaken a sense of omnipotence, spectacles that transcend the everyday works of reality'.[5] The purpose of reproducing nature, in its most tremendous form, was to symbolize the divine presence.

The German-born Bierstadt came to the United States when he was two, and returned to Germany in his twenties to study in Düsseldorf and undertake a European tour. In 1859, two years after his return to the United States, he joined an expedition to the Rocky Mountains. The oil sketches, and also photographs, which he made on the journey supplied material for paintings almost as spectacular as those of Church.

There is another side to Bierstadt's art. Small works, like his sketch of a *Surveyor's Wagon in the Rockies* (1859), show him grappling with the kind of material which resisted traditional formulae. The wagon and its horses, and a rider beyond, seem suspended in the endless space of the plains. The mountains visible beyond them are too remote to serve as spatial markers. Reality itself becomes phantasmagoric.

There is a similar feeling in some of the sketches made by another landscape painter of the period, Sanford R. Gifford (1823–80), when he accompanied a United States Geographical Survey expedition to Utah and Wyoming in 1870. Gifford's *Valley of the Chug Water, Wyoming Territory* has an absolute photographic accuracy in rendering quasi-abstract forms that creates a paradoxically dreamlike sensation in the viewer. His painting is extremely close to some of the work of the landscape photographer William Henry Jackson (1844–1942), who accompanied the same expedition.

Jackson and Gifford were both content to accept the new landscapes they were discovering as requiring no alteration or rearrangement in the name of art. The aesthetic impulse and the purely scientific one coincided. Nevertheless, 1870 was about the last moment at which artists, or indeed Americans in general, could see the wilderness as an inexhaustible resource still to be explored, nature virgin and untouched. It was in fact Jackson's photographic views of the Yellowstone, given to every member of the House of Representatives and of the Senate, which prompted the passage of an Act of Congress in 1872, declaring this region to be the first National Park. This, almost as much as the conclusion of the Civil War, marked the passing of an era.

American realist painting now took a different direction, concerned not with landscape but with the human figure. The United States of the first half of the nineteenth century did, of course, produce genre painters as well as landscapists. William Sydney Mount (1807–68) and George Caleb Bingham (1811–79), for example, both possessed distinctive visions of American society. Bingham in particular, with his paintings of the free men who lived and worked on the great Missouri River (*Fur Traders Descending the Missouri*, 1845; *Raftmen Playing Cards*, 1847), used genre as the vehicle for a major American myth, that of the life of the frontiersman, free of civilized constraints.

A distinctive feature which links Mount's work to that of Bingham is the interest in classical construction. Novak tellingly compares a painting by Mount, *The Power of Music* (1847), with Piero della Francesca's great *Flagellation* (1455) in Urbino. The composition is based on Piero's device of a box-within-a-box. Similarly, the central dancing figure in Bingham's *Raftmen* is a paraphrase of the Christ in Raphael's *Transfiguration* (taken from an

13 **Sanford R. Gifford** *Valley of the Chug Water, Wyoming Territory* 1870
The literal – yet curiously abstract – landscape forms create a dream-like feeling.

14 **George Caleb Bingham** *Raftmen Playing Cards* 1847
Bingham transfers a favourite genre subject, popular since the seventeenth century, to an exotic frontier setting.

15 **William Sydney Mount** *The Power of Music* 1847
The sentimental overtones of the subject matter divert
attention from the fact that the composition is based on a
device used by Piero della Francesca – a box-within-a-box.

OPPOSITE ABOVE

16 **Albert Bierstadt** *Surveyor's Wagon
in the Rockies* 1859
Bierstadt here had to look beyond traditional landscape
formulae. The wagon and its horses seem suspended in the
endless space of the plains.

OPPOSITE BELOW

17 **Eastman Johnson** *Cranberry Harvest,
Nantucket Island* 1880
A monumental genre scene notable for its combination of
rhythmic finesse and crisp characterization of individual
figures, such as the woman standing in the centre waiting
for her child.

engraving). Yet, though classical in one restricted sense, these painters are
also sentimental. Their realism of subject, place and atmosphere is thus
heavily qualified.

The painter whose career symbolizes the transition between the old, taken-
for-granted realism of the years before the Civil War and the new, much more
sophisticated variety which was to follow is Eastman Johnson (1824–1906).
Johnson was a less gifted painter than his younger contemporaries, Winslow
Homer and Thomas Eakins. In particular, he failed to sustain any real arc of
development, declining in his later years into a complacent portraitist of local
worthies. However, in mid-career he produced some paintings which still seem
quintessentially American, not only because of their subject matter but
because they encapsulate the idea that there is an American truth in art, quite
different from other kinds of truth that might flourish in Europe. For the new
facts of the landscape painters who preceded him, Johnson substituted
something subtler: a distinguishable social and moral atmosphere.

He began as a kind of journeyman, making use of such limited opportunities
to learn as were then available to aspiring artists in the United States. He first
trained as a lithographer; that is, he began in an established tradition of popular
illustration. Leaving this, he earned a living as a portraitist in crayons. He did
not start to work in oils until he was in his mid-twenties, and he soon realized
that he needed more help than America could give. In 1849 he left America and
enrolled in the Düsseldorf Academy. The Düsseldorf School of realists was at
that time well-known to Americans, and exercised greater influence than Paris
over artists in the United States.

What Johnson discovered in Düsseldorf may have been a surprise to him.
Founded in the early nineteenth century under Nazarene influence (its first

18 **Eastman Johnson** *Life in the South
(Old Kentucky Home)* 1859
An early painting showing the impact of the artist's
studies in Düsseldorf. Painted just before the Civil War,
it is an ambiguous work which appealed to both factions
in contemporary American politics.

head was Peter Cornelius), the Düsseldorf Academy was at that time deeply
divided along political lines. Many of the paintings produced by leading
Düsseldorf artists during the 1840s contained an element of social protest; and
during the abortive revolution of 1848 (only just over when Johnson arrived)
some prominent painters had been members of the Burgwehr, the citizen army
which manned the barricades. It was these politically radical painters who
tended to have the most thoroughgoing commitment to realism. Johnson seems
to have absorbed the lesson that serious art need not be idealizing or romantic,
nor was it necessary for it to stick to historical subject matter: it could be a
direct reflection of a particular milieu, contemporary with the artist himself.

Johnson seems, nevertheless, to have felt constricted by the Düsseldorf atmosphere and training. In 1852 he moved to Holland, to study Rembrandt. After spending three years there, mostly in The Hague, he returned to America, arriving home in 1855.

When he got back, he found there had been a change in the American market for art, even in the comparatively brief time he had been absent. The appetite for crayon portraits had been killed off by the daguerreotype. On the other hand, Americans had begun to envisage a more self-consciously national art, which reflected back to them their own ideas and feelings about what it was to be American. Like Bierstadt a few years later, Johnson went on to paint scenes of life in the West. He then moved East again to produce an ambitious genre painting that firmly established his reputation with the American public.

Life in the South (1859) is painted in typical Düsseldorf style – detailed, rather busy, with interlocking narratives which the spectator can follow by examining the attitudes and gestures of the different figures. It also owes something to Mount, both in its intricate compositional schema and in sentiment. Very much of its own time, it is an ambiguous work which appealed to both factions in current American politics. Those who were later to support the Confederacy saw it as idyllic; those who would rally to the Union perceived in it an attack, deftly coded, on the already controversial institution of slavery.

Compared with the paintings of Johnson's best period, done in the fifteen years that immediately followed the Civil War, *Life in the South* may appear weak and sentimental. Nevertheless, however ambiguously, it has the courage to deal with slavery. After the war, Johnson for a period concentrated on subjects which unequivocally expressed the unique flavour of life in the Northern States. Perhaps part of his inspiration was the fact that aspects of this life had recently been so deeply threatened. He showed activities specifically of their time and place – the maple-sugar harvest, corn-shucking bees, cranberry picking. His cranberry series culminates in the recently rediscovered *Cranberry Harvest, Nantucket Island* (1880). This has a much simpler and stronger formal design than *Life in the South*. The motion of the rows of stooping figures progressing from right to left is opposed by the stillness of the monumental female in the centre, who stands upright, looking the other way.

Though the composition is disciplined, *Cranberry Harvest* still allows room for anecdotal touches. The pickers are not brutalized by their labour, but remain lively and human. The woman in the centre is waiting for her child to be brought to her. There are courting couples; one old man has brought a chair to sit on while he picks. French paintings of similar type – such as those by Jules Breton,[6] a rather academic follower of Gustave Courbet – invite us to contemplate a collective image. Here the pickers are individuals, on equal terms with the artist himself.

19 **Winslow Homer** *The Gulf Stream* 1899

A powerful, poetic evocation of human danger and solitude amidst the hostile
forces of nature, one of the most celebrated images in American art.

CHAPTER 2

Thomas Eakins
and Winslow Homer

THERE IS a close affinity between the group of post-Civil War rustic scenes painted by Johnson and some of the early work of Winslow Homer (1836–1910), more than a generation younger. Like Johnson, Homer began his career as an apprentice in a lithographer's shop. He made illustrations for sheet-music, and was thus very close to the roots of popular art. Many of these illustrations were near-copies of prints imported from England; Homer was thus aware of the English mid-century realist style, with its emphasis on the humorous and the anecdotal.

After completing his apprenticeship he became a successful independent illustrator, supplying drawings for periodicals such as *Ballou's Pictorial Drawing Room Companion* and for *Harper's Weekly*. In these, and especially in the work he did for *Harper's*, Homer had to rely much more on his own observation. In 1861 he sketched Abraham Lincoln in New York on his way to the inauguration in Washington. Later he went to the front and made drawings of Civil War scenes.

The Civil War drawings, and the paintings he had now begun to do, show a new visual influence: that of photography,[1] which in the hands of men like Matthew Brady and Timothy O'Sullivan had become an important means of documentation, bringing the American public closer to the realities of the conflict. The photographic influence showed itself in Homer's work in a diminution of the purely anecdotal element, and in an emphasis on simple, static, often silhouetted forms – the camera was not yet able to record moving images successfully. These characteristics can be seen in the best-known of Homer's Civil War paintings, *Prisoners from the Front* (1866), which contrasts a ragged group of Confederate prisoners with a dapper, self-possessed Union officer.

No doubt coincidentally, there is a striking resemblance between *Prisoners from the Front* and the French realist masterpiece, Courbet's *Bonjour Monsieur Courbet*, painted a little less than ten years earlier. Courbet uses an identical compositional device: silhouetted figures are strung out across the canvas, parallel with the picture plane, with a group on the left opposed to a single

20 **Winslow Homer** *Prisoners from the Front* 1866
Ragged Confederate prisoners face a dapper Union officer
in an image influenced by the still, static nature of early
photography.

21 Winslow Homer *Snap the Whip* 1872
The mountainscape in the background was an afterthought,
absent from the preliminary sketch. Its sloping shape echoes
the diagonal made by the line of the boys and it has been
suggested that Homer borrowed this idea from the Japanese
printmaker, Hokusai. If so, this is an early example of
japonisme in American art.

figure on the right. In 1866, the year his painting was completed, Homer
visited Paris, where *Prisoners from the Front* was hung in the American section
of the Universal Exposition. French newspapers ignored the parallel with
Courbet and instead stressed a likeness to the leading academic painter, Jean-
Léon Gérôme.

When Homer returned to the United States in the following year, he began
the series of paintings which closely resembled what Eastman Johnson was
doing at the same time. Their paintings show that the two artists kept a jealous
eye on one another. Many of Homer's rustic genre scenes painted at this period
are celebrations of youth and high spirits – for instance, *Snap the Whip*
(1872). Childhood and the life of children took on a special significance in
America in the years following the Civil War, and these images symbolized the
will to rebuild and to make a stronger and more vigorous nation.

Homer also painted quieter scenes, often featuring pensive young women.
These later aroused speculation about a possible amorous relationship, in some
way frustrated or unfulfilled – a relationship which might explain why Homer
never married. Recent research has shown that the truth is more bizarre.[2]
Works such as the watercolour *Reading* (1874) were in fact posed for by a
young man wearing a woman's dress. The model, Joseph Keenan, later grew

up to be a police sergeant. What all observers have felt is a haunting sense of unease in these supposedly idyllic works. They were preliminary to a crisis in Homer's career.

In 1881 he decided to leave for Europe again. On this occasion he made, not for Paris, the acknowledged capital of art, but for an English fishing village, Cullercoats in Northumberland, where the river Tyne empties into the North Sea. It was the start of a new and increasingly reclusive pattern of life. When he returned to the United States, in November 1882, Homer chose to settle at Prout's Neck in Maine, a remote northern promontory sticking into the Atlantic. He had some family connections with the place, but clearly the overriding attraction was the fact that it provided an environment very like Cullercoats.

The period Homer spent in England was marked by a change of style. His work became less specifically realistic, more symbolic and romantic. This change has been attributed to purely artistic influences: contact with the drawings of the late Pre-Raphaelite artist Sir Edward Burne-Jones, and the opportunity to study the Elgin Marbles from the Parthenon in the British Museum.[3] Such influences are difficult to prove. What is unmistakable is a change of attitude. Homer now chose different subject matter and treated it in a different way, more painterly and more dramatic. He tended to show men locked in a heroic struggle with the elements, particularly with the sea; women were depicted as beings whose role it was to wait and endure. The mood was often one of endeavour, but also of ultimate helplessness in the face of the power and indifference of nature. These stylistic changes persisted and intensified after Homer's return to the United States.

22 **Winslow Homer** *Reading* 1874
It has only just been discovered that this and a few other similar works by Homer were in fact posed for by a boy wearing female dress. The discovery has raised questions about the nature of Homer's sexuality.

The most famous image from this very different second phase of Homer's career did not come from what he saw around him at Prout's Neck, but was inspired by one of his regular visits to the Caribbean. *The Gulf Stream* (1899) shows a solitary black in a dismasted sloop, adrift on a stormy sea full of sharks. Even on the simplest level, this image can hardly be described as a purely realistic one. It is clearly an archetype of solitude, conjured up by the artist's imagination, and not something directly seen.

When asked to name the greatest American artist of his time, Thomas Eakins (1844–1916) chose Homer without hesitation. Most lovers of American art would now cite Eakins himself as the finest American painter of the nineteenth century. Despite Eakins's admiration for his older colleague, the two were significantly different. Eakins, though he had his own vein of poetry, was constitutionally incapable of painting a work like *The Gulf Stream*, where what was to be portrayed did not present itself before his eyes in literal fashion.

Eakins's artistic education was much more thorough and systematic than that of either Johnson or Homer. Born and raised in Philadelphia, then still incontestably the cultural capital of America, he showed an early talent for drawing. His professional training began at the Pennsylvania Academy of the Fine Arts, the country's oldest art institution. He also studied anatomy at Jefferson Medical College – the training not of an artist but of a medical student. In later years, his anatomical knowledge was to be at least as great as that of most physicians, and his obsession with the subject can be linked to the strain of scientific investigation which ran throughout his work.

In 1866 Eakins left the United States for Paris, where he was to live and study for three years. He arrived at an important moment of transition in French art. The first stirrings of Impressionism were already being felt, though the movement had not yet acquired a name. Eakins seems to have been quite unaffected by the impulse towards change, and indeed largely unaware of it. He entered the studio of Jean-Léon Gérôme (1824–1904), who, at just over forty, was already one of the best-regarded academic artists in Paris and a celebrated teacher. Under Gérôme's guidance he laid the foundations of a sound technique, which was always to be based on accepted academic principles.

One of the most curious features of Eakins's period of study in Paris, as reflected in his letters home, was his apparent indifference to the Old Masters. Soon after his arrival, he wrote to his sister Frances, describing his first visit to the Louvre:

> I went next to see the picture galleries. There must have been half a mile of them, and I walked all the way from one end to the other, and I never in my life saw such funny old pictures. I'm sure my taste has much improved, and to show it, I'll make a point never to look hereafter on American Art except with disdain.[4]

The vow scarcely carries much conviction, given the tone of what precedes it. Eakins seems to have thought of his stay in Paris chiefly as a way of sharpening his technical resources; his basic sensibility was already formed. The painters he mentions in his correspondence are almost always French contemporaries who played a prominent part in the official Salons – men like Ernest Meissonier, Thomas Couture, Gustave Doré and Léon Bonnat (Eakins studied for a while with Bonnat as well as with Gérôme, but found him a less satisfactory teacher). Yet Eakins was not deliberately provincial. He soon adjusted to student life in Paris; he was already a good linguist, and his French became completely colloquial. He strolled the boulevards and went frequently to the opera, knowing he would probably never hear such good singers again – he was always passionately fond of music.

In Europe Eakins travelled widely, visiting Germany, Switzerland and Italy. Just before he returned home he spent some months in Spain, where the Old Master paintings in the Prado, often opposed in style to those he had seen in the Louvre, had an important effect on him. He was particularly struck by Velázquez and Ribera, whose work corresponded to his own pictorial instincts. His enthusiasm for Velázquez was the beginning of an important current in American art – a taste for the realism of the painterly Baroque – although, in Eakins's case, Velázquez's painterliness seems to have counted for less than his fidelity to observed fact. In Eakins's work, that fidelity took on a specifically American character, in terms both of the fact observed and of the manner in which it was rendered.

Eakins finally arrived back in Philadelphia at the beginning of July 1870. Apart from a brief visit to the American West, he was to spend the rest of his life in his native city. The paintings done immediately after his return often seem to be explicit statements about his American affiliations. For example, there is the outdoor portrait of a boyhood friend, *Max Schmitt in a Single Scull* (1871). As Eakins's biographer Lloyd Goodrich remarks:

> This was a scene completely familiar to the artist, observed first hand, and
> recorded with fidelity to reality. The light and atmosphere were those of
> America: clear air, strong sunlight, high remote sky, brown trees and grass –
> things which Eakins had never seen in Gérôme's class or in the Prado.[5]

23 **Thomas Eakins** *Max Schmitt in a Single Scull* 1871 Schmitt was a boyhood friend of the artist, who became a champion amateur oarsman. Eakins himself appears in another scull, in the distance to the right. Surviving perspective drawings for other rowing pictures show how carefully Eakins composed these apparently informal outdoor scenes.

Elaborate perspective drawings for other rowing pictures of this type show how carefully Eakins planned his compositions. What seems almost photographic has a strong underlying formal geometry. Despite Goodrich's assertions, there are also traces of Gérôme's influence, even though the subject matter is so different. Tonality, composition and system of lighting suggest comparisons with some of Gérôme's orientalist scenes, which show boats gliding on the still waters of the Bosphorus. But these are real-life American scenes, not exotic fantasies.

The first phase of Eakins's development culminates in a painting very different from *Max Schmitt* in emotional tone, setting and subject matter, but marked by the same unswerving commitment to realism. This is the justly celebrated *The Gross Clinic* (1875). Painted as a tribute to one of the leading American surgeons of the time, this looks not to Gérôme but to Rembrandt, particularly *The Anatomy Lesson of Dr Tulp*. It shows Dr Samuel Gross conducting an operation before an audience of students: a piece of dead bone is being removed from a young man's thigh. Though the painting is not as inherently gruesome as its seventeenth-century Dutch predecessor, the forthrightness of some of the details upset contemporary critics, who objected to the blood on the surgeon's hands, and on the hands and cuffs of one of the doctors assisting him. The fuss aroused by the painting heralded a long period of friction between Eakins and the society that surrounded him.

24 Thomas Eakins *Arcadia* 1883
One of comparatively few paintings in which Eakins
portrayed the male figure completely nude, though his
photographs demonstrate his fascination with the subject.

The most damaging dispute arose, not over one of Eakins's paintings, but over his teaching methods. Since his return from Paris there had been a number of tussles between the artist and the conservative management of his old school, the Pennsylvania Academy of the Fine Arts, but he was nevertheless appointed professor of drawing and painting there in 1879. In 1882 he was promoted to director. Eakins was a teacher of genius, but the innovations he introduced provoked growing opposition in traditional and rather prudish Philadelphia. The Academy admitted women students as well as men, and there were protests over Eakins's insistence that the model, whether male or female, should be studied completely nude:

> I am sure [he wrote] that the study of anatomy is not going to benefit any grown person who is not willing to see or be seen seeing the naked figure and my lectures are only for serious students wishing to become painters or sculptors.[6]

His protestations did him no good. In 1886, after a rather sordid intrigue which involved disloyal members of his own staff, he was forced to resign his post. The scandal spread, as he defended himself and his opponents struck back. One further charge seems to have been that he used some of his female pupils as models, without their mothers' knowledge or consent.

From this point onwards, Eakins – though certainly not ostracized by Philadelphia society – had, for many people, a whiff of the sulphurous about him. Lloyd Goodrich, when interviewing some of Eakins's surviving sitters and their relatives, found that there was a well-established tradition that the painter had frequently, and not always tactfully, importuned good-looking female sitters to pose naked for him.

If he did so, it was without success. Despite his well-documented obsession with the nude figure, Eakins's oeuvre offers very few female nudes. There is a small series devoted to the theme of *William Rush Carving His Allegorical Figure of the Schuykill River*. Rush was not Eakins's contemporary, but had lived and worked at the very beginning of the nineteenth century, and the various versions of this composition, effectively a historical and costume piece with a nude at its centre, are not among the artist's most intensely seen works: for Eakins, seeing was everything.

There are more male nudes, or near-nudes, among his paintings. Among them are the uncharacteristically Grecian *Arcadia* of 1883, with three nude youths in a landscape, and the ambitious but curiously unmoving *Crucifixion* (1880), which is devoid of religious atmosphere. In both cases Eakins seems to have been using a traditional theme as a pretext: it is not the announced subject but the nude that is primary. His depictions of boxers and wrestlers, which continue the 'sporting theme' of the paintings portraying oarsmen, also seem to have been inspired by the wish to paint the nude, now in a convincingly contemporary situation.

The most elaborate and most intensely felt of the works showing male nudes is *The Swimming Hole* (1884–85). This is simultaneously very American (the subject matter has a touch of Tom Sawyer and Huckleberry Finn), very formal (thanks to the strictly pyramidal composition) and very personal (the figures were posed by Eakins's students, and the painting includes, in the lower right corner, a portrait of the artist himself).

25 Thomas Eakins *Crucifixion* 1880

The model was John Laurie Wallace, one of Eakins's favourite pupils, who was only sixteen when the picture was painted. According to one contemporary account, the cross was sometimes set up on the roof of Eakins's house, with Wallace clinging to it. Neighbours thought the figure was a corpse. Lloyd Goodrich comments: '*Crucifixion* is a strictly objective portrayal of a human being in his last moments. Of customary religious feeling there is no trace.'

The Swimming Hole is one of the paintings most closely connected with Eakins's interest in photography. During the 1880s, in particular, he was not merely an enthusiastic photographer but a genuinely experimental one. His studies of figures in motion parallel similar work done by Etienne-Jules Marey in France and Eadweard Muybridge in the United States. Eakins corresponded with Muybridge on these experiments.

Though scarce among Eakins's paintings, nudes make up a high proportion of his photographic work. The majority of the surviving photographs feature males, not females. Eakins's images of the nude include the motion studies mentioned above and also figures posed in the studio. In addition, there is a series of candid pictures of his male students taken in the open air: these supplied much of the material upon which *The Swimming Hole* was based.

This painting and the photographs of male nudes connected with it raise similar questions as for Homer about Eakins's sexuality. Such questions are reinforced both by the painter's presence in the picture and by a small number of photographic images, clearly taken at his own direction, which show him nude, in a full frontal pose. It may be that these were intended to show the young men whom he asked to pose that there was nothing to be ashamed of. Yet they also hint at a homosexual urge – notwithstanding the fact that Eakins made a long–lasting and apparently devoted, though childless, marriage.

Eakins's paintings of nude and semi-nude males are the nearest he ever came to that suspect quality, glamour. By contrast, his portraits of women are constrained and self-conscious. The subjects usually look older than their real age, and there is no hint of eroticism about them. This may of course be the fault of the times and of the provincial society in which Eakins lived. The conventional way of depicting females in commercial portrait photographs was not wholly dissimilar.

A powerful but not charming painting of a young woman, *The Concert Singer* (1890–92), shows Eakins's qualities and defects as a painter of women, and indeed his qualities and defects considered in general. This was the second occasion on which he had tackled the same theme, a full-length likeness of a woman singing: the earlier work, *The Pathetic Song*, had been painted in 1881.

Here the singer is a twenty-three-year-old woman, Weda Cook, in a grand but rather dowdy pink brocade dress adorned with lace and pearl beading. Creases in the dress, and the fact that the bodice does not fit as well as it might, are all faithfully reproduced. When one visitor to his studio asked Eakins why there was a wrinkle across the bodice, the artist retorted: 'Why, what's the matter with that? It's there, isn't it?'[7]

Precisely the same degree of attention, no more and no less, is given to the sitter's own traits. The angle of her head does nothing to disguise her receding chin. She is seen from that particular viewpoint because Eakins was intent on catching the precise physiological effect of the activity she was engaged in: singing. Weda Cook said later that, whenever she came to take up her pose (and sometimes she came to the studio three or four days a week), Eakins asked her to sing the song 'O Rest in the Lord', so that he could observe the movement of her mouth and throat.[8] Not surprisingly, she grew thoroughly fed up with the piece.

26 Thomas Eakins *The Swimming Hole* 1884–85
This painting is closely linked to Eakins's interest in photography. One group of his images, clearly all taken on the same
occasion, shows his students wrestling and boxing outdoors in the nude, then cooling off at the actual site of *The Swimming
Hole*. In the photographs the arrangement of figures is random and informal, whereas in the painting they are carefully
arranged to form a pyramid – just as they are in John Singleton Copley's *Brook Watson and the Shark* (Ill. 8), painted more
than a century before. Eakins himself appears in the lower right-hand corner, swimming towards the rocky outcrop which
supports the other figures.

27 **Thomas Eakins**
The Concert Singer
1890–92
Weda Cook was twenty-three and a well-known local Philadelphia singer (a contralto) when she began posing for this portrait. The sittings lasted for two years and sometimes, during the first year, Cook posed as often as four times a week. She said afterwards that Eakins looked at her 'as if through a microscope'.

He was similarly meticulous about rendering precise gradations in the colour of her skin. Her arms and shoulders, for instance, are considerably paler than her hands, because they have been less exposed to sunlight.[9] Though hardly flattering, the result is subtle in its handling of tone.

The effect of stiffness and gawkiness, already present in the pose, is not mitigated by the composition, with the figure bolt upright in a space too wide for it. Eakins, who knew the work of Edgar Degas – 'that fellow knew what he was about', he commented to one of his students, citing a Degas drawing of a dancer[10] – has borrowed, but rather timidly, a typically Degasian device, itself based on snapshot photography. The hand of an otherwise invisible conductor, beating time, appears in the lower left-hand corner of the canvas. However, *The Concert Singer* has neither the spatial concision nor the overwhelming air of vitality to be found in Degas's likenesses of café-concert singers. The difference in atmosphere is not explained by the fact that Eakins's subject matter is a good deal more genteel. Though famous for his misogyny, Degas relished the animal vitality of his subjects; Eakins seems to have been cut off from feelings of this sort.

Eakins is a wonderfully gifted but also a disconcerting artist – perhaps incomplete in a profound, psychological sense. Contemporaries, even those most favourable to him, noticed something unfulfilled about his work and personality. Some fascinating notes describing a meeting with him were made by Mariana Griswold Van Rennselaer, a sophisticated American with well-developed taste in the visual arts. One of the first writers on art to sense Eakins's potential importance, she went to interview him for a planned article in *The American Art Review* (which in the end was never published):

> He is most modest and unassuming [she wrote to the editor, Sylvester B. Koehler], like a big enthusiastic schoolboy about his work. I do not believe he knows how good it is or how peculiar . . . He seemed to me much more like an inventor working out curious and interesting problems for himself than an average artist . . . If you met him in the street you would say a curious but most eccentric mechanic.[11]

Eakins's peculiarities of temperament were his own, but the quasi-scientific bent of his art was significant for the future of American realist painting in many of its aspects. In a sense, his work stands upon a cusp. His fascination with photography, and his tendency – which he shared with Degas – to use the camera as a means of seeing things afresh, of getting rid of the accumulated visual assumptions inherited from the Old Master tradition, made him a proto-Modern. On the other hand, in his attachment to the academic methods he learned from Gérôme – such as the use of elaborate perspective studies – he was deeply conservative.

His work embraces two aspects of realism which had long been opposed to one another. He often seems committed to a kind of forced objectivity, a deliberate refusal to comment. In many paintings, even his *Crucifixion*, he seems to want to present the visual world without emotional overtones or undertones. This lack of the affective element was to appear in the work of some Precisionist artists, and then more forcefully in Photorealism. Yet there are also paintings by Eakins which seem to take a very different view of the function of realism in art: in *The Gross Clinic* – as the obvious comparison with Rembrandt's *Anatomy Lesson* suggests – the spectator is deliberately forced into a confrontation with aspects of life which he or she might prefer to avoid. Realism becomes almost the opposite of hedonism.

A further complication is added by Eakins's probable sexual orientation (which, as we have seen, he shared with Homer). It supplies an explanation of Eakins's increasingly isolated path, just as it explains the physical reclusiveness of Homer's later years. Mrs Van Rennselaer, without finding precise and brutal words for it, seems to have suspected something of the kind, as one can detect from her description of Eakins as 'a big enthusiastic schoolboy'. Homer and Eakins, who now seem so central to the development of American art, and to the American realist tradition in particular, were in fact for most of their lives marginal artists in the American art world of their day, isolated in psychological terms because of their probable homosexuality, and even isolated physically from fellow practitioners and the American art-world in general. Their true importance – and that of Eakins in particular – was not recognized for a long time.

THE CAREERS of Homer and Eakins were paralleled by those of a group of still-life painters, active at the same period. Despite the already well-established tradition of still-life in American art, much less is known personally about these artists than about contemporary painters of the figure. The status they were accorded seems to have been very little above the artisan level. Though their work never enjoyed intellectual prestige, some had moments of popular success beyond the reach of more ambitious artists such as Eakins; yet after their deaths – and in some cases considerably before – these men were completely forgotten.

The first to be rediscovered was William M. Harnett (1846–92), who began to attract interest in the mid-1930s. The rediscovery of Harnett's followers John F. Peto (1854–1907) and John Haberle (1856–1933) followed, at first simply as part of an effort to separate genuine Harnetts from spurious ones.

The work done by these artists is not unique to American art. They belong to the main tradition of European still-life painting; more specifically to its northern branch, which descends from the Flemish painters and illuminators of the late fifteenth century.[1] Their most direct ancestors were the group of seventeenth-century Dutch and German painters who specialized in *trompe-l'oeil* techniques. What is unique about them is their central position within their own visual culture. In Europe, art of this type was almost extinct by the mid-nineteenth century; it had survived tenuously in the United States. Raphaelle Peale (1774–1825), a member of a celebrated family of Philadelphia artists, made several works of this type at the very beginning of the century; he had a few successors in the 1840s, often rather obscure provincial painters, before the appearance of Harnett and Peto.

In the late nineteenth-century American environment, *trompe-l'oeil* techniques took on fresh significance. They symbolized the opposition between high culture and popular culture. Paintings of this type were often displayed, not in art galleries or in drawing rooms, but in places of business and in taverns. They also laid a strong stress on masculine rather than feminine imagery (the hunt, smoking and drinking, the pursuit of money), which was novel in American art.

Before discussing the implications of this development, it is helpful to look at the careers of Harnett and Peto. About Haberle little is known, apart from what can be deduced from his painting.

Harnett was born in Ireland in 1848, but raised in Philadelphia. He began his career as an engraver, specializing in silverware. He entered the Pennsylvania Academy of the Fine Arts and attended night classes for two years. In the early 1870s he moved to New York, where he continued to work as an engraver and studied at the National Academy of Design, at the Cooper Union and with the portraitist Thomas Jensen.[2]

Unlike Eakins, Harnett came from an impoverished background and could not depend on financial support from his family. By the early 1870s he was already making a modest living as a still-life painter, producing many small still-lifes of the type now called 'bachelor paintings', because they seem to present an image of a man living alone, pleasing no one but himself: they often feature a pipe and/or a mug of beer. Harnett also began to produce works which were deliberate 'eye-deceivers', based on traditional *trompe-l'oeil* effects. One

CHAPTER 3

Still-Life and Populist Trompe-L'Oeil

28 **John F. Peto** *Office Board for Smith Bros. Coal Co.* 1879 *Trompe l'oeil* paintings were often commissioned as a form of business advertisement; minimal depth made the effect easier to achieve.

29 William M. Harnett
Still-Life 1877
One of a number of small still-lifes by Harnett and Peto (Ills 28, 33–35) featuring smokers' requisites. They were often called 'bachelor still-lifes', their subject matter presumably appealing to men.

was *Five Dollar Bill*, dated 1877. This was the start of a minor genre which has a special place in the history of American art.

In 1876 Harnett returned to Philadelphia, and the following year he re-enrolled at the now greatly changed Pennsylvania Academy of the Fine Arts. It was at this period that he became friendly with Peto. Eakins was now teaching at the Academy, but his influence over Harnett appears to have been exclusively technical: he seems to have helped him to refine both his actual technique and his feeling for luminosity. Harnett was now starting to make a better living: he was able to ask up to six hundred dollars for a painting. He saved enough money to contemplate a trip to Europe, an enterprise he described as 'the one cherished dream of my life'.[3] He went first to London, but found it hard to make a living, and was then invited by an American patron to go and work in Frankfurt. From Frankfurt he made his way to Munich, which was then almost as much of a mecca for American artists as Paris itself.

Inspired by the historicizing taste in Germany, Harnett painted a number of dullish still-lifes full of antiquarian objects, things which were themselves apparently ordinary, but which bore the marks of use and experience. His technical powers, however, were already at their height, and he gave ample evidence of them in the most celebrated products of his European years, the four successive versions of *After the Hunt*. The fourth and last was painted in Paris, on his way home to America, and was exhibited in the Paris Salon of 1885.

The Paris version of *After the Hunt* is a dazzling piece of visual deception, with complex roots in the history of art. In part it derives from the so-called 'hanging still-lifes' produced by some Dutch artists and later perfected by the eighteenth-century French painter Jean-Baptiste Oudry. These generally took the form of a suspended trophy of dead birds, or dead animals and birds, sometimes accompanied by the implements of the chase. They were not necessarily designed to fool the eye – Oudry's work, for example, does not attempt this. Harnett also had a more contemporary source of inspiration: a group of elaborate photographs of similar compositions made about 1867 by the celebrated Alsatian photographer Adolphe Braun, apparently with the aim of demonstrating that photography could rival painting.

What Harnett added to these sources was the element of illusion. Because the objects he was painting were already close to the picture-plane, he was able to paint them in such a way that they broke through its surface and seemed to take on an identity of their own. Yet the artist, not surprisingly, always disliked the implication that he was simply a maker of facsimiles. 'In painting from still-life,' he said, 'I do not closely imitate nature. Many points I leave out and many I add.'[4]

The imitation was, however, quite faithful enough to fascinate his contemporaries. Unsold in Paris, *After the Hunt* was later bought by an American businessman and became the chief attraction of a New York saloon. A caustic English observer, the correspondent of the London *Commercial Gazette*, vividly described its effect on the customers:

> Men come and stand before this picture for fifteen minutes at a time, and the remarks passed upon it are curious indeed. As a rule, city men are enraptured with it, and go into ecstasies over the feathery plumage of the birds and the furry coat of the rabbit, over the wonderful representation of the butt-end of an old snap-lock gun, over the extraordinary imitation of the brass work of the horn. But gentlemen from the country, and especially from Chicago, who see it for the first time, declare that nobody can take them in, and that the objects are real objects, hung up with an intent to deceive people.[5]

A further significant detail is added in a pamphlet issued by the proprietors of the tavern in 1903. The painting had become so popular that special hours had to be set aside for ladies to view it – from nine to eleven in the morning, when the saloon itself was not in operation.[6]

These details offer hints that the cultural situation Harnett found when he returned to the United States was different from that in Europe. The popular response to art was more vivid, and it was triggered by particular qualities. American critics, it is true, tried to apply what they considered to be universal standards. This is the attitude which comes through in one of the few exhibition reviews to discuss Harnett's work. It was written in 1879, just before the artist's departure for England, and refers to a painting Harnett showed that year at the National Academy of Design. Finding Harnett less to his taste than some now-forgotten rivals, the reviewer added loftily:

> The real fact is that this charge of inferiority is justified by the consideration that this imitative work is not really as difficult as it seems to the layman, and though

30 William M. Harnett *After the Hunt* 1885
The fourth and last version of the composition – three were painted when Harnett was in Munich – was done in Paris and exhibited at the Salon of 1885. It later became a popular attraction in a New York saloon, where the *trompe l'oeil* effect was enhanced by the use of a shadow box. It is Harnett's greatest virtuoso effort and remains his most celebrated work.

there are degrees of it, it is evident that only time and industry are necessary to the indefinite multiplication of them.[7]

Posterity has often tended to see in Harnett's mature works not imitation but a kind of abstraction. In the third and final phase of his career, he produced some very elaborate compositions, but others impress through their drastic simplicity. Each of the latter essentially concentrates on a single object, hung on a board and brought close to the picture plane. All the items depicted are endowed in one way or another with symbolic meaning – an old violin, a meerschaum pipe, a horseshoe or a revolver.

The response elicited by some of these in Harnett's own time was predictable from that already accorded to *After the Hunt*. When *The Old Violin* was shown in the Cincinnati Industrial Exposition of 1886, a policeman had to be employed to protect it from the curiosity of the public.[8]

Late twentieth-century reactions to these paintings are very different. Educated by encounters with modern art – for example, the *Flag* paintings of Jasper Johns – spectators now find in them a sort of iconic authority: that is, the paintings become secular versions of religious images. This is perhaps especially the case with *The Faithful Colt* (1890). The gun it depicts was no rarity to the men of Harnett's generation. An 1860 army revolver, it was a typical product of burgeoning American industry. Nevertheless, it also epitomized the romance of the frontier hero; it was the favourite weapon of the Wild West. Harnett endowed it with all these romantic resonances by carefully reproducing the signs of use and wear – the rust on the barrel, the cracked ivory of the butt.

The gun is shown hanging from its trigger guard on a nail driven into what is evidently a barn door. There are a couple of extra nails in the wood, in addition to the one which supports the revolver itself. Below and to the right is a newspaper clipping, one corner turned up to increase the illusion of depth. The sparse arrangement devised by the artist has extraordinary formal authority. It turns the Colt into a totem object, presented for contemplation and worship: the whole legend of the American frontier is summed up in the image.

This painting anticipates some of the key notions of American Modernism after 1945: in particular, the liking for centralized images which deny traditional ideas of nuanced composition. These images appear not only in the work of Jasper Johns, but in that of artists as different from him and from each other as Mark Rothko and Andy Warhol.

Harnett's friend and younger contemporary John F. Peto produced work which has often been confused with that of the older artist. Sometimes this confusion seems to have been deliberately induced. At the beginning of the Harnett revival, a number of Peto paintings appeared bearing false signatures, which seem to have been affixed shortly after Harnett's death. Like Harnett, Peto trained at the Pennsylvania Academy of the Fine Arts, entering it in 1877, at the beginning of Eakins's dominance. For a decade after this, Peto continued to live and work in Philadelphia; then in 1887 he made his way to Cincinnati. Significantly, this move was in response to a commission to paint a large *trompe-l'oeil*, in the manner of Harnett's *After the Hunt*, for a Cincinnati tavern. As a result of this trip, Peto met his future wife.

31 William M. Harnett *The Old Violin* 1886
The painting, which was later to be the subject of a popular chromolithograph, caused a furore when exhibited at the Cincinnati Industrial Exposition and had to be protected by a policeman stationed beside it.

OPPOSITE

32 William M. Harnett *The Faithful Colt* 1890
The quasi-religious depiction of the revolver, a popular symbol of the Wild West and its frontiersmen, provoked, on its rediscovery in 1935, an affinity in modern audiences for Harnett's work and a revival of his reputation. When the Wadsworth Atheneum purchased it soon after its reappearance, it was the first work by the artist to enter a public collection.

33 **John F. Peto** *The Cup We All Race 4* *c.* 1900
It has been suggested that the painting was intended as a
hidden jibe against the temperance Methodists who surrounded
Peto at Island Heights, New Jersey. As with Harnett's *The
Faithful Colt* (Ill. 32), it seems like a foreshadowing of the Pop
Art of the 1960s, although, unlike Harnett's overtly symbolic
works, Peto chose common, everyday objects.

After his marriage he began to spend more and more time in New Jersey, at
the small resort community of Island Heights. Here he was much in demand,
but as a musician rather than as a painter; he played the cornet at local camp
revival meetings.[9] In 1889 Peto built a house at Island Heights and began to
live there permanently, settling into the life of an obscure provincial artist.

Not all of Peto's paintings are still-lifes. There are unpretentious landscapes, and even a self-portrait showing the painter in his studio. Still-life
does, however, form the core of his output. He was not quite as skilful in
trompe-l'oeil as Harnett, but some of his efforts are extremely convincing, such
as the early *Office Board for Smith Bros. Coal Co.* (1879), a good example of a
'rack picture', with letters, papers and other small objects seemingly taped or
pinned to a board, designed in this case as a coded summary or portrait of
business activity.

Like Harnett, Peto also understood the symbolic value of isolated objects.
The Cup We All Race 4 (*c.* 1900) is a battered tin mug hanging from a hook
screwed into a board. Characteristically, Peto chooses a humble object, with
none of the romantic overtones of a violin or a Colt. This quotidian quality is

the real point. The title deliberately stresses this fact; it seems to have been carved into the board by a child inexpertly wielding a penknife.

Peto's 'non-deceptive' still-lifes also almost invariably feature everyday objects, in contrast to Harnett, who liked exotic bric-a-brac. One particularly charming homage to the poetry of the everyday is *Market Basket, Hat and Umbrella*, which demonstrates how close Peto's sensibility sometimes comes to that of the eighteenth-century French still-life painter, Jean-Baptiste-Siméon Chardin. Compared with that of other American artists in the same group, Peto's work has a peculiarly luminous look: his powdery surfaces and blurred edges show that his attention was fixed less on the objects he was painting than on their role as catalysts for the play of light. The bluntness of his brushwork, which derives from this preoccupation, suggests an affinity with later American artists such as Edward Hopper and Wayne Thiebaud.

Peto has a melancholic feeling for processes of damage and decay, exemplified in his still-lifes of books, injured, tossed aside, sometimes stripped of their covers. His paintings of this type have a kind of rhythmical instability of arrangement which in itself speaks of the passage of time. It is no accident

34 **John F. Peto** *Market Basket, Hat and Umbrella* after 1890

If *The Cup We All Race 4* (Ill. 33) has affinities with Pop Art, Peto's modest but beautifully incandescent painting has an undoubted resemblance to the work of the eighteenth-century still-life painter, Chardin.

that Peto associated these feelings with books above all: as one authority on his work remarks, Peto 'gazed on books as metaphors of artistic experience'.[10] For all the apparent restriction of his subject matter, he uses these books, and still-life in general, as a way of apprehending a world eternally in flux.

Almost entirely self-taught, John Haberle may well have thought of himself as even more of an outsider than either Harnett or Peto. A clue to his attitudes is supplied by a painting defiantly entitled *Reproduction*. This is a 'money' picture, similar to others done by Harnett and Peto, but both title and imagery make it clear that it is also a deliberate defiance of the establishment. The immediate inspiration seems to have been Harnett's well-publicized brush with the United States Secret Service, which objected to one of his paintings of five-dollar bills on the ground that it was a counterfeit within the meaning of the law.[11] Harnett accepted the warning and abandoned this kind of subject. At some point Haberle received a similar warning, but this only made him more stubborn in pursuing the path he had chosen. *Reproduction* is a gibe at the authorities, which at the same time defies the spectator to deny its reality.

The main image in *Reproduction* is a worn 1880 ten-dollar bill. There are also two one-cent stamps, a tintype self-portrait of the artist and two newspaper clippings. These, unlike the clippings in Harnett's and Peto's paintings, are perfectly legible. The larger of the two reads as follows: 'a work of the kind yet . . . / it is done entirely with a brush / John Haberle the Counter |feiter (Special to the World) New Haven., Dec. 12 / |de|ceives the eye into the belief that the ...' Beneath is a crude illustration depicting a bearded counterfeiter with a family resemblance to the artist, at work by lamplight with a pistol and a dagger hanging on the wall behind him. The second, smaller clipping reads: 'A COUNTERFEIT. / A Remarkable Painting of a ten-dollar/ sil|ver Uni|ted States' bill / A D|eception that would humbug Barnum.' The clippings simultaneously announce and unmask the deception.

Recent commentators have been at pains to tease out the *Vanitas* theme in the American still-life and *trompe-l'oeil* painting of the late nineteenth century. This reference to mortality was inherent in the European still-life tradition, and Harnett at least was not averse to using traditional *Vanitas* symbols, such as the skull. Yet it can also be said that many of these works achieve their force because they eschew transcendental overtones. They are reflections of a new American materialism, barely mitigated by moments of sentimental nostalgia. They stress the materiality of the material world, yet at the same time, paradoxically, cause us to question the evidence of our senses. The paintings of money add ironic reinforcement to both of these points.

These artists proposed a popular, democratic art which was different from the idealizing high art approved of by professional aesthetes. In a society where aesthetic matters were, by established pioneer tradition, considered to be largely the business of women, they produced art which often seemed to exclude females and to address itself specifically to men. There is a persistent legend that Harnett's patrons were philistine businessmen of little sensibility. One of his patrons, however, was the greatest 'eye' of his time – that ruthless and grim-faced businessman, Henry Clay Frick.

35 John F. Peto *Still-Life with Lard-Oil Lamp* 1900s
Both Peto and Harnett (Ills 29–32) painted still-lifes of second-hand books, which seem intended as a comment on the way in which time erodes the apparent solidity of established knowledge.

36 John F. Haberle *Reproduction* 1888
The artist seems to have painted this, his best-known work, as a satirical retort to the efforts made by the United States Secret Service to stop artists producing pictures that featured such accurate representations of US currency. Harnett (Ills 29–32) had been briefly under arrest for counterfeiting in 1886.

CHAPTER 4

Realism and the American Impressionists

Of those Impressionists not French by birth, it was the Americans who were the closest to the original movement. However, the element of scientific investigation inherent in true Impressionist doctrine was precisely what they were most inclined to omit. They were interested neither in the actual mechanics of vision (which fascinated Claude Monet), nor in a clear-eyed presentation of the realities of contemporary life, which artists like Degas and Edouard Manet took from the naturalist French literature of their time – from, for example, the novels of Gustave Flaubert and Emile Zola. It is significant that no literature of this kind existed in the United States. The chief thing that the American Impressionists took from the movement was a new attitude to landscape, which they painted with a new directness and informality.

Only one American artist – not a landscapist – took part in the succession of exhibitions held in Paris that eventually established Impressionism as a distinct style, opposed to the art of the official Salons. This was Mary Cassatt (1844–1926). Cassatt's background, social position and career were very different from those of the artists so far discussed. The world she inhabited was far removed from that of William Harnett, for example. The idea that her work might find a role as an attraction in a saloon would undoubtedly have horrified her – not that there was ever any risk of such an eventuality. The distance between her and the slightly fusty *petit-bourgeois* comfort of the world Eakins inhabited was also very great.

Cassatt did nevertheless have a common training with Eakins. Like him (and like both Harnett and Peto), she studied at the Pennsylvania Academy of the Fine Arts. She also had a period of study in Paris, even working for a while with the same master, Gérôme. There the resemblance stops. Cassatt came from a rich family and, after overcoming some mild initial resistance, was able to shape her life to suit herself. The process was eased by the fact that she seems to have shared the conventional tastes of women of her class and period in everything but matters to do with painting.

After initial study in Paris in the 1860s, Cassatt returned home to Pennsylvania, but soon decided that she wanted to live and work in Europe. She settled in France, and persuaded her parents and her sister Lydia to follow her there. The extended family group – relations and friends – provided her with her themes. As a woman artist she could not explore the kinds of subject matter – backstage scenes, café-concerts, even brothels – which became typical of other members of the Impressionist group, and especially of her chief mentor within it, Degas. There are other indications that she preserved a stubborn separateness, despite her close involvement with Impressionism. For example, she kept her legal residence in Philadelphia throughout her life and made it plain that she considered herself an American, not a French artist.[1] Writing about Cassatt's work in her own lifetime, in 1910, the French critic André Mellério was at pains to stress this. 'Here', he wrote, 'is a direct and significant expression of the American character.'[2]

Degas and Cassatt were drawn together by mutual admiration. Cassatt saw examples of Degas's work in the window of a Paris picture-dealer. He, in turn, noticed one of her early paintings at the Salon. 'There is someone who feels as I do,' was his comment.[3] Admiration ripened into friendship, and it was Degas

37 **Mary Cassatt** *Girl Arranging Her Hair* 1886
Cassatt's treatment of subject matter typically identified with her mentor, Degas, is less voyeuristic than his, but arguably even more realistic in its direct presentation of everyday details.

38 Mary Cassatt
The Oval Mirror 1901
Degas considered this 'the finest work
that Mary Cassatt ever did'. It makes
use of pictorial metaphor uncharacteristic of the artist: the dressing-table
mirror of the title provides a joint
halo, suggesting that the true subject
is the Madonna and Child.

who, in 1877, invited Cassatt to show with the Impressionists. It was not
merely compatibility of taste that eased her way into the group. Like some
other members – Degas himself, Berthe Morisot, Gustave Caillebotte – she was
well-bred, educated and provided with a private income.

Cassatt's work, like that of Degas, breaks many of the rules of classic
Impressionism. She did not work in broken touches; nor did she eschew the use
of black. Like Degas, she was deeply attached to the art of the past. Her mothers
and children, the subjects she painted perhaps most frequently, are heavily
indebted to the Renaissance masters Raphael and Correggio, for example,
whom she studied in Italy and in the Louvre. *The Oval Mirror* (1901), which
Degas considered 'the finest work that Mary Cassatt ever did',[4] shows this
innate classicism very clearly. What drew the two artists together, however, was
not a taste for the Old Masters, but a passion for real stringency of line. Both
were inspired draughtsmen, anxious to set down the thing seen, exactly and
without fudging. In devising compositions, both were influenced by
photography and by the radical croppings featured in Japanese *ukiyoe* prints.

The Japanese influence makes Cassatt's prints – which many now consider
her best work – less confrontational than her drawings and pastels. These have
a forthrightness of approach which disconcerted her contemporaries, especially
in America, where Cassatt's reputation grew only slowly. Her first one-person
exhibition in the United States did not take place until 1891 and consisted
only of prints. Her second, in 1895, was coolly received. The *New York Times*
described her paintings thus: 'These last are frequently hard, and have a
tendency towards the brutal … A rude strength, at times out of keeping with
the subject, is noticeable, and takes away in a measure from the charm of
femininity.'[5]

This contains a core of truth. Cassatt's hardness – the tough downrightness
of her outlines, for example – has been concealed from posterity by her

domestic subject matter, and by our own sentimentality about the content of her paintings.

Through her influence over her wealthy collector friend Louisine Havemeyer, Cassatt became one of the main channels whereby French Impressionist art reached America. She also advised other important American collectors, such as Mrs Potter Palmer of Chicago. In a sense, however, her impassioned advocacy of the work of the 'core' Impressionists set up a barrier. By stressing the unique merits of the French version of the style, she tended to delay its absorption into the mainstream of American art.

An American painter on the fringes of French Impressionism whom Cassatt liked at first (though later she had little time for him) was John Singer Sargent (1856–1925), twelve years younger than herself. Born in Florence, the son of prosperous American expatriates, Sargent did not visit the United States until he was a young adult, and all his artistic training took place abroad. The formative influence on his early work was the fashionable French portraitist Emile-Auguste Carolus-Duran (1838–1914), whose studio Sargent entered in 1874. Carolus-Duran, though fashionable, was also a progressive, a friend of Manet and – following in Manet's footsteps – a disciple of Velázquez. His advice to his pupils was: 'Search for the half-tones, place your accents, and then the lights ... Velázquez, Velázquez, Velázquez, ceaselessly study Velázquez.'[6]

Sargent clearly took him at his word. One of his important early commissions, *The Daughters of Edward D. Boit* (1882), is closely related to *Las Meninas*, which Sargent had copied on a visit to Spain in 1879. The handling also shows the effect of Sargent's close study of Frans Hals – he made a special visit to Haarlem in 1880. The Boit work, however, is less realist than its models, as can be seen not only from the work itself but from Henry James's sensitive reaction to it. James calls the painting a 'view of a rich, dim, rather generalized French interior ... which encloses the life and seems to be the happy play-world of a group of charming children'.[7] Sargent was, after all, attempting to depict the universe of James's own novels – although in these the vision is more specific and more subtly nuanced.

Yet at this period Sargent was also quite closely in touch with Monet. In the 1880s, in addition to portraits, he painted a series of brilliant Impressionist scenes in which Monet's influence is paramount. In 1883 Berthe Morisot actually tried to get Sargent to exhibit with the Impressionist group,[8] but he refused, apparently out of prudence.

Prudence did not save him from a considerable scandal the following year, when his society portrait *Madame X (Madame Pierre Gautreau)* was seen at the Salon. A dazzlingly self-conscious portrayal of an equally self-conscious and artificial personality, it caused such an uproar – because of what it seemed to say about the subject's moral character – that Sargent transferred his activities to England, where he rapidly became the most sought-after portrait painter of his time, the celebrator of the late Victorian and Edwardian plutocracy. In conformity with English taste, many of these portraits borrow formulae from eighteenth-century English painters such as Reynolds and Thomas Gainsborough. For all the sharp-focus glitter of many of the details, they can hardly be regarded as contributions to realist art. They transfer the sitters to a deliberately heightened sphere.

ABOVE
39 **John Singer Sargent** *Madame X (Madame Pierre Gautreau)* 1884
This decolleté portrait of a Franco-American society beauty caused a scandal at the Paris Salon. The outraged sitter demanded that the artist withdraw the work from exhibition, but Sargent replied that 'nothing could be said of the canvas worse than had been said in print of her appearance'. He retained the canvas and in later life thought it was the best thing he had ever painted.

ABOVE RIGHT
40 **John Singer Sargent** *The Daughters of Edward D. Boit* 1882
This is clearly indebted to Velázquez's *Las Meninas*, which Sargent copied on a visit to Madrid in 1879.

Sargent eventually wearied of the drudgery of portraiture and – despite intense pressure from would-be clients – more or less gave it up, though he continued to make glamorized portrait drawings as an easier alternative. In the paintings he made for himself during the final phase of his career, he reverted to a species of realist vision. The watercolours he made on his now-frequent travels, in Spain, Italy and elsewhere, have much of the informal directness of Winslow Homer's work in the same medium. What they lack is the precision and tightness or else the drab subject matter often popularly associated with realism in art. Their realism lies in their spontaneous, snapshot-like character. They exist simply as records of particular moments, things rescued from the flux of time.

With his international clientele, Sargent enjoyed success at a much higher level than that achieved by American Impressionists such as William Merritt Chase and Childe Hassam, who spent most of their careers at home.

William Merritt Chase (1847–1916), born in Indianapolis, studied in New York at the National Academy of Design and later at the Royal Academy in Munich. His reason for going to Munich rather than Paris was that the

41 John Singer Sargent *Paul Helleu Sketching with His Wife* 1889
Though the informal composition seems to ape the loosely structured Impressionist manner, this cannot conceal its underlying geometry. The taut design is based on the long diagonal of the canoe, contrasted with the shallow inverted *U* of Helleu's bowed legs.

42 John Singer Sargent *Study of a Nude Model* after 1900
The subject is Luigi Mancini, one of a family of handsome Italians whom Sargent employed as models for his Boston Library murals.

43 William Merritt Chase
The Tenth Street Studio
1880
The plethora of objects is intended to mirror both the aesthetic superiority and the financial success of the artist.

curriculum seemed more 'serious': 'I could saw wood in Munich instead of frittering in the Latin merry-go-round.'[9]

He enrolled at the Academy in 1872. The chief influence there was the sober realism of Wilhelm Leibl (1840–1900), which was rapidly becoming pervasive in German art. Chase's early work shows that he absorbed this obediently, but not quite as thoroughly as some fellow Americans, such as Frank Duveneck (1849–1919), who also studied in Munich. There was a hedonistic side to Chase, which manifested itself as soon as he got back to New York after six years in Europe. He was already reasonably well known, through paintings sent back from Germany to important American exhibitions. Once he had returned, he was careful to increase his personal visibility. He took a large studio in a prestigious building and filled it with exotic bric-a-brac (the studio itself provided material for art); he dressed his black servant as a Nubian prince; and he paraded the streets with a pair of wolfhounds on a leash.

While now basing himself in New York, Chase continued to travel. In 1881 he went to Spain to study Velázquez and other Spanish masters, and he made further trips to Europe in 1882 and 1885. The 1885 visit included a memorable interlude with the combustible James Abbott McNeill Whistler.

Chase made friends with him, painted his portrait (very much in Whistlerian style) and then, after an interval, quarrelled with him.

Chase's mature work is eclectic. There are still traces of Leibl's realism; there is a touch of classicism (perhaps mediated by some of Whistler's work); and there is the impact of French Impressionism, now becoming more widely known in America. Chase seems to have had little personal contact with leading members of the original Impressionist movement. He met Sargent in Paris in 1881 and 1882,[10] but after that made only occasional visits to the city – he seems to have preferred London, Madrid and Florence. Yet there is one group of paintings in which the influence of Impressionist *plein air* painting is overt: the landscapes painted at Shinnecock, Long Island, during successive summer visits in the late 1880s and early 1890s. These landscapes are realist in a special sense. What makes them so is not merely Chase's skill in catching particular effects of light and atmosphere, but an informal and at first sight unstructured quality. For all their apparent modesty of aim, such paintings provided prototypes for other, later attempts to describe the true nature of American scenery, especially in the Northeast. They offer an effective answer to the rhetoric of a Bierstadt or a Church.

44 William Merritt Chase *Near the Beach,*
Shinnecock c. 1895
Remarkable as an attempt to make a truthful depiction of an apparently unstructured landscape with no traditionally 'picturesque' elements.

45 Childe Hassam *Rainy Day, Boston* 1885
Hassam's early low-toned work anticipates the work of Robert Henri (Ills 49–51). With its plunging perspectives, it also has a surprising affinity to some of Richard Estes's city views (Ills 215–17). The wide expanse of foreground suggests the influence of the camera.

OPPOSITE
46 Childe Hassam *Allies' Day* 1917
An adroit adaptation of Manet's *Rue Mosnier with Flags* for patriotic purposes.

Childe Hassam (1859–1935) was a crucial decade younger than Chase. He started his career as Homer had done, working as a freelance illustrator, and began painting in 1878, the year in which he joined the Boston Art Club's evening classes. One of the important early influences on his work was that of the Dutch proto-Impressionist Johan Barthold Jongkind (1819–91). In 1878–79 Hassam was already working directly from nature. Later he was to protest: 'I have to debunk the idea that I learned to paint in France. I learned to paint in Boston before I ever went to France.'[11]

The mistake was a natural one, since much of Hassam's work has a distinctly French accent. He picked this up in the three years from 1886 to 1889, which he spent in Paris. Like many important American artists, he studied at the Académie Julian; but the chief gift that Paris made to him seems to have been a feeling for contemporary urban life as a subject for art. It can also be argued that the years in Paris simply brought out something which was inherent. If Hassam's late flag paintings of New York, showing the city bedecked during World War I, are among his most brilliant and delightful, his most original work probably came earlier. His *Rainy Day, Boston* (1885) to some extent anticipated the work of Robert Henri and other members of The Eight. The flag paintings of 1917, like the well-known *Allies' Day*, are simply accomplished reflections of what Manet had done many years earlier, in the two versions of the *Rue Mosnier with Flags*.

CHAPTER 5

The Ashcan School

As a designation for a group of American artists, the term 'Ashcan School' does not appear until 1934, when Holger Cahill and Alfred H. Barr, Jr employed it in their book *Art in America*. Before that, however, journalists had seized on the notion that these artists used ashcans as a metaphor for the grimier realities of urban life. As early as 1906, for instance, the *New York World* quoted Robert Henri (1865–1929) as saying: 'It takes more than love of art to see character and meaning and even beauty in a crowd of east side children tagging after a street piano or hanging over garbage cans …'[1]

Garbage cans were, of course, not only sordid but in a certain sense also emblems of modernity. The Ashcan School painters represent the crucial moment of transition between the artistic values of the nineteenth century and those of Modernism itself. Before Modernism, the assumption was that art would be representational, if not actually realist. After Modernism, to be realist meant making a conscious and often difficult choice.

The transition was symbolized by a single important event: the Armory Show of 1913, which completely changed the American art scene by introducing Cubism and the whole mainstream of Modernist development. The Ashcan School and their friends and allies were the chief organizers of this event, though it seems clear that they did not recognize what a drastic change the exhibition would bring with it. In fact it was the Armory Show that deprived Henri and his associates of their hard-won, and comparatively recent, leadership of the American vanguard.

The Ashcan School's leadership was itself founded on an exhibition – much smaller and less ambitious than the Armory Show. In 1908 eight artists, later to be known simply as The Eight, held a collective show at the Macbeth Galleries, at 450 Fifth Avenue in New York. The exhibition was a protest against prevailing policies at the National Academy of Design, then the chief showplace for leading American artists; it was a sensational success with the fashionable New York audience, if not entirely so with the critics. People queued to see it, lining the corridor outside the gallery before it opened each morning at nine.[2] Later, the exhibition was shown for a second time at the Pennsylvania Academy of the Fine Arts – an appropriate venue, since many of the participants had close connections with Philadelphia, and had lived and worked there for significant periods.

The artists who took part in the Macbeth Galleries exhibition, in addition to Robert Henri (who was generally regarded as the moving spirit), were John Sloan, William J. Glackens, George Luks, Everett Shinn, Ernest Lawson, Arthur B. Davies and Maurice B. Prendergast. Only five of The Eight can plausibly be described as realists. Of the others, Lawson (1873–1939) was a painter of landscapes, loosely Impressionist in style but with little grip on observed reality, whose work became more and more stereotyped as his career progressed. Davies (1862–1925) was a kind of Symbolist, a painter of poetic fantasies. The work of Prendergast (1850–1924) offers a close equivalent to what the Nabis were producing at the same time in Paris. What brought all these men together was not a commitment to realism as such, but opposition to the feeble academic art of the time, and resentment at the slights of an academic cabal.

Among the five who were committed to realism, Henri was to some extent isolated from the rest. He was more sophisticated, better educated, more

47 **William J. Glackens** *Chez Mouquin* 1905
Mouquin's restaurant at 28th Street and 6th Avenue was a favourite New York meeting-place for members of The Eight. The intimate, close-up view of the figures is uncharacteristic of the artist.

articulate and more ambitious. In one sense, he saw himself as a direct heir of Thomas Eakins: he was indeed probably the first artist to understand Eakins's centrality to the American tradition, though this understanding may have come late. When the Metropolitan Museum put on an Eakins memorial exhibition in 1917, Henri wrote an open letter to members of the Art Students' League, urging members to study the show and learn from it:

> Thomas Eakins was a man of great character. He was a man of iron will and his will was to paint and carry out his life as he thought it should go. This he did. It cost him dearly but in his works we have the precious result of his independence, his generous heart and his big mind. Eakins was a deep student of life, and with a great love he studied humanity frankly. He was not afraid of what his study revealed to him.[3]

Yet it was also true that Henri consciously belonged to a different generation. He admired some of the European artists who had influenced Eakins – in particular the great Spanish realists, Velázquez and Ribera. However, he passed well beyond Eakins in his admiration for artists like Manet and Whistler, both of whom had a profound impact on his own work. He had no time for Eakins's admired master, Gérôme; he absorbed the whole lesson of Impressionism, even if he ultimately rejected it, turning instead to painters like Hals and Rembrandt and to the non-Impressionist side of Manet. His artistic influences were so multifarious, and so visible, that it is fair to assert that Henri for the most part saw reality indirectly, through the mirror held up to it by art, and that this marks a crucial difference between Eakins and himself. His work, unlike that of the earlier artist, is seldom a direct confrontation with the facts. Any realistic element in his work is heavily qualified, because it is largely second-hand.

For Henri, therefore, Eakins was less a stylistic exemplar than a kind of father-figure. In order to understand the importance of this side of the relationship, one also has to understand elements of Henri's own biography. Henri was not his original name. His father, John Jackson Cozad, was first a successful professional gambler and then a land speculator, who in 1873 founded the town of Cozad, Nebraska. Dreams of a prosperous future in the fast-developing West collapsed just under a decade later, when Cozad killed a drunken cattleman in a fight. He and his family left Nebraska in a hurry, and changed their name in order to confuse the trail. Cozad himself became Thomas H. Lee; his son now passed himself off as an adopted child and took a name different from that of his father. Though Henri remained on good terms with his parents throughout their lives (his father supported him financially when he decided to train as an artist), this abrupt break in continuity during his vulnerable adolescent years must have fostered a later search for roots.

He studied first at the Pennsylvania Academy of the Fine Arts, entering in 1886, hot on the heels of Eakins's dismissal. Eakins was still a pervasive influence, however. Henri was later to recall that, when he was a student at the Academy, he regarded Eakins's *The Gross Clinic* as 'the most wonderful painting [he] had ever seen'.[4] Significantly, he chose Eakins's most Rembrandtesque, Old Masterly work. The most influential figure on the teaching staff of the Academy during Henri's period there was Thomas

Anshutz (1851–1912), who had played a prominent part in the cabal against Eakins, but who nevertheless continued the latter's teaching methods in only slightly modified form.

A few years before Henri became his student, Anshutz painted his most remarkable picture. *Ironworkers' Noonday Rest* (1880) is a formal, classical composition, but one which takes its material from everyday life, like Eakins's *The Swimming Hole*. Yet there is an important difference between the two works. Eakins depicts a rural idyll; Anshutz's painting is a celebration of proletarian America. It is the first fully realized statement of industrial subject matter in American art.

In 1888, feeling that the Pennsylvania Academy had no more to teach him, Henri left for Paris. He entered the Académie Julian, and studied under the academic arch-*pompier* William Bouguereau. Paris had much more influence on him than it did on Eakins. He became aware of Claude Monet and admired his paintings of *Haystacks*, exhibited at the Durand-Ruel gallery in 1891. He

48 **Thomas Anshutz** *Ironworkers' Noonday Rest* 1880
The first fully realized statement of industrial subject matter in American art by an associate, then opponent, of Eakins at the Pennsylvania Academy of the Fine Arts.

49 **Robert Henri** *La Neige* 1899
Painted when Henri was living and working in Paris,
La Neige was purchased from the Salon of 1899 by the
French government.

began to read the novels of the French naturalist school – Zola, and the much
lighter-weight Paul de Kock. He saw the fashionable periodical *La Vie moderne*,
which was backed by Auguste Renoir's patroness, Mme Charpentier.

After three years in Paris, Henri was forced to return home by a temporary
crisis in his father's financial affairs. He refused to settle in Atlantic City, where
his family were now living, or in New York, and chose instead to live and work
in Philadelphia. It was at this point that Henri, now a strong personality in his
own right, began to exert a significant influence over his contemporaries. He fell
in with a group of young men who were then working for various Philadelphia
newspapers. His effect on them was described by one of the group, John Sloan
(1871–1951):

> In Philadelphia in the nineties, there was a group of newspaper artists, plain and
> rather normal young men making their livings as craftsmen – and we became
> painters because Robert Henri had that magic ability as a teacher which inspires
> and provokes his followers into action. He was a catalyst; he was an
> emancipator, liberating American art from its youthful academic conformity,
> and liberating the individual artist from repressions that held back his natural
> creative ability.[5]

Yet Henri's band of disciples brought something to the union as well. To be an
artist reporter was to be a member of an extremely specialized group, whose
heyday lasted for barely a decade – from 1890 to 1900 – before the profession
was superseded by advances in techniques of photographic reproduction. It was
the newspaper artist's job to give visual embodiment in his sketches to what the
paper described. As often as possible he made rough drawings on the spot;

50 Robert Henri
Herself 1913
A Hals-like portrayal of an
Irish peasant woman, painted
on Henri's first visit to
Ireland.

sometimes he had to work from verbal descriptions given by eye-witnesses. He
needed not only great fluency and speed but a highly trained visual memory in
work which constantly drew his attention to everyday things.

Henri's connection with Sloan and the rest seems to have led him towards an
eventual renunciation of the Impressionist techniques with which he
experimented in the mid-1890s. Sloan noted, for example, that: 'We were
opposed to Impressionism with its blue shadows and orange lights, because it
seemed "unreal".'[6] Nevertheless there always remained a gulf between Henri
and his disciples. Where they emphasized the grittiness, and sometimes the
squalor, of contemporary urban life, he made little use of such themes. In one
way or another, his pictures often put a certain emotional distance between
himself and the chosen subject matter. This was the case throughout his career.
La Neige (1899), purchased by the French government for the Luxembourg, is
a hushed view of Paris under snow, almost devoid of human activity. *El Picador*
(1908) is not a reaction to an individual but a paraphrase of Manet's *Torero
Saluting*, painted forty years earlier. *Herself* (1913) is an Irish peasant woman
seen through the eyes of Hals.

During the period from 1895 to 1900 Henri divided his time between
Philadelphia and Paris. *La Neige* was painted during the last of his Paris
sojourns. Eventually he settled in New York and became a charismatic teacher
at the New York School of Art, where he completely eclipsed the original
founder, William Merritt Chase. His friends from Philadelphia followed him,
and the Ashcan School as we know it was born.

Sloan, William J. Glackens (1870–1938), Everett Shinn (1876–1963) and
George Luks (1867–1933) had all been newspaper artists. What they brought

51 Robert Henri *El Picador* 1908
Essentially a derivative artist, Henri is in
this case paraphrasing Manet's *Torero
Saluting* of 1866.

52 **John Sloan** *Hairdresser's Window* 1907
Exhibited in 1908 at the Macbeth Galleries exhibition, which
established the collective reputation of The Eight, this was
especially singled out by one hostile critic for its 'vulgarity'.

with them was the immediacy of observation and appetite for contemporary
facts required by their original profession. They lacked Henri's technical
sophistication, though like him they painted in a fluid, tonal manner derived
from Velázquez, Hals and Manet. However, their work has a greater
authenticity than his: a sense of places, events, people and objects genuinely
experienced. There are parallels – though probably no contacts – with the work
of the contemporary English Camden Town painters, such as Walter Sickert.

Sloan's *Hairdresser's Window* (1907) is a typical Ashcan School work –
demotic and democratic, but also essentially detached and without any strong
moral overtone. The box-within-a-box composition can be traced back to some
of the genre scenes of Mount, while the figures are not far from caricature. The
same slightly caricatured vitality appears in Luks's *The Spielers* (1905), which
shows two slum children dancing in the street. Luks was the most notoriously
bohemian member of the circle, and in some ways the most mysterious: little is

53 George Luks
The Spielers 1905
The boldness with which
the image of slum children
dancing is put down on
canvas echoes Luks's dictum:
'Technique do you say? My
slats! Say, listen you – it's in
you or it isn't. Who taught
Shakespeare technique? …
Guts! Guts! Life! Life!
That's my technique.'

54 Everett Shinn
Mouquin's 1904
An exterior view of the
restaurant whose interior is
seen in Glackens's painting
(Ill. 47).

known about his early life, though he claimed to have been taught at one point
by Renoir. The energy displayed by the children is a reflection of Luks's own
abounding appetite for life.

Not all Ashcan School paintings, however, are vignettes of low life. Like the
'Intimist' wing of the Nabis group in France (Pierre Bonnard and Edouard
Vuillard), the Ashcan School painters liked to paint people who were familiar to
them in equally familiar surroundings. The subjects in Glackens's restaurant
scene, *Chez Mouquin's* (1905), are known individuals, not street types. The
Impressionist derivation is obvious: there are similar scenes in the work of
Degas and of Henri de Toulouse-Lautrec. Glackens's vision, however, is not as
judgmental as theirs; his sitters are more at ease with themselves. The painting
is reportage, with no touch of social satire, no tinge of bitterness. Shinn, in an
exterior view of the same restaurant painted the previous year – the place was
popular with all members of the group – offered an informal snapshot of New
York in bad weather. The liveliness of the scene makes a fascinating contrast
with the repressive quietude of Henri's *La Neige*.

One artist who did not participate in the exhibition of The Eight at the Macbeth Galleries, but who is nevertheless always associated with the Ashcan School, is George Bellows (1882–1925). From 1904, Bellows was a pupil of Henri's at the New York School of Art, and Henri was the dominant influence in his early work; yet there was also, from the very start, a strong influence from Eakins. Things that Henri only paid lip service to, Bellows put into practice.

The attraction of Eakins's work expressed itself in two ways – through Bellows's choice of subject matter, and through his attitude to composition. *Forty–Two Kids* (1907) is a reprise, in a more informal vein, of *The Swimming Hole*. A recent critic has referred to 'the inspired novelty of the close-up, comic-strip quality of the naked boys, as well as of the deft calligraphy of the brushwork with which they are rendered'.[7] Other paintings show Bellows's interest in the kind of geometrically planned compositional system to be found in a number of Eakins's most satisfactory paintings, among them *The*

55 **George Bellows** *Forty-Two Kids* 1907
An informal paraphrase of Eakins's *The Swimming Hole* (Ill. 26), influenced by snapshot photography. When it was first exhibited, at the New York Academy in March 1908, one reviewer described the boys as 'looking more like maggots than like humans'. Shown in the same year at the Pennsylvania Academy, it was denied a prize because of its potentially offensive nature, despite the fact that the jury voted for it eight to two.

56 George Bellows
Dempsey and Firpo 1924
From a celebrated series of paintings of boxers, a subject also favoured by Eakins. The use of underlying geometric forms is conspicuous, but more dynamic than similar compositional devices in the work of Eakins.

Swimming Hole. Bellows's *Dempsey and Firpo* (1924), one of a series of paintings of boxers, owes much of its visual authority to the subtle way in which the painting has been constructed to achieve a sense of dynamism. He also seems to have been influenced by Anshutz: *Men of the Docks* (1912) has an affinity with *Ironworkers' Noonday Rest*.

Of all the artists who were overtaken by the events triggered by the Armory Show of 1913 (and he participated in its organization in addition to exhibiting in it), Bellows was in certain respects one of the most unfortunate. Though he was still young, the Armory Show immediately relegated him to the position of being a conservative, or at least a middle-of-the-road artist.

This was even more of an injustice than it seems at first sight, as there were aspects of Bellows's work which were in advance of their time, rather than abreast of or behind it. He can, for instance, be thought of as the true progenitor of the American social realists of the 1930s and 1940s. *Cliff Dwellers* (1913) abandons the amused detachment of the artists of the Ashcan School, and looks forward to the work of Ben Shahn and Reginald Marsh. More important than this, it is a landmark work because of the use it makes of material drawn from popular visual sources. A modern commentator, Marianne Doezema, observes:

> *Cliff Dwellers* seemed convincing to some members of its first audience in part because it seemed to reaffirm commonly held conceptions of tenement district life – that its inhabitants were alien and inferior. But to late-twentieth-century eyes, the painting's departures from the 'real' seem obvious. It is first and

foremost a pictorial construction, in which spatial manipulations enhance
the evocative quality of the scene – most prominently the sense of chaotic and
oppressive crowding. In addition the bony angular bodies of the children in
the foreground and their exaggerated, awkward postures were part of a visual
language that signified the real life nature of the subject. Such distortions
derive from established conventions especially prevalent in mass media.[8]

In other words, in this painting Bellows was consolidating a tendency already
visible in the work of Sloan, Glackens, Shinn and Luks, who transferred ideas
and visual conventions generated by their hasty newspaper work into their
more considered activity as fine artists. As in some of the paintings of Harnett
and Peto, popular or mass culture had begun to make its contribution to the
development of a specifically American form of realism.

57 **George Bellows**
Cliff Dwellers 1913
This painting anticipates
the work of the social realists
of the 1930s, stressing the
effects of urbanization and
industrialization on the lives
of immigrants who inhabited
the tenements of New York's
lower East Side.

CHAPTER 6

Precisionism: the Realist Impulse and the New Avant-Garde

WHEREAS THE Ashcan School dealt with people, usually in urban settings and often observed with a lively sense of movement, Precisionism was an art of stillness, whose main subjects were buildings and machines. The human presence is implied in Precisionist paintings, but usually not directly stated. If figures are present, they play a minor part in the composition. With its preternatural clarity, its smooth, undifferentiated surfaces and its ability to discover strong formal relationships beneath under ordinary appearances, the style marked a turning point in the development of the realist impulse in American art. Essentially, it was an attempt to reconcile three trends: the new Modernist spirit, which had originated in Europe and was now taking root in the United States; the influence of photography; and the ingrained American desire to confront reality directly.

Each of these was subject to further modifying factors. For example, the Modernist art which made the most impact in the United States was Cubist, and also to some extent Futurist. Elements of both styles are present in Marcel Duchamp's *Nude Descending a Staircase* (1912), which was one of the major sensations of the Armory Show. However, these avant-garde styles arrived in America before American art had fully absorbed the influence of Paul Cézanne. Watercolours made by Charles Demuth and Charles Sheeler at the beginning of their careers show how important Cézanne's vision was to the new generation of American artists.

In turning towards Modernism, Americans did not entirely abandon the art of the past. Like artists in Europe, they found a new set of artistic heroes among the Old Masters. Velázquez, Rembrandt and Hals, the major influences of the period from 1880 to 1910, were replaced by Piero della Francesca, Masaccio and Giotto. Many artists now aspired to the grand classicism of Italian fresco painting.

The debt owed to photography by Precisionist painting is too obvious to need emphasizing. What does need to be emphasized is that this was a different kind of photography, more artful and more self-conscious than the material used by Eakins.

During the period immediately before World War I, photography everywhere – but perhaps most conspicuously in the United States – had been engaged in a struggle to be recognized as an independent art form. The Pictorialists, as they were called, used soft focus, deep shadows and brilliant highlights, and their work was often heavily manipulated during the printing and developing processes. What the camera saw was raw material, to be changed and altered by means of darkroom skills.

Alfred Stieglitz, originally part of the Pictorialist movement, eventually became the leader of a revolt against it. He championed what was termed 'pure photography', where the results were achieved chiefly through the careful selection of viewpoints and isolation of images. The photographs taken by Stieglitz and his followers tried to educate people to look at the world in a new way, and they made no pretence of being like traditional drawings and prints (as had often been the case with Pictorialist work). However, Stieglitz maintained photography's claim to be an art form in its own right, with its own vision, particular to itself. It was therefore ironic that the developments in painting became dependent on aspects of what he and his followers were doing.

58 **Charles Sheeler** *Suspended Power* 1939
Unit No. 2 being installed at the Tennessee Valley Authority's hydroelectric plant in Guntersville, Alabama. Sheeler deliberately depopulated the plant and tidied up the setting in order to achieve the curiously disturbing, threateningly phallic effect. *Fortune*, the magazine which commissioned the painting, took a somewhat different view, likening its hushed atmosphere, in the text accompanying the reproduction, to the halls of the Vatican.

The realist aesthetic of Precisionism was affected not only by its connections with a new sort of photography but by the often radical changes taking place in American society during the 1920s and 1930s. In American life, as in Precisionist art, industrial and rural images were increasingly sharply opposed. Precisionist painters responded to the industrialization of America by developing their own version of the machine aesthetic, which was now also widespread in Europe: machines and industrial buildings, rather than being thought of as ugly and brutal, became objects of study and appreciation. Yet at the same time there was nostalgia for the 'simple', rural, American values of the past. Old farm buildings, such as barns, and simple American antiques, such as Shaker chairs, became totem objects. What seemed to link the two kinds of subject matter was a cult of pure, uncluttered forms, made to fulfil a particular purpose and regarded as beautiful because of this. It was a world with no place for the lively, untidy humanity portrayed by the artists of the Ashcan School. Where Precisionist paintings included figures, these appeared only as markers, dwarfed by impersonal buildings or by huge industrial artifacts.

The Precisionists were a much looser grouping than the Ashcan School, whose members remained linked throughout their careers by strong bonds of friendship as well as by common attitudes to art. Whereas the Ashcan School, though still unnamed, made an immediate public impact thanks to the exhibition held at the Macbeth Galleries in 1908, Precisionism emerged only very gradually. The existence of common interests and stylistic similarities among a new group of American artists was not generally identified until the 1920s. At this time it became customary to use the adjective 'precise' to describe a particular aspect of current American painting.[1]

Among the artists so labelled were Charles Sheeler, Georgia O'Keeffe, Niles Spencer and Ralston Crawford. There was a consensus of sorts concerning a range of characteristics which these and other painters seemed to have in common. This consensus did not, however, achieve full definition until the beginning of the 1960s, by which time what it described was in the past:

> ... as exemplified in the work of Sheeler, Spencer, and Crawford, the work of the Precisionists is unique in its visual sobriety and acuity. Peopleless and emotionless, their paintings reflect little involvement with the social issues which attended the technological transformations of the day.[2]

This description is accurate as far as it goes, but does not fully acknowledge Precisionism's key role in the history of modern American realist art. This role is best understood by examining the career of Charles Sheeler (1883–1965).

Like so many American artists of the late nineteenth and early twentieth centuries, Sheeler came from Philadelphia. He studied first at the School of Industrial Art, then at the Pennsylvania Academy of the Fine Arts, where Anshutz was one of his teachers. Like Henri before him, he was thus in the direct line of artistic descent from Eakins, though at this point the latter's work did not interest him. He had the opportunity of seeing Eakins at work on the portrait of *Professor Leslie Miller* (1901). Watching him transfer a perspective drawing of his signature on to the painting, Sheeler concluded brashly that 'the man couldn't be a great artist, for we had learned somewhere that great artists painted only by inspiration, by a process akin to magic'.[3]

Sheeler was then under the influence of the flamboyant American Impressionist, William Merritt Chase. Chase led parties of students on trips to Europe, and the young artist travelled with him to London and Holland in 1904 and to Spain in 1905. The emphasis, as always with Chase, was on the study of Hals and Velázquez. In 1908 Sheeler made a third European tour in the company of his parents and of his great friend and fellow artist Morton Schamberg (1881–1918). They went to Italy, and Sheeler was greatly impressed by the precise design and solid architectonic forms of fifteenth-century fresco painters such as Masaccio and Piero della Francesca. Later they moved to Paris, where Sheeler and Schamberg saw the work of the Post-Impressionists and of the emergent avant-garde. In particular, Sheeler paid a visit to the apartment of the American collector Michael Stein, brother of the more famous Gertrude. He was stirred but also baffled by what he saw there:

> They were strange pictures which no amount of description, of which I had considerable in advance, could prepare me for the shock of coming upon for the first time ... But this much was evident in spite of this bewilderment, that something profound was in the making.[4]

New artists like Picasso and Henri Matisse were available at the Steins', but the artist who seems to have moved Sheeler particularly was Cézanne. When he returned to America, he continued to seek out Cézanne's work, probably visiting the small show of Cézanne's watercolours held at Stieglitz's 291 Gallery in 1911, and having access to the group of Cézannes which the Philadelphia collector Dr Albert Barnes had already started to amass. Around 1913 Sheeler took a photograph showing the interior of his own studio; among his own paintings is a framed reproduction of Cézanne's *The Smoker*.

In 1913 Sheeler sent five mildly Cézannesque paintings to the Armory Show, and these were enough to place him firmly in the American vanguard. He was less impressed by this success than by the distance he felt between his own work and what was taking place in Paris. He said of Matisse's *The Red Studio* (1911): 'We had never thought a picture could look like that – but there it was to prove it. Pictures like this offered further evidence that a picture could be as arbitrarily conceived as an artist wished.'[5]

During the second decade of the century Sheeler's interests and sensibility developed in two directions, apparently opposed but in fact closely linked. Around 1912 he and Schamberg, with whom he was sharing a Philadelphia studio, decided to turn to commercial photography as a way of making a living without compromising their art. Schamberg's specialty was portraiture. Sheeler's was architectural work and, later, works of art.

Soon, however, he began to think of photography as an artistic medium in its own right. His first photographic images made purely for their own sake featured details of a little house in Doylestown, Pennsylvania, which he and Schamberg had rented as a holiday retreat. Built about 1768, this modest dwelling was an excellent example of the simplicity and purity of American colonial architecture, all the more so because it had preserved intact many original details, such as iron hardware. Sheeler's landlord, a local landowner, was an enthusiast for early Americana, and drew the artist's attention not only to the merits of colonial architecture but to those of typical American artifacts of the eighteenth and early nineteenth centuries. Sheeler was to be a collector of these, and especially of Shaker furniture, all his life.

Sheeler's photographs taken in rural Pennsylvania were his first fully mature work – in advance of the paintings he was making at the same time. They show the fascination with the abstract patterning of ordinary things which was later to be a striking feature of his painted compositions. His use of tight framing and close-up frontal views in some of these images recalls compositional devices favoured by Harnett and Peto. For example, the identification of the actual subject with the picture-plane in Sheeler's photograph *Side of White Barn* (1917) offers a close parallel with the rack-pictures produced by the two masters of still-life.

Even before he took up photography seriously, Sheeler was in touch with Stieglitz, who was the arbiter of the New York avant-garde, especially in matters photographic. Stieglitz was greatly impressed with the new images and started to promote Sheeler as an up-and-coming new photographer. In 1918, as one of the judges, he was largely responsible for Sheeler's being awarded both first and fourth prizes in the thirteenth John Wanamaker photography exhibition, organized by the famous department store. This was more marked recognition than Sheeler had yet received as a painter.

Stieglitz was not Sheeler's only contact with the New York avant-garde. He was also increasingly friendly with the pioneer collectors Walter and Louise Arensberg, whom he got to know in 1916 and who soon became patrons of his. An area of mutual sympathy was Americana: the Arensbergs shared Sheeler's passion for simple American antiques. Their earliest purchases from him were abstracted studies of American barns - the equivalents, in terms of drawing, of the photograph *Side of White Barn*, though the photographic image has a more powerful presence.

Schamberg died of influenza in 1918, and Sheeler decided to move to New York. This brought him even more decisively into the Arensberg circle, and he actually lived in their apartment throughout the summer of 1921. The Arensbergs were celebrated for their hospitality; they liked to bring together all the leading avant-garde figures of the day, and especially the Dadaists. Duchamp, then living in New York, was a close friend of theirs, and Sheeler was greatly impressed by his personality. He later described him as 'built with the precision and sensitiveness of an instrument for making scientific machinery'.[6] What he admired was not Duchamp's ironic sense of humour, which seems to have passed him by, but his rigorous powers of analysis. Sheeler said of Duchamp's *Nude Descending a Staircase*, which belonged to the Arensbergs, that it was 'the very antithesis of what we had been taught. For in it the statement was all important and the means by which it was represented were skilfully concealed'.[7] In making this statement Sheeler was setting his own course for the future.

However, that course was not to be a conventionally avant-garde one. As the facts of his career demonstrate, Sheeler was not alienated from the society which surrounded him. His most interesting and productive years, from the mid-1920s to the mid-1940s, find him working in conjunction with the social tendencies of the time, and not resisting them, as Ben Shahn or the Soyer brothers were to do.

59 Charles Sheeler
Side of White Barn 1917
In this photograph, the identification of the actual subject with the picture-plane offers a parallel to some works by Harnett (Ills 29–32) and Peto (Ills 28, 33–35).

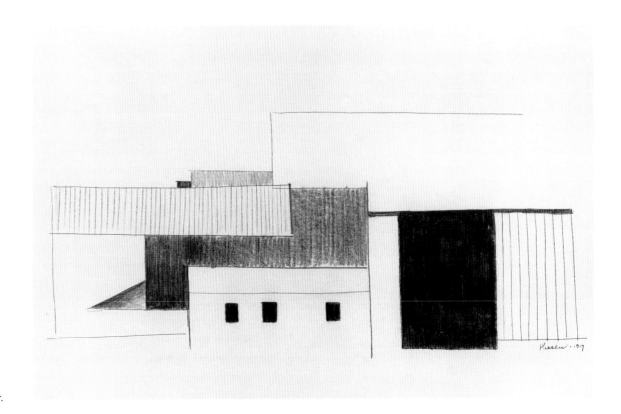

60 Charles Sheeler
Barn Abstraction 1917
Inspired by the vernacular architecture of Bucks County, Pennsylvania, the drawing also shows the impact of Cubism on Sheeler.

Events soon tended to attenuate Sheeler's links with the extreme avant-garde. In 1921 the Arensbergs left New York for California. In 1923 Duchamp departed for Paris. And in the same year Sheeler quarrelled with Stieglitz over some mild criticisms he had made in a review of Stieglitz's work. All of this tended to throw Sheeler into a completely different milieu, much closer to the mainstream.

Sheeler's earliest works in a fully developed realist manner fall into three categories. There are deliberately sparse still-lifes, intended, as he said, to show 'the absolute beauty we are accustomed to associate with objects suspended in a vacuum';[8] these have a certain kinship with some of Peto's work, but in the 1920s the latter was still awaiting rediscovery, and Sheeler was certainly unaware of him. Secondly, there are unpeopled interiors, often directly dependent on photographs made in Doylestown up to a decade earlier. Thirdly, there are cityscapes of New York, also derived ultimately from photographs or from the experimental film *Manhattan* (1920), which Sheeler had made in collaboration with his fellow photographer Paul Strand.

It was the skyscraper paintings that pointed most directly to the path Sheeler was now to follow. Their theme was excitement about the new and powerful America which had just emerged from World War I. They aimed to join what had been learned from the work of the French Cubists to a new vision of contemporary reality. The next step forward was to make representations of industry itself and of industrial objects which seemed to symbolize a new vision of the world.

Sheeler's first attempt at this kind of subject matter produced what is still, perhaps, his most famous painting. It sprang directly from his work as a commercial photographer. Around 1928 he was asked to make some pictures of the new liner SS *Majestic* for a shipping line brochure. The photographs were never published, but one was the source of *Upper Deck* (1929), which presents a complex composition of ventilators and manifolds whose industrial nature is clear, though the marine connection is only marginally apparent.

This painting provided a stepping-off point for other industrial images. The first major enterprise of this kind was already in train, as a photographic commission, by the time *Upper Deck* was painted. Late in 1927 the advertising agency N. W. Ayer arranged to send Sheeler to Detroit, to take pictures of the new Ford Motor Company plant at River Rouge. This plant had been purpose-designed to build the new Model A Ford, the replacement for the Model T, and was just going into production.

When he arrived, instead of concentrating on the cars themselves, or the workers, or the narrative of the assembly line process, Sheeler found inspiration in the new, totally unornamented buildings and in the great machines they housed. These he made into the stuff of myth, forceful and heroic. The photographic images he produced were immediately successful, much praised and widely published. Where Sheeler himself was concerned, they were perhaps too successful: they blocked his activity as a painter, because it seemed impossible to produce anything which had equivalent force. These doubts were resolved only when he made a sidestep and began work on *Upper Deck*. This enterprise, in turn, somehow freed him to work on paintings of the River Rouge plant itself.

OPPOSITE ABOVE
61 Charles Sheeler
Skyscrapers 1922
Like many of Sheeler's paintings,
this is closely based on one of his
own photographs. Comparison
between the painting and its
photographic source indicates how
he simplified and generalized the
shapes recorded by the lens.

OPPOSITE BELOW
62 Charles Sheeler
Upper Deck 1929
The most celebrated of Sheeler's
paintings, based on a photograph
made aboard the liner SS *Majestic*.

63 Charles Sheeler
Windows c. 1952
This raking view belongs to a later phase
of Sheeler's work in which he tended to
emphasize the dynamism of skyscraper
structures in addition to their verticality.

64 Charles Sheeler *American Interior* 1934
A study of some of Sheeler's own possessions. There is a typical Shaker table in the left foreground on which sits a Whieldon mug.

Thanks to his photographs, he was able to look at the visual material in a new way. It is worth quoting a recent description of *American Landscape*, the first painting in the River Rouge series, because it neatly contrasts the traditional and non-traditional elements in the work:

> The emphatic verticals of the crane, the smokestack, and their reflections rhythmically mark off spatial intervals, and the implied motion of the smoke rising and the crane lifting and dropping all suggest a grand epic: the story of the Rouge as the story of American industry. Yet the picture is without narrative climax or heroic focus. Rather, the additive composition, the compressed bands of space, the complex massing of details, are a product of the deliberately unselective camera eye. The flattened space of the picture and the expansion of the subject beyond our field of vision is an abstracting photographic device Sheeler had used inventively since *Side of White Barn*.[9]

One can say, in fact, that in some of the River Rouge paintings Sheeler deliberately revives elements of pre-Civil War American realism – when artists were still excitedly exploring the idea of the frontier, and finding ways to present things and experiences which seemed completely fresh and new – and, at the same time, looks forward to the dialogue with photography and the photographic vision which was to be typical of American realist art post-1960.

Sheeler's second major industrial series was commissioned by the Henry Luce organization, publishers of *Time*, *Fortune* and *Life*. He was asked to produce paintings (not photographs) on the theme of 'Power', the idea being to sell the idea of industry to an American population which still, in many regions of the country, remained predominantly agrarian and rural. During 1939 he travelled the United States in search of subject matter, using a camera as a sketchbook. The six works which resulted, five paintings and a tempera, were published in *Fortune* in December 1940.

In this series, architecture takes second place to the exploitation of significant detail, so as to produce images perhaps more ambiguous than the client envisaged. The painting that perhaps best expresses Sheeler's attitude to the machine is *Suspended Power*, which shows a giant turbine dangling in mid-air, in the process of being installed in the Tennessee Valley Authority's plant at Guntersville, Alabama. *Fortune*'s commentary on the image suggested that it had a hallowed air, and likened the hushed atmosphere of the painting to the halls of the Vatican. In fact, the turbine is portrayed as a phallic aggressor ready to plunge into the pit beneath it:

> In *Suspended Power*, perhaps more than in any other image in the series, the artist presents with great subtlety a metaphor for the moral dilemma of the machine age: the potential violence of a technology presented as the nation's social and economic salvation.[10]

During the period of these industrial commissions, Sheeler continued to be preoccupied with the American domestic interior. Paintings based on his own house show sealed spaces filled with domestic objects in vernacular style. Items from his collection of Shaker furniture feature prominently. These paintings were interpreted by progressive critics as an attempt on Sheeler's part to have his cake and eat it:

Still another picture is called *Americana* and shows how a cute Yankee painter can get away with cubism in a country that says cubism is against the law. Old-fashioned hook rugs are on the floor … and they have the kinds of patterns you see in early cubist pictures, accented by the lights and shadows that filter through a ladder-backed chair that stands against the light.[11]

During the middle span of his career, when he was doing his best work, Sheeler was very much in step with the society of his time, in the sense that he received patronage from major corporations - either directly, or through advertising agencies - and also from prominent individuals such as Gertrude Vanderbilt Whitney and Abby Aldrich Rockefeller. For example, he made two paintings of

65 **Charles Sheeler** *American Landscape* 1930
A view of the Ford Motor Company's River Rouge plant near Detroit, where Sheeler had spent six weeks in 1927 taking photographs for the Philadelphia advertising agency which handled the Ford account.

66 Elsie Driggs *Pittsburgh* 1927
The artist said of her return to Pittsburgh, to recapture childhood experiences: 'My reaction was totally visual ... I was moved. I was taken over by this great powerful still-life of masses, tubular shapes and cones.'

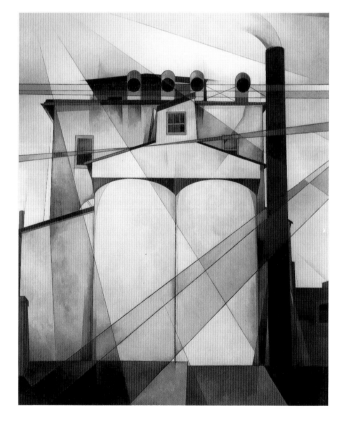

67 Charles Demuth *My Egypt* 1927
The slanting diagonals or 'ray lines', as Demuth called them, seem to have been suggested by the similar 'force lines' used by the Italian Futurists to suggest the energy inherent in inanimate objects.

historic houses in Colonial Williamsburg for Mrs Rockefeller, as well as a drawing of Central Park in New York, to preserve a favourite view of hers which was about to be altered by new landscaping. This phase of public acceptance reached a fitting climax in a retrospective exhibition held at The Museum of Modern Art in 1939. It included photographs as well as paintings and drawings. The photographs, necessary to give a complete picture of Sheeler's career, were included against the advice of his dealer, Edith Halpert of the Downtown Gallery, who had done much to promote Sheeler's work. (It is significant that she also triggered the rediscovery of William Harnett and his school.) The press notices, though generally favourable, proved her right: critics stressed Sheeler's dependence on the camera, implying a certain lack of originality.

Whether for this reason or for others, such as the rise of Abstract Expressionism, Sheeler made a sharp change of direction in the 1940s. His new paintings, though still based on photographic imagery, were no longer realistic in any strict sense. With their flat, bright, unmodulated areas of colour and their play of overlapping planes, they reverted to the simplified and only half-understood Cubism of Sheeler's earliest work. Efforts have recently been made by his admirers to emphasize the importance of these paintings, done in the late 1940s and 1950s. The truth is that they represent a decline. They are the products of a painter who was running out of creative energy and who felt alienated by the newest developments in American art.

A substantial group of other painters have, at one time or another, been categorized as Precisionists: the question is whether they were also realists. Few show Sheeler's complete commitment, sustained during more than two decades, to the closely observed representation of physical facts.

One of the exceptions is Elsie Driggs (1898–1982), who worked in a Precisionist style only briefly. Driggs trained at the Art Students' League in New York, being taught by the Ashcan School painter George Luks among others. In 1921 she travelled to Europe, and in Rome she met Leo Stein, another brother of Gertrude and an almost equally avid collector of avant-garde art. Stein's most influential act, as far as Driggs was concerned, was to introduce her to the work of Piero della Francesca, who had such an influence over almost all the classicizing artists of the period (in Europe and Latin America as well as the United States).

Returning to America in 1924, Driggs produced Precisionist renderings of factories and machinery for the rest of the decade before moving on to different, less tight and precise ways of working. Her best-known Precisionist painting is a somewhat menacing view, *Pittsburgh*, produced in 1927. The visionary quality of this image derives from a childhood memory of passing through Pittsburgh by night, aboard a train. It anticipates ideas found in Sheeler's *Upper Deck*, which dates from a year later.

The same visionary quality can be discovered, much accentuated, in one of the most celebrated of Precisionist images, *My Egypt* (1927) by Charles Demuth (1883–1935). Like Sheeler, Demuth (who came from Lancaster, Pennsylvania), studied at both the School of Industrial Art in Philadelphia and the Pennsylvania Academy of the Fine Arts, where he was a pupil of Anshutz. During his student years he went twice to Paris, spending five months there in 1907. He then paid a more extended visit to the city after leaving the

68 **Charles Demuth**
Modern Conveniences
1921
The 'ray lines',
visible in *My Egypt*
(Ill. 67), also appear
in this earlier
painting, whose
starting point is the
simplest kind of
vernacular
architecture.

Academy, from 1912 to 1914. During this period he was drawn into the circle of the Steins, meeting Gertrude as well as Leo, who had not yet moved to Rome, and making the acquaintance of leading members of the avant-garde, among them both Picasso and Matisse.

When Demuth returned from Europe, he almost immediately came into contact with the Arensbergs, and through them with Duchamp. His own work, however, remained more conservative than these contacts might lead one to expect. His main inspiration was Cézanne, as appears from a series of crystalline watercolours painted in Bermuda and Provincetown. Another inspiration seems to have been either the Orphism of Robert Delaunay or Italian Futurism: it is probable that Demuth derived from one or other of these the characteristic 'lines of force' visible in *My Egypt*, and also in earlier Precisionist compositions such as *Modern Conveniences* (1921), based on the view from the garden of Demuth's own house in Lancaster. These lines define shifts of hue which in turn endow mundane subject matter – *My Egypt* shows grain elevators – with an ethereal, otherworldly air.

The next step from Demuth's views of industrial subjects is represented by the work of Joseph Stella (1877–1946). In Stella's celebrated views of Brooklyn Bridge all pretence of realism has been abandoned. The structure of the bridge becomes the pretext for a series of poetic exercises, a virtuoso play of lines and forms.

Other painters connected with the Precisionist ethos included Niles Spencer (1893–1952), Preston Dickinson (1889–1930), George Ault (1891–1948) and

BELOW LEFT
69 **Niles Spencer** *Apartment Tower* 1944
Spencer methodically simplified architectural details to an even greater extent than Sheeler (Ills 58–65).

BELOW RIGHT
70 **George Ault** *Brooklyn Ice House* 1926
Ault's paintings present a somewhat less optimistic view of urban architecture than those of other Precisionists, as revealed in this stark and desolate view of Brooklyn.

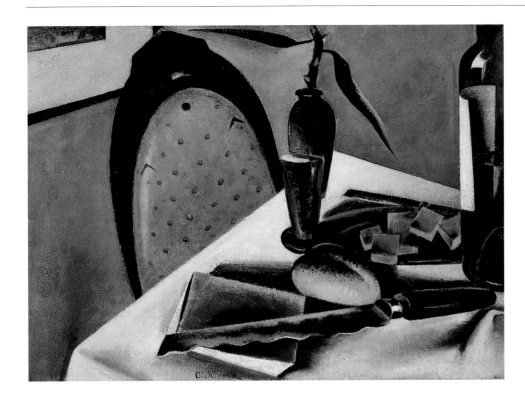

71 Preston Dickinson
Still-Life with Yellow-Green Chair 1928
Closely related to some of Sheeler's domestic interiors (Ill. 64).

Louis Lozowick (1892–1973). Much younger than the rest, and a belated follower of the style, was Ralston Crawford (1906–1978). He outlived them all except Georgia O'Keeffe (1887–1986), remarkable for her longevity as in every other respect.

Spencer travelled to Europe, like Sheeler and Demuth, but not until 1921. When he got there he, like so many other American painters of the epoch, felt the twin impact of French Cubism and Italian Renaissance fresco painting. Inevitably, he was also impressed by Cézanne, the source for so much in Cubism. Spencer's preferences – for Juan Gris and Georges Braque rather than Picasso, for Giotto rather than Piero – tell us what to expect from his own work, which resembles that of Sheeler but is simpler, rougher-hewn and much more concerned with texture. A painting like *Apartment Tower* (1944) seems in fact to be oversimplified. The spectator feels that he or she is in the presence of something which the artist has indeed seen, but has been unable to realize fully in paint.

Dickinson's work wavers between fantasy and the kind of sub-Cubist bluntness visible in *Still-Life with Yellow-Green Chair* (1928). A similar bluntness, but also a deliberately naive handling of form, appears in the paintings of George Ault. *Brooklyn Ice House* (1926) looks primitive compared with either Sheeler's or Demuth's handling of similar subject matter. Like Spencer's work, it is an approximation, rather than a convincing representation, of what the artist has seen.

Born in Russia, Lozowick received his initial training – a rigorously academic one – at the Kiev School of Art. He did not arrive in the United States until 1906. In the early 1920s he returned to Europe and travelled widely, visiting not only Paris but Berlin and Moscow, where he met leading Russian artists, among them Kazimir Malevich, Vladimir Tatlin and Alexander

Rodchenko. He began a series of portraits of American cities while still working in Europe, stimulated by the interest in his adopted country which was widespread among European intellectuals. The *City* paintings are testaments to the technological optimism so prevalent at the time, but their realistic content is slight. In the 1930s Lozowick's political beliefs moved sharply to the left, and his work began to feature the social protest themes which preoccupied so many American artists at that time.

The belated Precisionist paintings of Ralston Crawford, produced in the late 1930s, were for the most part out of step with the ethos of their period. One painting, *Overseas Highway* (1939), did, it is true, become widely popular, because it offered a symbol of optimism and future possibilities which appealed to the great mass of the American public. A simple, powerful yet sophisticated design, it shows Crawford's talent for arranging shapes within a rectangle at its best, but also has a certain patness which helps to explain why throughout his career he made more impact as a printmaker than as a painter. To his more intellectually inclined contemporaries, Crawford was fated to seem forever out of step. They could forgive older painters, such as Sheeler, for continuing to push a technological agenda, but by the end of the 1930s technology was starting to take on a sinister aspect. This was not reflected in Crawford's typically pristine, dandified work.

72 Louis Lozowick
Seattle 1926–27
One of a series of visionary views of American cities, testaments to the technological optimism of the 1920s.

73 Ralston Crawford
Overseas Highway 1939
The artist's best-known work,
originally given wide currency
when used to illustrate an article
in *Life* about the San Francisco
Golden Gate Exposition.

74 Ralston Crawford
Sanford Tank No. 2 1939
Like Sheeler's *Barn Abstraction*
(Ill. 60), this assimilates ideas
borrowed from Cubism to
essentially realist subject matter.

75 Ralston Crawford
Testable 1946
One of a series inspired by the atom
bomb test at Bikini Atoll, which he was
the only professional artist to attend,
Testable is indicative of Crawford's
move towards abstraction at the end of
his career.

He continued to be an odd man out, even when he abandoned Precisionism for a more fragmented, abstract style. This is represented by a series of compositions inspired by the atom bomb test at Bikini Atoll, which Crawford was the only professional artist to attend. When he exhibited these works in December 1946, at Edith Halpert's Downtown Gallery in New York, they aroused surprisingly little interest despite their intense topicality. In a catalogue preface Crawford said defensively that his purpose had been 'to convey ideas and feelings in a formal sequence, not to reproduce nature'.[12] Given this attitude, it is perhaps not surprising that he elicited such a muted response.

The Precisionist artist who achieved a contemporary celebrity at least equal to that of Sheeler, and perhaps greater, was Georgia O'Keeffe. Like her Mexican contemporary, Frida Kahlo, O'Keeffe has become a feminist icon, and this has tended to overshadow her other qualities as an artist. Gender was not the only issue in her work, though it did play a part in it, and an even greater part in the way in which it was initially received. Alfred Stieglitz, successively O'Keeffe's dealer, lover and husband, shrewdly presented her as a seer and prophetess – the paintings were secondary to the total impact made by her personality.

One important respect in which O'Keeffe differed from all the artists so far described in this chapter was that Europe played no role in her artistic education – in fact, she never set foot there until she was sixty-five. What she knew of Europe she owed to Stieglitz. Even the Armory Show meant little to her. When it opened, she was teaching in Amarillo, Texas, then even more remote from New York, culturally and geographically, than it is today.

Born in the Midwest to a pioneering family of partly Irish, partly Hungarian descent, O'Keeffe spent part of her youth in rural Wisconsin and part in

Virginia. After studying in Chicago and New York, she began a career as a teacher of art, working in Texas, then in Columbia, South Carolina. In 1916 a friend showed the abstract drawings she had been making to Stieglitz. With his remarkable eye for talent, Stieglitz immediately took fire. In 1916, without telling O'Keeffe, who was still absent, he arranged a one-person show for her at the 291 Gallery – the last show before the gallery closed down. As an inevitable result, the two met. Stieglitz, who was unhappily married, became O'Keeffe's lover, and they began to live together. Throughout the 1920s Stieglitz, moving from one gallery situation to another, arranging exhibitions, sharing temporary quarters with other galleries, was to be a potent force in publicizing O'Keeffe's work. Its inherent qualities – strong colour, and bold and unconventional design – were given additional piquancy, in the public's eyes, by its apparently sexual content, and by gossip about the unconventional nature of the relationship between the artist and her devoted impresario. By the mid-1920s, she was able to achieve the highest prices of any artist in the Precisionist group.

Like many artists, O'Keeffe took a different view of her own work from that espoused by outside commentators. For one thing, she minimized its sexual content. Lewis Mumford saw one show of hers as 'one long loud blast of sex, sex in youth, sex in adolescence, sex as gaudy as "Ten Nights in a Whorehouse" and sex as pure as the vigils of the vestal virgin, sex bulging, sex tumescent, sex deflated'.[13]

He was referring to the enlarged representations of flowers which had helped to make the artist's reputation. O'Keeffe could only retort, with a certain injured dignity: ' … when you took time to really notice my flower you bring all your associations with flowers on my flower, and you write about my flower as if I think and see what you think and see of the flower – and I don't.'[14]

She was also anxious to play down the influence which the camera had had on her vision – understandably enough, since her mentor was a celebrated photographer, and emphasis on the photographic nature of her work called her own originality into question in more ways than one. According to O'Keeffe, the enlarged flowers, which allowed her to find a way of being simultaneously abstract and representational, came from the conjunction of two things in her mind – a small still-life by the French flower-painter Henri Fantin-Latour and the speed and dynamism of New York:

> That was in the 20s, and everything was going so fast. Nobody had time to reflect … There was a cup and saucer, a spoon and a flower, well the flower was perfectly beautiful. It was exquisite, but it was so small you really could not appreciate it for yourself. So then and there I decided to paint a flower in all its beauty. If you could paint that flower on a huge scale then you could not ignore its beauty.[15]

In fact O'Keeffe's most typical paintings of the 1920s and 1930s, not merely the flowers, are photographic in a special sense. They make full use of the optical freedom of the camera, as this had been exploited by Stieglitz and still more by Stieglitz's disciple Paul Strand (1890–1976). O'Keeffe got to know Strand very soon after she met Stieglitz, and they became close friends. Strand's views on photography (the quotation which follows dates from 1917)

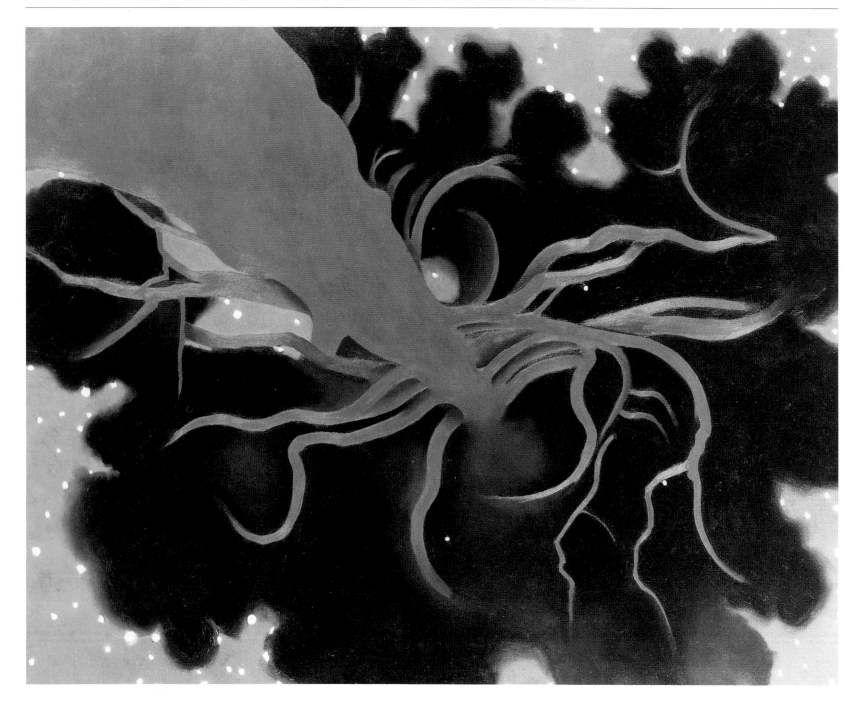

76 Georgia O'Keeffe *The Lawrence Tree* 1929
The pine tree which stands in front of the house in Taos, New Mexico, once occupied by the writer D. H. Lawrence. O'Keeffe said that she painted it 'as you see lying on that table under it at night – it looks as tho it is standing on its head with all the stars around'.

must have been perfectly familiar to her, as were the images he was making and the means used to achieve them:

> The photographer's problem is to see clearly the limitations and at the same time the potential qualities of his medium, for it is precisely here that honesty no less than intensity of vision is the prerequisite of a living expression. This means a real respect for the thing in front of him expressed in terms of chiaroscuro … through a range of almost infinite tonal values which lie beyond the skill of human hand. The fullest realization of this is accomplished without tricks of process or manipulation through the use of straight photographic methods.[16]

What seems to have seized O'Keeffe's imagination, as she moved into the Stieglitz circle, was the range of possibilities for optical manipulation offered by the camera, not merely its power to record external reality. She was probably the first painter to realize these possibilities to the full. Seen through the camera lens, things could be near or far, or both, with the middle ground eliminated entirely. Objects could be altered by the use of magnification, made almost unrecognizable by means of radical cropping, or seen unexpectedly from either above or below. Her work is full of such visual tropes. In *Corn, Dark I* (1924) the growing plant is viewed directly from above. In *Black Iris III* (1926) a single bloom is vastly magnified until it makes a monumental shape. In *The Lawrence Tree* (1929), painted in Taos, New Mexico, the observer is looking directly up the tree trunk, as if lying on the ground below.

O'Keeffe's closest points of contact with the other Precisionists, in terms of subject matter, are her views of New York skyscrapers. *Shelton with Sunspots* (1926) has a close affinity with some of Sheeler's architectural compositions, and with those of less gifted artists such as Spencer. Even here, however, one is aware of the special fashion in which she takes the camera into account. The sunspots of the title are an effect typical of a view seen through a lens.

As political and economic circumstances in America darkened, O'Keeffe found herself isolated within the New York art scene. In 1930, she took part in a public debate with Michael Gold, the editor of *New Masses*, the periodical which embodied the left-wing, populist philosophy of the time. Gold criticized her for failing to reflect the struggles of the oppressed. O'Keeffe's reply was twofold. Firstly, she said, with evident justice, that women were themselves still an oppressed class. Secondly, she asserted that

> The subject matter of a painting should never obscure its form and color, which are its real thematic contents … so I have no difficulty in contending that my paintings of a flower may be as much a product of this age as a cartoon about the freedom of women, or the working class, or anything else.[17]

A reporter who was present 'saw Gold as fussed, awkward and intimidated, O'Keeffe as mild, self-possessed and friendly', so one may conclude that she got the better of her opponent.[18] Nevertheless, the change in artistic climate, as well as her now strained and cooling relationship with Stieglitz, may have had something to do with her increasing tendency to withdraw to New Mexico to live and paint. Until Stieglitz died, she spent most of her summers there. Later she settled in New Mexico permanently. By 1950, when she held her first exhibition since Stieglitz's death four years previously, she had become what the *New York Times* called 'an enigmatic and solitary figure in American art'.[19] Her reputation was, however, to regenerate itself over the next three decades, and by the time of her own death she was not only a solitary but also a legendary personality – so much so that the legend tended to obscure the kind and quality of her achievement as a painter.

ABOVE RIGHT
77 **Georgia O'Keeffe**
Black Iris III 1926
One of the best of her series of enlarged flowers.

78 **Georgia O'Keeffe**
The Shelton with Sunspots 1926
O'Keeffe captures the effect of light as
it is seen through a camera lens.

CHAPTER 7

Regionalism

I N 1930 a painting called *American Gothic* was shown at the Art Institute of Chicago's Forty-Third Annual Exhibition of Painting and Sculpture. Reluctantly accepted by the jury, it was eventually awarded a bronze medal and a prize of $300. Later, the Friends of American Art of the Art Institute bought it for a further $300.[1] It was not long before it had established itself as a national icon, symbol of a vanishing rural America. Its success marks the real beginning of the Regionalist movement in American art.

American Gothic was the work of Grant Wood (1891–1942), a little-known artist from the small city of Cedar Rapids, Iowa. It is in many ways an ambiguous image. Does it celebrate its subjects or satirize them? Are they brother and sister, husband and wife, or father and daughter? Does it represent the present moment, or is it nostalgic? This last question is pertinent because the composition is obviously based on photographs of the kind made by itinerant photographers in the post-Civil War period. Such photographs not only used the same format, but often included emblematic objects, such as the pitchfork the man is holding.

Wood himself was always evasive about his intentions, once the picture had become famous. The most he would say was that it represented 'types' known to him all his life, and that he had not intended to ridicule them by pointing to faults such as 'fanaticism and false taste'.[2] Commentators have proposed a comparison with the writer Sinclair Lewis (1885–1951), whose novel *Main Street* (1920) Wood illustrated, citing a similar power to create universally recognizable American types. Going further, they have even wanted to discover, in the Regionalist movement with which Wood became associated, a mirror-image of much of the American fiction of the interwar years – not the work of expatriates such as Ernest Hemingway and F. Scott Fitzgerald, but that of William Faulkner, John Dos Passos and John Steinbeck. The further these comparisons are pursued, the more strained they become. This stay-at-home fiction is critical and often pessimistic, not celebratory. The typical Faulkner novel, for example, has been described as 'designedly a silo of compressed sin, from which life emerges as fermentation'.[3]

The Regionalist movement, however, was thought of as celebratory by its participants, a revival of the values of the Midwestern heartland of America – this in spite of the fact that the Midwesterners of the time were often resistant to, and sometimes deeply offended by, the way in which leading Regionalist artists chose to depict them. If Regionalism has true parallels, these can be found not in the United States but abroad, and must be drawn from the visual arts. It has some affinities with the Mexican Muralist movement of Diego Rivera, José Clemente Orozco and David Alfaro Siqueiros – not least because the majority of the Regionalist artists made public art – and also with Soviet Socialist Realism. However, its political values tend to be conservative rather than left-wing.

The most vocal Regionalist, and the self-appointed leader of the movement, was Thomas Hart Benton (1889–1975), who did not meet Wood until as late as 1934. Though he was a genuine Midwesterner by origin – he was born in Missouri, the son of a Democratic Congressman – his background as an artist was cosmopolitan. He studied at the Art Institute of Chicago, then in Paris, where he became associated with Stanton Macdonald-Wright (1890–1974)

79 **Jerry Bywaters** *Sharecropper* 1937
Influenced by Grant Wood's *American Gothic* (Ill. 90), but with a much sharper polemical edge, *Sharecropper* is the best-known image produced by a strong group of Texas Regionalists.

80 Thomas Hart Benton *The Lord Is My Shepherd* 1926
Painted before the Regionalist Movement got under way, this
is a double portrait of George and Sabrina West, a profoundly
deaf elderly couple who were Benton's neighbours when he
spent summer months at Martha's Vineyard.

and with the latter's protégé, Morgan Russell (1886–1953), who were the
founders of Synchromism, the first genuinely avant-garde movement in
American art. He also met members of the Parisian avant-garde, among them
Rivera, then still a Cubist, and Leo Stein.

Benton returned to America in 1911, settled in New York, and by 1917–18
was making near-abstract Constructivist paintings. Meanwhile, to support
himself, he worked as a set designer in the new movie industry. The studios
had not yet moved to Hollywood but were across the Hudson River, at Fort
Lee, New Jersey. This gave him his first experience of working rapidly on a
large scale.

During the decade of the 1920s he continued his flirtation with European
Modernism. Gradually, however, he became disillusioned with its lack of
narrative content. While still doing war service in the Navy, he had conceived
an ambitious project, an uncommissioned series of mural-sized paintings
called *American Historical Epic*. He initially planned to do no fewer than
seventy-five canvases, and by the late 1920s had completed eighteen of them.
They were influenced by descriptions he had read of Tintoretto's working
methods, which involved making three-dimensional models in order to obtain
an accurate idea of the spatial relationships between the figures. The paintings
have the aggressive plasticity and dynamism typical of Tintoretto's work; these
qualities were thenceforth to be the hallmarks of Benton's own style.

The *American Historical Epic* series is, however, much less specific in its
treatment of the figure than another series of paintings which Benton made at
the same period: portraits of local worthies from Martha's Vineyard, his
summer home. These have much greater human warmth than the glacial
townscapes and interiors which the Precisionists were producing at the same
period. The best known is *The Lord Is My Shepherd* (1926), a likeness of a
profoundly deaf elderly couple who were Benton's neighbours. It has been well
said that the painting 'conveys a sober mood of hard work and eternal
silence'.[4] Benton himself commented: 'I could, on hindsight, say that I saw
something in these deaf mutes from an artist's point of view that one didn't see
in a normal person.'[5]

Constitutionally restless, Benton spent much of his time in the 1920s
travelling in the American heartland, drawing and painting. He visited the
regions he had known as a boy, Missouri and northwest Arkansas, then
explored many parts of the South, especially Texas. A visit to the raw
settlement of Borger, Texas, in 1926, produced *Boomtown*, an early
manifestation of the sensibility which, three decades later, was to develop into
Pop Art: for example, the very centre of the bustling townscape, with its rash
of blaring signs, is occupied by the Red Star Theater, a symbol of the growing
importance of the movies in American culture, and of their power to unite the
hinterlands with the metropolitan centres of the long-settled East. However
different the lives they led, Americans had begun to dream the same dreams,
created for them by the cinema.

In their different ways, all the enterprises just described – portraits of
American types, widespread travel, and the narratives of the *American
Historical Epic* – served to prepare Benton for his first mural commission. In
1930, José Clemente Orozco (1883–1949), one of the three major Mexican

Muralists, who was living in the United States, secured a mural commission, without pay, for the New School of Social Research, then under construction in New York City. He owed the job to his mistress, Alma Reed, who was also his dealer. Benton at this time was also represented by Reed, and by playing the 'American' card he managed to get himself a second set of murals, for the New School's boardroom, on the same terms.

Benton's compositions are closer to Rivera's work as a Muralist than to Orozco's powerful expressionist style. They use the system of zigzagging, interlocking compartments, derived from contemporary newspaper design, which also features in some of Rivera's work. Benton, however, is bolder than Rivera in breaking up the flat plane of the wall surface, and makes more play with contrasts in scale. The dynamism of his compositions is in keeping with his theme, *America Today*.

The murals for the New School caused a considerable storm, but were nevertheless followed, two years later, by another project of the same type, once again located in New York. Benton was asked to make a series of paintings for the library of the Whitney Museum of American Art, then housed on 8th Street in Greenwich Village. The theme was now *The Arts of Life in America Today*, and the painter made it plain that what he had in mind were the popular arts, which he described as 'generally undisciplined':

> They run into pure, unreflective play. People indulge in personal display: they drink, sing, dance, pitch horseshoes, get religion, and even set up opinions as the spirit moves them.
>
> These popular outpourings have a sort of pulse, a go and come, a rhythm; and all are expressions – indirectly, assertions of value. They are undisciplined, uncritical and generally deficient in technical means; but they are arts just the same.
>
> The real subject of the work is, in the final analysis, a conglomerate of things experienced in America: the subject is a pair of pants, a hand, a face, a gesture, some physical revelation of intention, a sound, even a song. The real subject is what an individual has known and felt about things encountered in a world of real people and actual doings.[6]

The most original panel of the series, a lunette entitled *Political Business and Intellectual Ballyhoo*, does not really conform to this description. Nor does it adapt itself to any commonly accepted realist norms. A rousing satire on the intellectual left, with whom Benton had hitherto associated, it features Mickey Mouse and Mutt and Jeff in addition to the American eagle, and quotes the first line of a vulgar song: 'Oh, the eagles they fly high in Mobile.' The composition prefigures the work of 1960s Pop artists such as Andy Warhol and Roy Lichtenstein, both of whom were to use similar source material.

The Whitney murals got an extremely mixed press. *Art News* described them as 'a brilliant bit of bedlam',[7] but the critic of the New York *Sun* opined that 'The painting of these murals is quite as raw and uncouth as the subject matter.'[8] There was every sign that Benton had alienated many of the major tastemakers and patrons in New York. Teachers and students at the Art Students' League circulated a petition asking that the murals be destroyed, alleging racism in Benton's portrayal of African Americans. Benton lost all the

81 **Thomas Hart Benton** *Boomtown* 1927–28
In the late 1920s, Benton travelled widely in the south and west of the United States, stopping at the town of Borger, Texas. Thanks to an oil-strike in 1926, the population had swelled, in the course of only ninety days, from zero to 30,000.

82 **Thomas Hart Benton**
Palisades (American Historical Epic) c. 1919–24
From the 'First Chapter' of Benton's sequence, which consisted of five scenes showing the arrival of European settlers and their relations with the native Indians.

83 **Thomas Hart Benton** *The Arts of Life in America Today: Political Business and Intellectual Ballyhoo* 1932
'Political Business' is represented by the top-hatted broomstick on the right; 'Intellectual Ballyhoo' is symbolized by a caricatured group of readers of leftist magazines – suitably enough, these are on the left. Above them, Mickey Mouse and Mutt and Jeff stand beside a sign advertising a 'Greenwich Village Proletarian Costume Dance'.

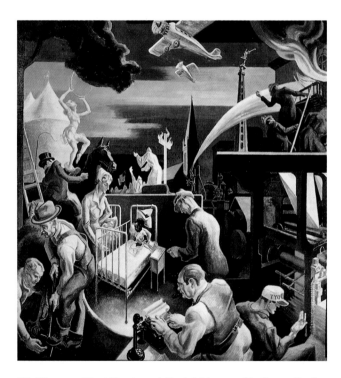

84 **Thomas Hart Benton** *A Social history of Indiana: Parks, the Circus, the Klan and the Press* 1933
Disconnected vignettes intended to suggest the variety of life in Indiana. Benton was able to get away with showing a Ku Klux Klan 'Klavalcade' because the Democrats were then in power in Indiana, and the Klan had flourished under a previous, Republican administration.

black students in his classes, plus many white liberals: a sure sign that cultured opinion was turning against him.

It was at this point that he was lucky enough to pick up another and much more important mural commission – a painting 14 feet high and 230 feet long for the Indiana Pavilion at the Chicago World's Fair of 1933. Benton got the job because nobody could think of an artist capable of doing it who actually came from Indiana – and here at least was a qualified artist who was a Midwesterner by birth, though not actually from the state itself.

The Indiana murals (the vast painting was broken up into a series of scenes or panels) confronted Benton with different problems from those he had met in his two previous commissions. His target audience was more conservative in taste than any he had encountered before; and in Indiana he was much resented as an outsider. In addition, he was no longer dealing simply with the American present. He had to treat history and the passage of time, just as he had originally attempted to do in *American Historical Epic*. He also had some tricky episodes to get around – for example, the association between Indiana and the Ku Klux Klan. Benton resolved this and other difficulties – it helped that he was a drinking man – by ingratiating himself with local legislators. There was at that moment a Democratic majority in Indiana, and the Klan had flourished under a previous, Republican administration.

Benton's Indiana series was a success, and established him not only as a muralist, but as an artist whose chief interest lay in depicting the American heartland. By this time both the American press and one or two ambitious dealers were looking for something new in American art, a fresh beginning for an art world still badly affected by the Depression. In particular, a young dealer named Maynard Walker had begun to sense the possibility of piecing together a new movement, featuring work by Benton, Grant Wood and another artist who seemed to use similar subject matter, John Steuart Curry. It did not matter to him that the resemblance was in fact superficial, and the three were very different in background and temperament. What Walker hoped for was a new market in the Midwest itself, to replace the now faltering gallery scene in the East. To this end, he put together a group show which he sent to the Kansas City Art Institute. In a statement made to *Art Digest*, Walker put forward the idea, then still quite novel, that there was now a new regional art:

> Very noticeably much of the most vital modern art in America is coming from our long-backward Middle West. Largely through the creative impact of a few sincere and vital painters, the East is learning that there is an America west of the Alleghenies and that it is worth putting on canvas.[9]

The show was a flop in Kansas, but it had one important consequence: it prompted a cover story for *Time* magazine, which was now, thanks to recent improvements in printing techniques, able to illustrate an inside story in colour. To launch this new facility, *Time* published an issue with a piece on 'The U.S. Scene' in December 1934. It carried a self-portrait of Benton on the cover, and the other artists featured were Wood, Curry, Charles Burchfield, Edward Hopper and Reginald Marsh. Benton was described as the leader of the new Midwestern group. Jealous colleagues thought he intended to use the article, and the nationwide publicity it brought with it, as a springboard to further his ambitions, which had always been huge: 'Once the front page was taken over by Regionalism, which was a political thing, [Benton] knew how to get back on to the front page.'[10] Benton himself commented that 'a play was written, and a stage created for us'.[11]

The *Time* story in fact offered the first really convincing example of the way in which mass circulation media – newspapers, news magazines and later television – could short-circuit the reputation-making process and push the traditional elite of tastemakers to one side. It is probable that Benton instinctively understood this, since one of his first reactions to his new celebrity was to open a breach with the whole of the Modernist circle in New York by publishing an article in which he attacked Alfred Stieglitz. Immediately afterwards, he embroiled himself in a quarrel with the whole of the leftist faction led by his inveterate enemy, the abstract painter Stuart Davis, by expressing indifference to the recent destruction of Rivera's unfinished mural at the Rockefeller Center. In an address to the left-wing John Reed Club, Benton said:

> I have not joined those who have been protesting the indignity put upon Diego
> Rivera's work in the Rockefeller Center because I do not find, in the seriously
> decadent condition of our own art, that what happens to Mexican art is of great
> importance.[12]

Reactions to this and other provocations were so violent that Benton decided to shake the dust of New York from his feet, at least for a while. He made a lecture tour in the Midwest (meeting Wood at long last in the course of it). The most serious results of the tour were a commission to paint murals for the Capitol building of his home state, Missouri, and an invitation to come and teach at the Kansas City Art Institute (also in Missouri). 'I made up my mind,' he later declared, 'suddenly to leave New York and go home to Missouri for good.'[13]

His decision was made public with considerable fanfare. A headline in the New York *Sun* for 12 April 1935 announced 'Mr Benton Will Leave Us Flat',[14] and other papers carried the story throughout the country. In September, he arrived in Kansas City to start a new life.

The immediate task in front of him was the new set of murals for the Missouri State Capitol building in Jefferson City. Entitled *A Social History of Missouri*, these were to form a continuous strip running right round the walls of a large room. The compositions restated themes already used for the Indiana murals. With his innate pugnacity, Benton could not resist inserting details which were bound to be controversial. At one point he showed a woman wiping a baby's bare bottom – a sight still guaranteed to shock the prudish. In another scene, he attempted to illustrate the links between machine politics and the Missouri business world. In it, Tom Prendergast, the notoriously corrupt local political boss, is shown listening to a speech made by a local businessman. In the front row of the audience, looking straight at Prendergast (who is placed on the platform behind the speaker), is a leading member of Kansas City's best-known banking family. The implication is that he and Prendergast are allies.

When finished, the murals were met by the usual outburst of controversy attracted by all Benton's large projects – the painter would have been

85 **Thomas Hart Benton** *Politics, Farming and Law in Missouri* 1936
Mural for the Missouri State Capitol in Jefferson City. The crowded composition contains a vignette (to the left) which scandalized some local viewers: a woman wiping a baby's bare bottom. Benton retorted, 'There wouldn't have been any military history if there weren't any babies to put diapers on.'

disappointed if this had not been the case. He must in any event have been prepared for a mixed reaction, since the murals had been painted *in situ*, and the public had been free to come and make comments. On one occasion Benton replaced a plough with one of different and sturdier design, after an elderly farmer had criticized his original effort. At question-and-answer sessions after the paintings were completed, he was happy to defend his own version of realism. He said of the murals that they showed

> ... the conditions under which history is made rather than history itself ... Had I treated the theme as a succession of events, I would have had to receive my impressions at second hand. I never put anybody in a picture of this kind unless I have had an opportunity to get acquainted with him or sketch him from life.[15]

The main criticism which the murals aroused locally was that they showed 'crudeness and lack of feeling'[16] – in other words, that they were insufficiently idealized. The attacks they inspired were, however, mild in comparison to those aroused by Benton's hard-hitting autobiography, *An Artist in America*, published in 1937. This inspired a campaign, masterminded by one of his most persistent local critics, to get him fired from his teaching post, now up for renewal. The board of trustees of the Kansas City Art Institute at first failed to confirm his contract, then reluctantly did so after being subjected to considerable public pressure (1938). Benton continued to teach there for another three years, but in 1941 his position once again began to deteriorate – a new director had been appointed, and he and Benton did not get on. Then Benton fatally compromised himself by launching an attack on the staff of the local museum, the Nelson-Atkins Art Gallery, airing the obsessive hatred of homosexuality which was the least admirable aspect of his character. This gave Benton's detractors the opportunity they had long been looking for, and he was forced out. He never again did any regular teaching and, while he remained a celebrity, he was increasingly isolated on the American art scene, which was now being taken over by the rising generation of Abstract Expressionists.

John Steuart Curry (1897–1946), the third member of the main Regionalist triumvirate, is a more marginal figure than either Benton or Wood, both of whom, in their different ways, made an enduring impression on the American psyche. His connection with the movement was in part opportunistic. Though born in Kansas, he studied art in the East, at a school of illustration in New Jersey. In the first half of the 1920s he had quite a successful career as an illustrator, making drawings for periodicals such as *Boy's Life* and the *Saturday Evening Post*. By 1924 he was sufficiently prosperous to buy himself a studio at Otter Ponds, in the art colony of Westport, Connecticut. However, his career did not sustain itself as he had hoped, largely because he was still a very imperfect draughtsman. To remedy this, he went to Europe in 1926 and spent the best part of a year studying there. He frequented artistic hangouts like the Dôme in Montparnasse, but does not seem to have had any intimate contact with the Parisian avant-garde. In 1928, after his return to Westport, he produced the painting which made his reputation, rather as *American Gothic* made Wood's.

Curry's account of the genesis of the work is almost touchingly simple: 'I was in a state of desperation, trying to get along at illustration, or anything I could do. I took a month off and painted this picture. It was painted without notes or sketches from memory of a baptism that took place in 1915.'[17]

In the fall of 1929, Curry showed *Baptism in Kansas* at the Corcoran Gallery of Art in Washington, D.C., and scored an immediate success. Edward Alden Jewell, the critic of the *New York Times*, praised it as 'a gorgeous piece of satire'.[18] Curry was offered a subsidy of $50 a week by the great patron Gertrude Vanderbilt Whitney. Later, in 1931, she purchased *Baptism* for her new Whitney Museum of American Art. At the opening, this was the work the *New York Times* photographer chose to place her against, as an example of what she was trying to promote.

Not surprisingly, in view of the fact that Easterners interpreted his work as satire, Curry found himself coolly received in his native Kansas. In 1931 the dealer Maynard Walker sent a one–man show of Curry's work to the Art Institute of Chicago, and this then travelled on to the Mulvane Museum in Topeka. From Topeka a local spokesman wrote to tell Walker that 'the public resented [Curry's] so-called crude angle'[19] towards the region of his birth. What now seems like a nostalgic, slightly humorous evocation of Curry's youth was perceived locally as tactless mockery, or at the very least as an unwelcome reminder of a less sophisticated epoch which had now passed into history. Later, his images of tornados and manhunts were also seen as negative stereotypes. Kansas's need to assert its own self-worth and faith in the future came into direct conflict with Curry's need to reclaim the past.

Nevertheless a campaign was begun to get Curry back to Kansas to undertake some major project. One campaigner was Grant Wood, who felt that Curry should return to his roots in order to reinvigorate local culture. He invited Curry to his Stone City Art Colony in 1933, and the two artists were photographed together, wearing suitably rustic bib-overalls. One of these photographs was used as an illustration to the *Time* article on 'The U.S. Scene' published at the end of the following year – the key event which provided Regionalists with a national identity.

From this time onwards Curry himself, abetted by various friends, tried to persuade fellow Kansans that they had misjudged him. A group of local newspaper editors came over to his side, and it was they who raised a fund to pay for a set of murals in the Kansas State House in Topeka. Even after that, it required much lobbying before Curry was awarded the job. Even less than with Benton's murals in Missouri, however, was there any kind of unanimity about what the artist should be asked to portray. Some of the most famous incidents in the past of the state, such as Carrie A. Nation's temperance campaign, with its violent attacks on saloons, were too controversial to depict. Others featured personalities who seemed likely to invite ridicule. One such (actually suggested for inclusion) was 'Doc' Brinkley, an eccentric physician who specialized in goat-gland transplants for purposes of rejuvenation, and who, after losing his medical licence, ran for governor as a write-in candidate and won, only to be disqualified by horrified election officials.

Curry had been given two spaces in the building – the East Corridor, which was to be tackled first, and the central Rotunda. In the corridor he decided to contrast what he called the 'Tragic Prelude' with the pastoral tranquillity of modern Kansas. One of his tragic figures was the Spanish conquistador Francisco Vázquez de Coronado, who was alleged, though without much certainty, to have made his way to the grassy plains of Kansas as early as 1541. One reason for Coronado's popularity was that he seemed to challenge the claims to historical priority made by the East Coast. When Curry started to paint his mural, the conquistador had already become a centrepiece for historical pageants, held not only in Kansas but in other states whose territories he was said to have traversed. In addition to nourishing local pride, the legend was thought to be a good stimulus for the tourist industry. Appropriately enough, Curry made use of a costume hired from a Hollywood studio for his portrayal of this rather ill-documented hero.

Another and much more contentious choice was the anti-slavery campaigner John Brown. Brown was not born in Kansas, nor did he meet his end there. His place of birth was Torrington, Connecticut, and he was tried and hanged in Charlestown, Virginia, after his abortive raid on Harper's Ferry in 1859. It was this raid and its aftermath which turned him into the John the Baptist of the Union cause. The raid on Harper's Ferry had, nevertheless, been preceded by an earlier adventure, Brown's intervention in the conflict between

86 **John Steuart Curry** *Baptism in Kansas* 1928
Curry said that the picture was 'painted from memory from a baptism that took place
in 1915', but many viewers, among them the critic of the *New York Times*, read it as a
satire on contemporary life in the Mid-West. Not surprisingly, Curry's fellow Kansans
were offended by this, and therefore by the picture itself.

87 **John Steuart Curry** *Kansas Pastoral* 1937–42
Intended as a celebration of modern agriculture, but the bull
in the centre of the long wall was severely criticized in the
local press for not being true to life.

pro-slavery and anti-slavery forces that took place in the Kansas Territory in
the mid-1850s. His five sons were homesteaders in Kansas, and it was they
who summoned his aid. Accompanied by four of his sons and a son-in-law,
Brown led a raid on a settlement called Pottawotomie, in the course of which
five of his opponents were killed.

In evolving his image of Brown for the mural, Curry made use of a well-
known contemporary photograph and of various posthumous paintings based
on this. The general conception derives from an earlier sketch by Curry, made
for a mural destined for the Department of Justice building in Washington,
D.C. This showed a group of freed slaves and was rejected by the bureaucrats
because of what they called the 'hallelujah pose' of the central figure. Curry
now substituted Brown for the liberated slave, and made the pose more
purposeful by putting a rifle in one of Brown's hands and a Bible in the other.
On either side of him are representatives of the Confederate and Union forces,
while in the background looms a symbolic Kansas tornado. Wild-eyed and
patriarchally bearded, Brown becomes a modern surrogate for Michelangelo's
Moses. With some justification, Curry thought the image was his best work; he
made a powerful lithograph after it.

Neither this group nor the *Kansas Pastoral* on one of the long walls found
favour with the local audience. The militant figure of Brown was considered
too disturbing; the *Pastoral* was criticized for being badly drawn. A local
newspaper claimed that the bull in the centre had assumed an impossible
stance, and offered a comparative photograph of a prize bull to prove it.

The real difficulty was that many people felt that Curry had persisted in misrepresenting them, just as he had done in the *Baptism*. They wanted Kansas shown as modern and progressive; Curry showed it as essentially rural, and enmeshed in the problems of the past. Unhappy with the work he had already done, they were even less happy with the scenes he proposed for the second phase of the job. In the Rotunda he intended to portray the droughts and grasshopper swarms, the soil erosion and accompanying dust storms, which routinely plagued the state. In the Kansas of the 1930s, erosion had become an ever more serious problem, and Curry was a public crusader for soil conservation, a cause associated in many minds with interference from central government in Washington.

In order to fresco the Rotunda as he wished, Curry had to obtain permission to remove some of the marble panels with which it was lined. Action groups sprang up to prevent this. Often they made it plain that the real cause was not love of the panels themselves but distaste for what Curry had already done and dismay at what he intended to do. The Kansas Council of Women, for example, issued the following statement: 'The murals do not pertain to the true Kansas. Rather than revealing a law-abiding, progressive state, the artist has emphasized the freaks of its history – the tornadoes, and John Brown who did not bow to legal procedure.'[20]

The pressures were too great. In 1941 the Kansas State Senate voted to maintain the marble as it was, effectively putting an end to Curry's work in the State House. Even after the vote was taken, he remained the butt of

88 **John Steuart Curry** *Tragic Prelude* 1937–42
The central figure is the anti-slavery campaigner, John Brown. In Curry's own words, 'In this group is expressed the fratricidal fury that first flamed on the plains of Kansas, the tragic prelude to the last bloody feud of the English-speaking people.'

89 **Grant Wood** *Woman with Plants* 1929
Portrait of Wood's mother. The plant she is holding,
a snake's tongue or sansevieria, symbolizes both her
prowess as a gardener and the hardiness of the
pioneer spirit.

90 **Grant Wood** *American Gothic* 1930
Based on photographs of the kind made by itinerant
photographers of the post-Civil War period. The models
were the artist's sister, Nan, and his dentist, Dr B. H.
McKeeby.

acrimonious attacks in his native state, vilified for his disregard for local
sensitivities and values. When he died in 1946, he was a disappointed and
broken man.

Unlike Benton and Curry, Grant Wood remained throughout his career in
the Midwest where he was born. In this sense, he was the most truly regional
artist among them. Like them, however, he eventually fell from favour and was
shabbily treated by those among whom he lived and worked.

Until he found fame with *American Gothic*, Wood's career followed a
pattern in which New York and the opinion-formers of the East Coast had
played no part. Born on a farm near Anamosa, Iowa, Wood moved in 1901,
after the death of his father, to Cedar Rapids. His training as an artist was
fragmented, with the emphasis almost as much on craft and design as on fine
art. It included stints at the Minneapolis School of Design and Handicraft, a
life-drawing class at the University of Iowa, and night classes at the Art
Institute of Chicago – Wood lived in Chicago from 1913 to 1916, working
part-time at the Kalo Silversmiths Shop.

After a brief period of war service, spent in Iowa and in Washington, D.C.,
Wood returned to Cedar Rapids and took a job as an art teacher. For most of
the 1920s he divided his time between teaching and trips abroad. During these
trips he studied briefly at the Académie Julian in Paris (a rather Seurat-esque
life study survives from this period), and also made numerous small
landscapes in a conservative version of Impressionist style. He seems to have
remained completely isolated from the European avant-garde movements of
the time, even more so than Curry. The paintings he produced in Europe, and
similar paintings made at home, were well received in Cedar Rapids, a place
which prided itself on its reputation as a local cultural centre; and Wood found
many local patrons, selling his work for unambitious prices. He also acted as
an artistic jack-of-all-trades, builder, decorator and designer: in fact, a well-
liked arbiter of local taste.

A single event pushed him into a decisive change of style. In 1927, soon
after he had left teaching and decided to work as a freelance, he received an
important decorative commission: to create a large stained-glass window for
the hall of the new Cedar Rapids Veterans' Memorial Building. The committee
responsible decided that this could be properly executed only by specialist
workshops in Munich, and Wood went to Germany to supervise the work. In
Munich he saw the great collection of early German and Flemish paintings
housed in the Alte Pinakothek, and was greatly struck by them. He was
afterwards to claim that the sharp-edged clarity of these paintings, and the
artists' commitment to a realistic depiction of the life of their own time, had a
decisive influence, leading him towards a complete change of style. It is also
possible – though Wood never mentioned this – that he saw work by
contemporary German painters of the *Neue Sachlichkeit*, among them 'Magic
Realists' such as Christian Schad and Franz Radziwill.

There is also another possible influence on Wood's change of direction.
Shortly before he left for Munich, he had become interested in American naive
painting. A mural made in 1927, for a hotel in Council Bluffs (formerly
Kanesville), Iowa, is directly based on a panorama painted in 1849 by an
untrained artist named George Simons. At this time, too, Wood was attracted

91 **Grant Wood** *Stone City* 1930
This combines elements borrowed from nineteenth-century
naive art with the fashionable Art Deco style, in order to
produce an idealized 'all-American' pastoral landscape.

to other kinds of Victoriana, notably the old daguerreotypes and tintypes
which were common forms of family heirloom among his friends.

American Gothic, though it made Wood's reputation nationally, was not the
first painting in his new style. *Woman with Plants*, painted in the preceding
year, is a portrait of his mother. Mrs Wood is shown in old-fashioned country
garb, wearing an apron trimmed with rickrack braid over a simple grey dress.
She holds a snake's-tongue or sansevieria plant, an allusion both to her
prowess as a gardener and also, since the plant is well-known for its hardiness,
to the strength of the pioneer spirit.

The sudden success of *American Gothic* changed Wood's life – in the long
run, not for the better. He began to think of himself as the pioneer of a new
kind of art, based on an American regional sensibility. The manner he had
initially applied to portraits or quasi-portraits was extended to landscapes and
narrative paintings. The landscapes, such as *Stone City* (1930), combine
elements taken from nineteenth-century naive painting – crisp definition of all
objects, near and far, and the use of the bird's-eye view – with others, such as
the stylized treatment of foliage and rhythmic patterning of larger forms,
which came from the Art Deco style then making itself felt in much American
design and architecture.

The Deco element was also clearly evident in his most complex narrative
work, *Parson Weems' Fable* (1939), as is the tendency to refer back to naive
art – in this case to the limners or 'face painters' of the late eighteenth and
early nineteenth centuries. Mason Locke Weems, the clergyman who fabricated
the well-loved but apocryphal story about George Washington and the cherry
tree, is shown pulling back a curtain to reveal this invented incident.
Washington, wielding his axe, is represented (as in some naive child portraits)

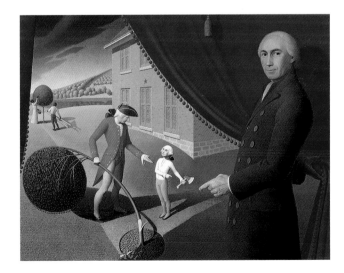

92 **Grant Wood** *Parson Weems' Fable* 1939
An ironic comment on the well-loved, but apocryphal story
about the young George Washington and the cherry tree.

as a miniature adult, wearing a formal powdered wig. The painting is significantly unlike the work of the Midwestern novelists to whom Wood is carelessly compared. Far from exalting instinct, as a writer like Sherwood Anderson did, *Parson Weems' Fable* is detached, ironic and judgmental. The curtain, for example, is a distancing device of an almost Brechtian sort.

Despite the complexity of the images that Wood created in his new manner, and the play of sly humour to be found in his mature work, his actual career-pattern often makes him seem rather naive and self-deluding. After a very prolific period in 1930–32, during which he established his national reputation, he allowed himself to be turned into a public figure who spent too much of his time lecturing and propagandizing and too little actually painting. He produced more prints than paintings, because the medium made fewer demands on him - and perhaps, too, because it seemed to him more democratic. He also painted murals, or rather designed them, since the actual painting was the work of his pupils; he had now gone to teach at the State University of Iowa in Iowa City.

At the University, Wood was at first able to present himself as a liberal force, a breath of fresh air in a department still largely devoted to nineteenth-century academic methods. In 1935 he published a tract entitled *Revolt Against the City*, outlining his beliefs. In the course of it he drew a parallel (a rather specious one so far as his own practice was concerned) between Regionalist art and Regionalist literature – by which he meant now-forgotten books by Iowa writers, such as Ruth Suchow's momentarily popular *Home Folks* and the slightly better-remembered poems of Paul Engle. Wood went on to assert that the Depression had actually been good for American art, because it fostered self-reliance.

This tract, however, marked the high point of his national influence, as what he said had to be supported by his reputation as an artist. This soon started to decline. His first one-man show in New York, also held in 1935, was harshly criticized for decorative mannerism and sentimentality. This was followed by increasing damage to his authority on his home ground - his students, for example, rebelled against collective mural projects and wanted to paint independently.

In 1940, Wood involved himself in a bitter academic dispute. His department – greatly enhanced in reputation, thanks largely to his presence – was now populated by younger teachers, often from the East, who had been affected by the Modernist ideas current in New York. They were critical of Wood's hands-on, art-is-craft approach, and still more so of his inflexible teaching methods. Efforts were made not only to discredit him as a teacher but to undermine him as an artist. At the same time, Regionalism itself was in full retreat. World events had made a doctrinaire, pro-America, anti-European stance seem irrelevant if not actually intolerable. Wood was forced to take a year's leave of absence in 1940–41, and during this period a messy compromise with his opponents was patched together by the university administrators. Before it could take full effect, he became ill with inoperable liver cancer. His death in 1942 was followed by a memorial exhibition at the Art Institute of Chicago, where he had scored his first major success. It was a measure of how far his reputation had fallen that after this there was no major museum show of his work until as late as 1983. Only *American Gothic* retained its fascination, for the public if not for the critics. Deliberately archaic, even at the time it was painted, it continued to be accepted as an archetype of American rural life.

Wood, Curry and Benton are the artists identified with the Regionalist movement in the public mind, and featured as such in standard histories of American art. However, they are certainly not the only artists who belonged to the Regionalist current. Because the movement diffused itself across the United States, a great many built only local reputations in their own time, and are largely forgotten now. Some do not deserve this kind of oblivion.

In Texas, for example, there sprang up a vigorous group of young painters imbued with the Regionalist spirit. In some ways, they were more typical of what later commentators have taken that spirit to be than were the three 'great men' of the movement. They were more closely engaged with the society they lived in, and in general more critical of it. In these respects they bore a real resemblance to certain writers of the period, most of all John Steinbeck – though Steinbeck's characteristic settings are Californian, not Texan. One of the motivating forces in Steinbeck's *The Grapes of Wrath* (1939) is the Oklahoma dustbowl, which drives the Joad family to California to find work; and the dustbowl is also a major theme with the Texas painters of the same epoch.

The majority of the leading artists of the region were associated with the Dallas Artists' League, founded in May 1932; and Dallas (rather than Houston, which is usually regarded as more progressive and open to innovation) was the focus of their activities. One reason for this was the support that the League and its membership received from *Southwest Review*, a literary magazine based on Southern Methodist University in Dallas, which was already publishing a Regionalist agenda. Those connected with the magazine were determined to foster and identify a new culture, specific to the region. In this, one influence was the thought of John Dewey, who had urged American artists to discover 'the localities of America as they are'.[21] Among the artists who belonged to this distinctive, Texas-based Regionalist movement were Jerry Bywaters (1906–89), Alexandre Hogue (1898–1994) and Otis Dozier (1904–87).

Bywaters, an active member of the Dallas Artists' League, was born in Paris, Texas, and first studied painting at Southern Methodist University. Later he worked at the Art Students' League in New York under John Sloan, and then, in 1928, paid a three-month visit to Mexico, where he met Rivera. Immediately after his return, he wrote in *Southwest Review*:

> What excites me is that Diego Rivera has taught me a lesson I had not learned
> elsewhere in Europe or America. I now know that art, to be significant, must be
> understandable to the layman, and that it must be part of a people's thought.[22]

It is perhaps not surprising that Rivera should have had a more direct impact in Texas than in other parts of the United States, since Texas itself lies on the Mexican border and was once part of Mexico. On the other hand, Bywaters did not adopt Rivera's philosophy in full, any more than did his fellow Texans; and it is significant that, while he carried out various mural commissions, it is his easel paintings that sustain his reputation today. Rivera's chief lesson to Bywaters and his associates was a general one: not to be afraid of populism.

Alexandre Hogue, born in Memphis, Missouri, moved to Texas while still an infant. He identified himself with the local scene, despite studies in the North (at the Minneapolis College of Art and Design) and a stint in New York as a commercial artist. He returned to Dallas to live and work in 1925. His best work has much in common with that of Bywaters, not least a feeling for the harshness of the land. Both artists painted memorable images of drought-stricken landscapes which make Wood's work in this genre look decorative and complacent.

Different from these two, but almost equally typical of the Texas attitude to art, was Otis Dozier. Born in Lawson, Texas, Dozier had only a limited formal art training, in Dallas itself, but nevertheless rapidly absorbed the basic elements of the Modernist idiom. He seems to have acquired these largely through a study of the avant-garde magazine *The Dial*. In the 1920s this reproduced work by most of the great Parisian Modernists, including Matisse, Picasso, Fernand Léger and André Derain. His career is thus an early example of the impact of new printing technology, which led to the birth of the illustrated magazine and art book, now perhaps the main carriers of artistic information. Born a generation earlier, and with a career following the same pattern, Dozier would not have been able to acquire vital information so rapidly and easily, and would probably not have become a Modernist at all. Printed material was henceforth to play a major role in disseminating new styles throughout the United States. It was also to play a part in closing historical gaps. An artist working on the West Coast, who had never been to Europe, might be as much struck by the work of Caravaggio as by that of some contemporary – and might indeed convince himself that the former *was* a kind of contemporary – because he found him featured in a glossily illustrated new art book.

Another, more conventional influence on Dozier's work, and indeed upon that of all the Texas artists surrounding him, was a travelling show drawn from the collection of the new Whitney Museum, shown in 1933 at the Dallas Museum of Fine Arts. It included work by, among others, Demuth, Sheeler, Curry and Spencer. Significantly, Bywaters found Curry's work too shallow and illustrative.

Inevitably, the Dallas group also came into contact with Benton, the best-travelled as well as the most heavily publicized of all the Regionalists. They seem, however, to have taken more from his personal example, in promoting the cause of a visibly American and visibly regional art, than from what he actually produced. When Bywaters and Hogue painted a set of ten murals depicting events in the history of Dallas for the Old City Hall Building - under the auspices of the short-lived Public Works of Art Project (PWAP), set up in 1933 as part of Franklin D. Roosevelt's vast New Deal employment initiative – Benton saw the works soon afterwards and praised them highly, despite the fact that they do not show either artist at his best:

> If you want any art to grow in your locality, it will have to grow through the
> efforts of men such as Bywaters and Hogue. In spite of all cultural whoopings
> to the contrary, art cannot be imported. It has to grow. Keep your plant and
> water it.[23]

93 **Otis Dozier** *Still-Life with Striped Gourd* 1935
A Texas Regionalist here combines ideas borrowed from the
Cubists with elements of local folk art.

The individual flavour of the work produced by Texas Regionalists does indeed
owe much to local influences, but just as much to what was absorbed from
outside. Purely local, for example, was the influence of folk art, in which Texas
was very rich. This led the Texas Regionalists to flirt with the kind of
primitivism to be found in Otis Dozier's *Still-Life with Striped Gourd* (1935).
But this also owes something to the French Cubists, whom Dozier knew from
The Dial. Similarly, Bywaters's melancholy portrait of a *Sharecropper* (1937) is
somewhat in debt to *American Gothic* but may, with its strain of social criticism,
be equally dependent on the German artists of the *Neue Sachlichkeit*. His *On
the Ranch* (1941) points to a different range of influences: European
Surrealism, and especially the eerie desert scenes produced by Salvador Dali, on
the one hand; O'Keeffe and other painters working in New Mexico, on the other.

The most striking paintings made by Hogue at this period show his
passionate concern with the environment, and in particular with the horrors of
erosion. He returned to this theme repeatedly – for instance, in *Drouth Stricken
Area* (1934) and *The Crucified Land* (1939). The latter is even more obviously
indebted to Surrealism than some of Bywaters's work. The painting is suffused
with passion: the flayed landscape becomes a suffering human figure, a
tormented giant. Not surprisingly, Hogue came to resent the dominance of the
'unholy American trinity' of Benton, Curry and Wood, and to feel that the art
produced by himself and his associates was superior to anything they could
offer: 'In a brief ten years,' Hogue said to a radio interviewer in 1939, the year
in which *The Crucified Land* was painted, 'we have reached a regional maturity
which is the envy of other parts of the country.'[24]

94 Alexandre Hogue
Drouth Stricken Area 1934
One of a number of Texas Regionalist landscapes that deal with the horrors of erosion.

95 Jerry Bywaters
On the Ranch 1941
At this stage of his career, Bywaters had begun to be influenced by the fashionable Surrealism of Salvador Dali.

96 **Alexandre Hogue** *The Crucified Land* 1939
Here the flayed land is anthropomorphized; the point is driven home by the cross planted on it, which is also a scarecrow.

The most widespread expression of the Regionalist spirit, though certainly not the best, was the government campaign to supply murals for public buildings, mostly post offices, all over America. This started under the auspices of the PWAP, and continued under the patronage of the Treasury Section (or Section of Painting and Sculpture), set up in 1934. It is these programmes that most acutely raise the question of the influence exercised over Regionalism by Mexican Muralism on the one hand and Soviet Socialist Realism on the other. The answers are complex.

Mexican Muralism was known and admired in the United States. Rivera, Orozco and Siqueiros all executed important works there, and for a while Rivera was a major artistic celebrity. In 1931–32 he was the subject of a major retrospective exhibition at The Museum of Modern Art in New York, the second in the Museum's history (the first had been devoted to Matisse). However, there was always a feeling that Mexican Muralism was, in American terms, exotic, and that it reflected the ideas of a very different society.

97 Victor Arnautoff *City Life* 1934
The mural offended the authorities because the newsstand in the corner displayed copies of *The Masses* and *The Daily Worker*.

Socialist Realist painting remained largely unknown to American artists and the American public. The likeness between many Russian works of the 1930s and those produced under the patronage of the PWAP and the Treasury Section is nevertheless striking. It seems to have sprung not from actual knowledge but from shared ideas which transcended the boundaries set by very different political systems. The chief of these ideas were that art should be immediately intelligible, and that it should be both intellectually and emotionally accessible to the whole population rather than to an elite. In general, American murals, though often as conservative in style as their Soviet counterparts, were careful to avoid overt political content.

A striking exception to this rule was provided by some of the murals in the new Coit Tower in San Francisco, built as a memorial to the city's volunteer firemen. Commissioned in 1933 under the PWAP, when things were less strictly controlled than they were to become under the Treasury Section, these were the work of twenty-five different artists, some with strong left-wing credentials. Offence was given by paintings done by two ex-assistants of Diego Rivera, neither of them American-born or destined to settle permanently in

America. *City Life*, a huge mural by the Russian Victor Arnautoff (1896–1979), offended not only because of its Rivera-like style but because a newsstand in the painting displayed copies of *The Masses* and *The Daily Worker*. The elusive Clifford Wight (*c*. 1900–*c*. 1960), generally described as 'an English sculptor', painted a towering figure of a *Steelworker*, surmounted by the hammer-and-sickle and the slogan 'United Workers of the World'. This was going too far, and despite the artist's protests the emblem and its accompanying slogan were obliterated, though the figure itself was allowed to remain. The furore over the Coit Tower bred a determination in Washington that in future no government-sponsored mural project must be allowed to slip from the grasp of the central bureaucracy.

Under the Treasury Section, the previous happy-go-lucky decentralization gave way to what has been described as a 'rigid system of aesthetic watchdogging'.[25] The man in charge was Edward Bruce, and his deputy was Edward Rowan, formerly director of the Little Gallery in Cedar Rapids – a community gallery which had some of the characteristics of a modern arts lab, but no doctrinaire commitment to Modernist ideas. The two administrators 'set up a scheme of graduated stages for the conception, refinement and completion of a mural, and personally scrutinized designs at every step for iconographic and stylistic deviation from quality standards'.[26]

Bruce, in particular, was a man who knew his own mind. He disliked both retrograde academic art and all Modernism too obviously influenced by the School of Paris. For him, both of these were out of step with American reality. The kind of murals he commissioned – and by the time the Treasury Section was disbanded in 1943 there were more than a thousand of them – were usually what would now be called Regionalist in subject matter: they fell into officially approved categories, such as 'the Post, Local History, Past or Present, Local Industry, Pursuits or Landscape'.[27] They were supposed to deal with these themes in a direct, easily recognizable way.

Conflicts – and they were numerous – arose when Bruce and Rowan tried to impose their will not so much on the artist they had chosen for the task as upon a local community which happened to have strong opinions of its own, either about the style of the mural proposed or (more usually) about its actual subject matter.

Despite an announced policy of consultation and of using local artists wherever possible, the Section also tended to impose painters who were regarded as complete outsiders on communities ill-prepared for their arrival. It switched approved compositions arbitrarily from one location to another, sometimes with curious results. For example, when *Life* magazine ran a feature illustrating some of the proposed designs, the illustration labelled 'Shelton, Oregon' showed a trail-boss, with his cowhands and his herd, in the plains of the Dakotas. The caption writer attempted to explain the anomaly by noting that 'Richard Haines's design for a prairie campfire scene will be altered to show lumberjacks, with whom Shelton's residents are more familiar.'[28]

A number of disagreements arose in circumstances rather similar to those which triggered Curry's breach with the Kansas legislature. For example, the inhabitants of the mining town of Kellogg, Idaho, gave a thumbs-down to a sketch by Fletcher Martin (1904–79) showing two miners carrying an injured

98 **Clifford Wight** *Steelworker* 1934
Wight, little known, but generally described as 'an English sculptor', was an ex-assistant of Diego Rivera. The figure was once accompanied by a hammer-and-sickle and the slogan 'United Workers of the World'.

comrade to safety. Martin was the artist who later succeeded Benton at the Kansas City Art Institute. He had already made a reputation for painting violent, macho scenes, and is today best remembered for his painting *Trouble in Frisco*, which shows two brawny sailors fighting on the dockside. Edward Rowan very much admired his sketch for Kellogg, and made strenuous though unavailing efforts to get it accepted. When Martin expressed a willingness to redesign his work, Rowan forbade him to do so and suggested that he paint an additional mural instead of altering it.

In this case there was little the Section could do, confronted as it was by opposition across the entire social spectrum. The mineworkers' union at Kellogg condemned the proposed mural in a unanimous vote, and the Idaho Art Association issued a statement which was equally negative: 'To hang a picture depicting [a mining accident] would prove a torture to the families of the victims and would certainly be in the poorest taste.'[29] In other cases, however, the Section did succeed in imposing its wishes on an indifferent, reluctant or even openly hostile local community.

There seems to be no complete register, even today, of all the post office murals commissioned by the Section and of their authors, but it is clear that the biggest guns among the Regionalists played a somewhat limited role. In general, they were already occupied with more important and better-paid enterprises. Curry actually pulled out of a major PWAP commission to go and work in Kansas.

BELOW LEFT

99 **Grant Wood and assistants** *Breaking the Sod* 1937
Wood's pupils eventually rebelled against being asked to participate in his mural projects.

BELOW RIGHT

100 **Fletcher Martin** *Trouble in Frisco* 1938
This striking design is the best-known work by the artist who succeeded Benton (Ills 80–85) in his teaching post at the Kansas City Art Institute.

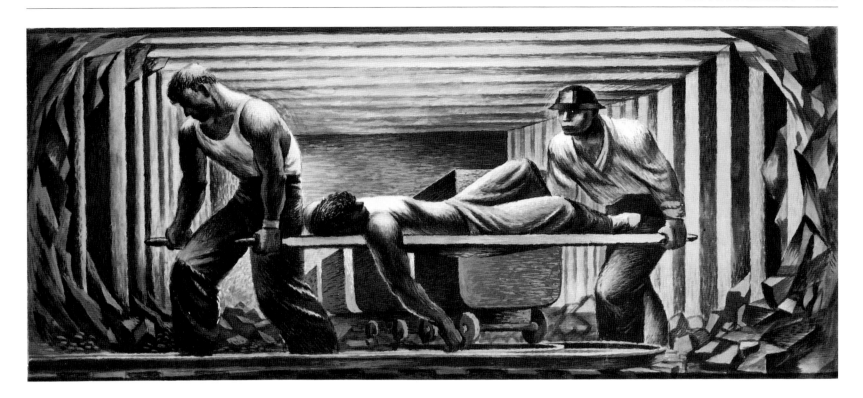

An examination of the lists of artists and commissions which have in fact been published, notably that covering Southern and Southwestern states included in Sue Bridwell Beckham's *Depression Post Office Murals and Southern Culture* (1989), indicates that the area where the Section's commissions and the local artistic situation were most closely aligned was probably Texas. Bywaters executed five murals at four different locations. Dozier carried out three, Hogue also three (two in Houston, one elsewhere). However, commissions were also given to out-of-state artists like Arnautoff (leader of the team which had decorated the Coit Tower in San Francisco, and now apparently forgiven for his behaviour on that occasion) and Martin.

Viewed from the standpoint offered by these numerous government commissions, handed out over a period of ten years, Regionalism seems to pose a paradox. The announced policy was to marry art to local feelings and local concerns. Yet the Regionalism of the post office murals was the nearest the United States ever came to imposing an official style. Where Regionalist artists were left face to face with local patrons, without the government serving as intermediary and ultimate arbiter, the result was often violent disagreement. It is surely significant that the three major names in Regionalism – Benton, Curry and Wood – all finished by alienating the very people in the Midwest whom they had said it was their intention to serve. Benton and Curry, in particular, never succeeded in overcoming an outsider status pinned on them from the moment of their return from the East. The movement, though sometimes bitterly attacked by artists and critics in New York, had more credibility there than in Missouri or Kansas.

101 **Fletcher Martin** *Mine Rescue* 1939
A sketch for a mural intended by the Treasury Section in Washington for the post office at Kellogg, Idaho. The subject was vehemently rejected by the local population, led by representatives of the mineworkers' union.

102 **Edward Hopper** *Hotel Lobby* 1943
The three people present are transients, as the setting
suggests, yet they also seem to be captives of an insuperable
inertia, an atmosphere typical of many of Hopper's interiors.

CHAPTER 8

Charles Burchfield and Edward Hopper

Two artists whose names were often linked with those of the leading Regionalists, but whose reputations survived the collapse of the movement in the early 1940s, were Charles Burchfield (1893–1967) and Edward Hopper (1882–1967). Both were fascinated by the texture of American life, but neither had a political or social agenda, or an ambition to make public statements about what it meant to be an American. For them, it was enough to paint what they saw, even if – or perhaps sometimes especially if – it had not previously been thought of as a subject for art. Both men had rather withdrawn, solitary, even melancholy temperaments, and it is this sense of personal isolation, of being within American society and yet not wholly of it, that gives special fascination to their work.

Burchfield's recently published *Journal* shows as clearly as his paintings that he was by temperament a non-joiner, content to live and work in almost total isolation from the rest of the American art world. The private quality of his art is emphasized by the fact that nearly all his work is in watercolour, and thus small in scale. He made only a few attempts to use oils, and these were unsuccessful. He lived a deliberately restricted life, first in Ohio, then in upper New York State. He left the borders of the USA only once, for a brief trip to Canada in 1941, and never went much farther west than Cleveland, which was the city where he received most of his artistic training, attending the Cleveland School (now Institute) from 1912 to 1916. His early work – produced before he left his childhood home in Salem, Ohio, to settle in Buffalo in 1921 – can hardly be described as realist; or rather it showed no signs of the realist impulse until the very end of that period. As a student in Cleveland, Burchfield was influenced by the tail-end of the *fin de siècle*. He read the Symbolist verse plays of W. B. Yeats, the transcendentalist poetry of Emerson and Walt Whitman, and the *Gitanjali* of Rabindranath Tagore. In 1915 he discovered the prints of Hokusai and Hiroshige, and he was also influenced by Art Nouveau poster design. These were not altogether happy years. Between 1916 and 1918 Burchfield suffered from profound emotional and psychological disturbances, accompanied by severe depression. He sometimes had experiences of disorientation and hallucination, which are reflected in his work.

He was not, however, cut off from his surroundings. Salem and its environs made a profound impression on him. When he revisited his home town in 1922 (thus only very shortly after he had separated himself from it), he noted in his journal: 'Nothing has changed or ever will change, this is mine forever.'[1]

In Buffalo, Burchfield got a job with a wallpaper manufacturing company, M. H. Birge & Sons, making designs and eventually running the design department. This obviously required a lot of thought about, and work with, pattern. Perhaps in slightly perverse reaction to this, the watercolours he produced in his own time grew markedly more realistic, elaborating a style which he had begun to explore before he left Salem. A watercolour like *The False Front* (1920–21), produced just before his departure from Ohio, depicts a visual environment which is not stimulating or picturesque in any conventional sense learned from European art. Burchfield seems to have accepted the subject simply because it was there, and because it somehow enabled him to express the sense of awareness he felt as he gazed at it.

ABOVE LEFT
103 Charles Burchfield
Hump Operations 1936
A number of similar railroad
subjects can be found in
Burchfield's oeuvre.

ABOVE RIGHT
104 Charles Burchfield
Promenade 1927–28
Burchfield finds aesthetic
interest in a row of banal,
turn-of-the-century houses in
the suburbs of Buffalo.

LEFT
105 Charles Burchfield
The False Front 1920–21
Though painted in Negley,
Ohio, before Burchfield left to
settle in Buffalo, the watercolour is already typical of his
deliberately anti-picturesque
approach.

In Buffalo itself, and later in Gardenville, the suburb to which he moved in 1925, Burchfield explored a variety of subject matter. It ranged from the banal turn-of-the-century bourgeois houses shown in *Promenade* (1927–28) to grittier subjects such as *Freight Yards* (1936) and *Three Boats in Winter* (1933). The bleak Buffalo waterfront, redolent of industrial decay, provided especially congenial material.

Though Burchfield did not become a controversial public figure, after the manner of Benton (nothing would have pleased him less), his watercolours found a reasonably steady market. Inevitably, because of their subject matter, he attracted the attention of the Regionalists and their supporters. Grant Wood, that indefatigable recruiter for the cause, paid Burchfield a visit in 1935.

Burchfield's reactions to the rise of Regionalism were ambiguous. He understood that his own work stood to benefit, at least in the short term, from association with this fashionable, much-discussed art movement. On the other

106 Charles Burchfield *Three Boats in Winter* 1933
In his *Journal*, Burchfield recorded the physical difficulties of working in wintry conditions on the shores of the Great Lakes.

hand, he did not really identify himself with it in any way, and resented the role of Regionalist forerunner which critics sometimes imposed upon him.

After the Regionalist movement began to weaken – and perhaps partly in response to this, but more likely because of his own inner promptings – Burchfield moved back to the more mystical, visionary manner of his younger years, sometimes actually making new versions of early compositions. By the mid-1940s he could no longer be counted primarily as a realist.

One contemporary artist with whom he did feel sympathy was Hopper, whom he first met in 1929. They were brought together by the fact that they shared the same New York dealer, and remained friends for the rest of their lives. Even so, there existed a certain reserve, at least on Burchfield's side. He once wrote to Alfred H. Barr, Jr, of The Museum of Modern Art in New York, that he felt that he and Hopper were 'at opposite poles of expression';[2] and this was before his own final change of style.

Hopper, who was ten years older than Burchfield, was slow to achieve his mature and characteristic manner. He did not become the Hopper most people know until he was in his forties. However, once he had established his style and range of subject matter, these varied hardly at all for the rest of his life. The flavour of these paintings is so powerful that they have played a part in shaping many people's vision of America – even that of people who know and care very little about the visual arts. In addition, although Hopper is not generally recognized as a powerful influence on other artists, elements of his way of looking at things recur in the work of American artists younger than himself.

Born in Nyack, N.Y., the son of the owner of a dry goods store, Hopper first studied commercial art (1899–1900), a profession which was later to stand him in good stead for some years, then worked under Robert Henri and Kenneth Hayes Miller at the New York School of Art. At the same period he had some contact with Chase, but did not admire his way of teaching. He thought Chase had rapport chiefly with the female members of his classes, and was inclined to show off to his students. Henri, on the other hand, influenced him profoundly. One of Hopper's best early paintings, *Blackwell's Island* (1911), is like a paraphrase of – and at the same time a reply to – a painting Henri had made eleven years earlier of the same motif.

This canvas is an exception in Hopper's early production, because its subject matter is specifically American. In 1906, after leaving the New York School, Hopper, with the financial help of his parents, went to Europe and spent the best part of a year in Paris. He did not enrol in an art school, but the city nevertheless had a major effect on him. Through his former classmate Patrick Henry Bruce (1881–1936), an expatriate painter later associated with Synchromism, he discovered the work of the Impressionists, but apparently not that of Matisse, who was to influence Bruce himself strongly from 1907 onwards. Hopper did not venture into the lively Paris avant–garde of the period, though the opportunity certainly existed. He said later:

> Whom did I meet? Nobody. I'd heard of Gertrude Stein, but I don't remember having heard of Picasso at all. I used to go to the cafés at night and sit and watch. I went to the theatre a little. Paris had no great or immediate impact on me.[3]

107 **Robert Henri** *Blackwell's Island, East River* 1900

108 **Edward Hopper** *Blackwell's Island* 1911
Hopper here tackles a motif Henri had used a decade
before (Ill. 107).

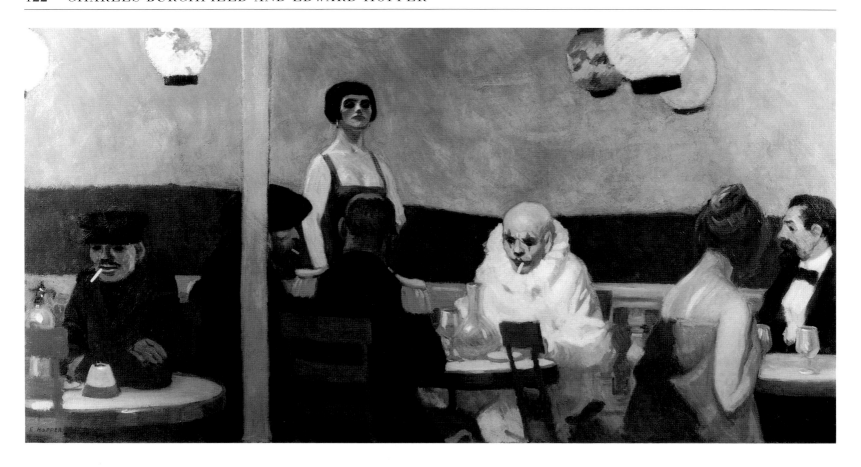

109 Edward Hopper *Soir Bleu* 1914
Hopper long retained nostalgic feelings for the period he spent
in Paris. This record of the Mi-Carême carnival is a
modernized version of one of Watteau's *fêtes galantes*.

When one looks at Hopper's early work, this last statement seems disin-
genuous. Quite a number of the early paintings are reminiscences of Paris, and
the city exercised a continuing fascination over him. He returned there in
1909, and once again in 1910, when he also went to Spain, visiting Madrid
and Toledo. This was his final trip to Europe, but his memories remained vivid
for a long while. 'It seemed awfully crude and raw here when I got back,' he
said later. 'It took me ten years to get over Europe.'[4] While living in New York
he continued to paint recollected scenes, rather than what was directly in front
of him. The most ambitious painting of the early period, *Soir Bleu* (1914), is a
sentimental evocation of the Mi-Carême festivities on the Parisian *grands
boulevards*, and also a tribute to the *fêtes galantes* of Watteau.

As a means of escape from his nostalgia for France, Hopper started painting
seascapes. There is a whole series showing the rocks and shore of Monhegan
Island, Maine. Influenced by Cézanne, these show a high degree of boldness and
abstraction, and demonstrate the now rapid development of Hopper's individual feeling for colour and light. At the same time, they are impersonal and
unspecific. What they lack is precisely the quality which seems most personal in
the bulk of Hopper's work – a sense of location, a feeling that a particular
moment must be fixed to the canvas because it can never be recaptured.

At the same period, Hopper was making prints which, in style and subject
matter, anticipated important aspects of his mature work.

The breakthrough came in 1923. The first work which showed what
Hopper would become was not an oil painting but a watercolour. *The Mansard
Roof* was painted in the fishing port of Gloucester, Massachusetts, in 1923. It is

110 Edward Hopper
House by the Railroad 1925
Usually thought to be the first fully formed example of Hopper's mature style, it embodies one of his typical moments of transience.

111 Edward Hopper *The Mansard Roof* 1923
Painted in the fishing-port of Gloucester, Massachusetts, this watercolour convincingly demonstrates the close stylistic link between Hopper and Burchfield (Ills 103–06).

close to some of Burchfield's work of the same period, though more brilliant in tone. Hopper exhibited it in a group show at the Brooklyn Museum, and the museum immediately purchased it.

In 1925 Hopper painted *House by the Railroad*, the first canvas where he is fully himself. It is filled with the clear, bleak light typical of many of his paintings. The building of the title is shown in isolation, in a way which makes it clear that this is something seen in passing. The painter, and therefore the spectator, can only guess at what goes on inside, behind the drawn blinds that cover nearly all of the windows.

Hopper specializes in the feeling of loneliness and detachment which fills *House by the Railroad*. He has innumerable ways of conveying it, and can conjure it up successfully even where the human figure is present. In *Office in a Small City* (1953), a man is seated at his desk in a brightly lit office on an upper floor. He is unaware of our presence; we see him through an uncurtained sheet of plate glass as if, once again, we were looking at – and now right into – the building from a passing train. In *Gas* (1940), the agent of motion is obviously an automobile. We are just drawing up to a country gas station, where a single figure is fiddling with one of the pumps. A brief, meaningless encounter will take place, and then we shall draw away again, leaving the attendant to his solitude. For its time (although the automobile was already an established feature of American life), the subject is unconventional. Before Hopper, gas stations were invisible to art; after him, they attracted many leading American artists: Pop painters and sculptors such as Ed Ruscha and George Segal, Photorealists such as Ralph Goings.

On those occasions when Hopper includes several figures in a single scene – an example is *Hotel Lobby* (1943) – he generally manages to suggest that the relationships between them are either non–existent or else distinctly uneasy. This painting combines both possibilities. On the right is a seated woman who reads a magazine and ignores everything around her. On the left we find an elderly couple, she seated, he standing. She glances up and seems to say something; he stares straight ahead and ignores her. The coat over his arm seems to indicate that he is impatient to leave.

This scene acquires a particular intensity from the fact that it takes place by artificial light. In the background the curtains are drawn, and a half-glimpsed restaurant is unlit and clearly not in use. The figures are in a kind of limbo: it may be late at night, or even very early in the morning, before dawn.

Hopper is always very skilful in using light to suggest times of day, which in turn help to set a mood. In *Office in a Small City*, the time seems to be late afternoon: almost time for the man at the desk to go home at the end of a perhaps profitless working day. In *Gas*, either the season is earlier or the hour is later. Dusk is beginning to gather, and a light is already on in the building behind the pumps. The darkening atmosphere adds to the general feeling of abandonment.

Both Hopper and his wife liked the theatre; it was one of the few things they spent money on, in an otherwise frugal existence. Theatrical influences have been detected in some of Hopper's paintings. A production of Elmer Rice's *Street Scene*, with decor by Jo Mielziner, has been seen as a probable source for Hopper's most famous image, *Early Sunday Morning* (1930).

112 **Edward Hopper** *Office in a Small City* 1953
The viewpoint indicates either that the office is seen from an adjoining high building,
or – more probably – from a passing train on an elevated track.

113 Edward Hopper *Early Sunday Morning* 1930
A quintessential evocation of urban loneliness.

It is typical of Hopper's temperament that actual theatre interiors, when he painted them, generally show an underpopulated auditorium, with the curtain down. *Two on the Aisle* (1927) uses a formula very like the one Hopper employed fifteen years later for *Hotel Lobby*. To the left, in a box, is a woman entirely on her own, absorbed in reading her programme. Down front, in the second row of the stalls, are an elegant couple who have arrived long before anyone else and are busy settling themselves. They seem to ignore the empty space around them and also each other.

Hopper is a pivotal figure in the history of American realist art. He looks back to Eakins and Homer and forward to artists like Robert Bechtle (usually classified as a Photorealist) and Wayne Thiebaud (often classified as Pop). His enormous popularity shows that he touches something deep in the American psyche; Americans clearly feel that he holds a truthful mirror up to themselves. This is understandable in one way. In a subtly understated fashion, Hopper represents a wide range of typically American subject matter. The paintings are full of small details which show that they could emanate from no other country. What does seem un-American about them, however, at least to an outsider, is that they are so often melancholic, or even downright pessimistic, in tone.

114 Edward Hopper *Gas* 1940
Probably the first appearance of
the gas station in serious art, *Gas* anticipated
the Pop artists of the 1960s, notably George
Segal (Ill. 197), and the Californian, Ed
Ruscha.

115 Edward Hopper *Two on the Aisle* 1927
Hopper and his wife, Josephine, were both
passionately fond of the theatre, yet despite the
essentially gregarious nature of theatre-going,
his paintings of the subject generally show, as
here, an underpopulated auditorium.

CHAPTER 9

Urban and Social Realism

Any painter whose subject matter is chiefly urban is apt to find himself or herself characterized as a social realist. This is misleading in the case of a number of prominent American artists of the 1930s and 1940s. Their subject was the city and its environs – specifically New York – but what they painted was seen in a relatively neutral way, leaving the social and moral commentaries to others.

There were also, by contrast, urban painters who were deeply concerned about the social problems of the day, and who wanted to comment on these directly and unambiguously. These artists were alienated by what they took to be the boosterism and sentimentality of Regionalist work, and by a narrow chauvinism which glorified what they felt to be unacceptable stereotypes. This was the attitude of a number of artists living in New York who were forced to confront the city's problems at first hand. The painter Moses Soyer, reviewing the Whitney Museum's Second Biennial Exhibition (1934–35), denounced what he saw as a distortion of both moral and artistic values:

> Artists … should not be misled by the chauvinism of the 'Paint America' slogan. Yes, paint America, but with your eyes open. Do not glorify Main Street. Paint it as it is – mean, dirty, avaricious. Self–glorification is artistic suicide. Witness Nazi Germany.[1]

The irony was that these vehement social realists were closer in style to the Regionalists than to the cooler urban painters. Many participated in the Federal mural programme, which is now often seen as a Regionalist-dominated enterprise.

The 'cool' urban realists of the period were the artists who belonged to the so-called Fourteenth Street Group. These rendered New York scenes and figures in a relatively detached and dispassionate way, though the consequences of the Depression are often clearly visible in the scenes they chose to depict.

The senior member of the group was Kenneth Hayes Miller (1876–1952). Originally a pupil of Chase, Hayes Miller was already an influential teacher at the Art Students' League in the years just before World War I. He taught there for forty years, from 1911 to 1951. His own work is an amalgam of two slightly incompatible impulses. On the one hand, while still quite a young man, he fell in love with Renoir's work of the 1880s – the so-called 'classical' period, best represented by the great picture of *Bathers* now in the Philadelphia Museum of Art. On the other hand, he came strongly under the influence of the great Renaissance fresco painters of the early fifteenth century, Masaccio and Piero della Francesca.

In the mid-1920s, some years before the birth of Regionalism, Hayes Miller began to paint pictures of women shopping. Though in contemporary dress, the figures are endowed with a kind of monumentality. Characteristic examples are *Shopper* (1928) and *Show Window No. 2* (1932). In both, the urban setting is conveyed by a background of plate-glass windows full of goods for sale. These are, in fact, among the earliest works to tackle the theme of consumerism, which came to dominate American art in the years after World War II. Hayes Miller's bourgeois figures are so determinedly neutral that they have been accused of vacuousness – though to me he seems a much better and

117 **Kenneth Hayes Miller** *Shopper* 1928
This shows the curious combination of influences in Miller's work – on the one hand, Renoir, on the other, Italian Renaissance masters, such as Piero della Francesca.

OPPOSITE
116 **Kenneth Hayes Miller** *Show Window No. 2* 1932
Universally acknowledged as an influential teacher, Hayes Miller has been underrated as an artist. His paintings are perhaps the very first to take American consumerism as their subject.

118 Isabel Bishop *Tidying Up* 1941
Bishop had instinctive sympathy for the shop-
girls and secretaries who populated the streets
around her studio during their lunchbreak.

stronger painter than most critics have taken him for, and an important originator. He is, for example, the true ancestor of the Magic Realists who carried the realist banner in the 1950s, at a time when all forms of realism seemed threatened with extinction.

In recent years, the reputation of his pupil Isabel Bishop (1902–88) has stood higher than that of Hayes Miller himself. Bishop's actual subject matter differs very little from his, but stylistically she is more refined, to the point where some works can seem too nervously vaporous and evanescent. Not an adventurous colourist, she triumphs through her draughtsmanship; always exquisitely refined, her drawings are among the strongest in twentieth-century American art.

Her background was upper middle-class. Born in Cincinnati and brought up in Detroit, she came to New York in 1918 to study illustration, later working under Hayes Miller at the Art Students' League. She then took a studio on 14th Street, later moving to Union Square, and started to explore her typical and, on the whole, very narrow range of subjects. She painted female nudes, and also depicted what she saw around her in the New York streets – young working women from nearby offices, shopping or eating in their lunch hour, and the bums and hoboes who were typical inhabitants of the quarter, which stretched as far as the Bowery.

119 Isabel Bishop
Ice Cream Cones 1942

120 **Isabel Bishop** *Dante and Virgil in Union Square* 1932
An unusually large and complex composition for the artist.
Dante and Virgil appear in the centre foreground as visitors
to downtown New York, seen as a modern version of Dante's
Purgatorio.

The essential difference between Bishop's work and that of her mentor,
Hayes Miller, lies in her treatment of light. Even in relatively early paintings
her figures are already surrounded by a tremulous envelope of light.
Sometimes, as in the ambitious *Dante and Virgil in Union Square* (1932), she
views her protagonists from a distance, and the crowd itself becomes a living
organism; sometimes she moves into close-up. Whether she paints the crowd or
the individual, the message is one about humanity, but never in a narrowly
political or social sense. As she herself once said: 'I had no political interest
whatsoever. These were observations of fact. I felt I was saying some small
thing which was true of American life – apart from politics and economics.'[2]

Bishop was closely associated professionally with Reginald Marsh
(1898–1954), who was also a pupil of Hayes Miller. Marsh's subject matter –
the ordinary life of New Yorkers – was basically the same as hers, but he
imbued it with a very different mood. He painted people on display – in the
streets, in dance halls, in burlesque theatres and on the crowded beaches at
Coney Island, where New Yorkers traditionally escape the summer heat. He
was at one and the same time an obsessive chronicler of the minutiae of
contemporary life and the creator of a dream world which linked bums and
taxi-dancers and tawdry amusement parks to the tumultuous work of some of
the Old Masters, notably Tintoretto and Rubens. He was one of the earliest
artists – perhaps indeed the very first – to explore the possibilities offered by
the new world of mass culture; and yet at heart he was a traditionalist, always
keenly aware of the art of the past.

121 **Reginald Marsh** *East 10th Street Jungle* 1934
Both Marsh and Bishop (Ills 118–20) were fascinated by the
hobos who hung around the Bowery.

122 **Reginald Marsh** *Ten Cents a Dance* 1933
The taxi-dancers who worked in New York dance-halls
modelled themselves on the movie-stars of the day such as
Jean Harlow.

Like Bishop, but unlike many of his contemporaries in the New York art
world, Marsh came from a prosperous, cultivated background. His paternal
grandfather made a fortune in the Chicago meat packing industry; his father
was a successful mural painter. Marsh himself was educated at Yale (class of
1920). His first ambition was to be a cartoonist, and he soon achieved success
in that field, landing a job on the *New York Daily News*, doing cartoon reviews
of vaudeville and burlesque performances. In 1923, when the *New Yorker* was
founded, he was one of the first cartoonists recruited by the magazine. In
1925, having married the daughter of the curator of painting at the
Metropolitan Museum of Art, he made a trip to Paris which fuelled his interest
in the Old Masters, and it was on his return that he enrolled at the Art
Students' League under Hayes Miller.

From his earliest years in New York, Marsh recorded everything he saw.
After his death more than two hundred sketchbooks were found, neatly
organized in chronological order. In addition to these he kept scrapbooks,
notebooks and calendars in which he documented every phase of his activity.
He was an enthusiastic snapshot photographer, and figures and groupings
from his photographs were regularly transferred to his teeming compositions.

Their identity is often difficult to detect, even with both photograph and
painting immediately in front of one, because Marsh suffered from a kind of
horror vacui. In his most typical paintings, such as *Coney Island* (1936), the
composition is stacked up vertically and at the same time pressed tightly
against the picture-plane. The mass of interlocking figures occupies so much of
the available space that the spectator's eye cannot find a way of escaping into
the distance. The ultimate model for compositions of this type seems to be
Rubens – for example the *Fall of the Damned* and the *Small Last Judgment* in
Munich, which, though different in subject, have a similar pictorial structure.

Though Marsh painted scenes intimately connected with the Depression
and its effects, such as *East 10th Street Jungle* (1934), what motivated him
was neither moral indignation nor the desire to condemn the present state of
American society. He was not a reflective artist; his desire, chiefly, was to
celebrate what he saw. Beneath this general celebratory impulse lay another:
Marsh clearly had a strong sexual drive, and one of the things which fascinated
him was the blatant sexuality of the new American society. This fascination
asserts itself in almost all his work – for instance in *Ten Cents a Dance* (1933),
which shows taxi-dancers waiting for partners in a New York dance hall. It has
quite rightly been pointed out that these dancers, and many of the other young
women shown in Marsh's work, offer an echo of the movie-stars of the period:
Jean Harlow, for instance, as she appeared on posters and on the covers of
movie magazines. Stars of this type did of course provide the women Marsh
painted with role-models. Yet he too, and quite independently, was enamoured
of the same image. Marsh's New York floozies of the Depression years are the
forebears of Warhol's portraits of Marilyn Monroe. In today's climate these
images are sometimes read as misogynist, but the real motive was admiration,
tinged with a certain irony.

Even where the commentary on society is more specific, and more obviously
political, than in the work of Hayes Miller, Bishop or Marsh, there are wide
variations of style among the American urban realists of the period. There is,

123 **Reginald Marsh** *Coney Island* 1936
This composition typifies Marsh's *horror vacui* – the whole surface is packed with figures. His sources were often snapshot photographs he took himself.

124 Raphael Soyer *Office Girls* 1936
A variation on a theme often used by Isabel Bishop
(Ills 118–20).

for example, a wide stylistic gap between the paintings made by the three Soyer brothers, Moses (1898–1973), Raphael (1898–1987) and Isaac (1902–81), and those of William Gropper, Ben Shahn and Jack Levine. This is true despite the fact that all these artists were Jewish, and either immigrants or the children of immigrants, and thus keenly aware, from personal experience, of the darker side of American life.

Born in Russia, the Soyer brothers arrived in the United States in 1912. Raphael, who was to become the best-known of the trio, and Moses were twins, but after a while decided to study at different art schools, so as not to influence one another too much. For this reason Raphael went to the Art Students' League, while Moses went to the Educational Association. There is, nevertheless, a strong stylistic resemblance, which also extends to the work of the youngest brother, Isaac.

The Soyers were admirers of the nineteenth-century realist tradition, as represented in France by Courbet and in America by Eakins. Though they sometimes chose similar subjects to those selected by Bishop and Marsh, their actual treatment of them is looser and more painterly. Raphael Soyer's *Office Girls* (1936) makes an interesting contrast with Bishop's treatment of the same theme: the composition, with close-packed standing figures, is similar, but surface and handling are entirely different.

In addition to being close to one another in style, the Soyer brothers were attracted to certain common themes. One was the idea of people passively waiting for something to happen. Moses Soyer (*c.* 1935) and Isaac Soyer (1937) both showed people waiting, apparently without hope, in an employment agency. Raphael Soyer produced the less specifically titled *Waiting Room* (*c.* 1940). There is thus a link with Hopper as well as with Eakins; the people in Hopper's paintings often show a similar passivity.

It is passivity, as well as a certain conservativism of style, that helps to mark off the work of the three Soyer brothers from that of Gropper, Shahn and Levin. These, too, are commonly called 'realists' by critics and historians of American art – and Shahn, for one, was certainly prepared to put himself, at least momentarily, at the head of a realist phalanx opposed to Abstract Expressionism. But their perceived realism seems to spring, not from their actual treatment of appearances, but from their insistent emphasis on the grittier and more sordid aspects of contemporary life.

William Gropper (1897–1977), for example, was essentially a caricaturist, who exaggerated aspects of reality for satirical or polemical purposes. Though born in America, he experienced the immigrant sweatshops of the Lower East Side at first hand, and was a long time in making his escape from them. They played a major role in shaping his view of American society. Despite the poverty of his background, he was not self-taught, but managed to pick up the rudiments of art education, often working part-time. Both Henri and Bellows were among his teachers. In 1919, when he finished his studies, his dazzlingly fluent skills as a draughtsman won him a job on the *New York Tribune*. This employment, in turn, brought him into contact with the world of left-wing politics. In addition to working as a cartoonist for magazines like *Vanity Fair* and *The Smart Set*, he became a contributor, generally unpaid, to left-wing

ABOVE LEFT
125 Moses Soyer
Employment Agency c. 1935
These two very similar
compositions, by Moses Soyer
and his brother Isaac (Ill. 126),
are comments on the near-
hopeless search for employment
during the worst period of the
Depression.

ABOVE RIGHT
126 Isaac Soyer *Employment
Agency* 1937

127 Raphael Soyer
Waiting Room c. 1940
These are travellers in a railway
station, rather than people in
search of work, but the
atmosphere is nevertheless very
similar to that in the other two
paintings by members of the
Soyer family (Ills 125-26).

128 **William Gropper** *Tailor* 1940
A reminiscence of the artist's family background: his father,
grandfather and great-grandfather had all been tailors.

periodicals, working for the Yiddish Communist daily, *Morning Freiheit*, and
also for *New Masses*, which showcased some of his best work.

Gropper twice visited Russia at this time: first in 1927, as an official guest
for the tenth anniversary of the Soviet Union (his companions included
Sinclair Lewis and Theodore Dreiser), and then in 1930 as a delegate to the
Kharkov Congress. In New York he became one of the organizers of the left-
wing John Reed Club and of the American Artists' Congress.

Given this frenetic level of political and professional activity, it is not
surprising that Gropper was slow in establishing himself as a painter. His first
one-person exhibition of paintings, at the ACA Galleries in New York, did not
take place until 1936. In spite, or perhaps even because, of his well-advertised
left-wing connections, it was an immediate success. For a while, Gropper was a
very fashionable artist. He was given a Guggenheim Foundation award in
1937, and in the same year the Metropolitan Museum of Art bought two of his
paintings. He was drawn into the mural movement, first doing a post office
mural at Freeport, Long Island (1936), then a series of murals for the
Department of the Interior building in Washington, D.C. (1938).

After this the tide began to turn. In the 1940s, Gropper first was chosen to
record the achievements of the American troops sent to participate in the North
African campaign, then had the appointment cancelled because of his record as
a 'premature anti-Fascist'. He continued to be a prolific draughtsman and
printmaker after the war, but did not really succeed in re-establishing himself as
a painter.

One reason for this was the changed political climate; another was the
radical change in the artistic situation brought about by the rise of Abstract
Expressionism. Yet another was the nature of his talent. Gropper's graphic work

129 **William Gropper** *The Senate* 1935
Political caricature in paint.

is more original, and likely to last better, than his painting. Whereas Honoré Daumier, another great caricaturist, survives the transition to oil-paint, Gropper seems to lose much of his brio in a different medium. *The Senate* (1935), which is really no more than a political caricature in paint, lacks the inventiveness, the surreal menace, the sense of real evil, which pervade Gropper's best drawings for *New Masses*. Although *The Tailor* (1940) is a direct reminiscence of Gropper's own family background (his father, grandfather and great-grandfathers had all been tailors, and he remembered sleeping on huge bundles of clothes in the sweatshops),[3] it remains curiously detached in feeling.

Ben Shahn (1898–1969) seems to have built a more durable reputation, though even this has been somewhat eclipsed in recent years. Shahn was born in Lithuania and settled in New York with his family in 1906. He got his early training in a lithography shop, before attending New York University, City College and finally (1933) life classes at the National Academy of Design. In 1925 and again in 1927 he travelled abroad; in Paris, the two artists whose work appealed to him most were Georges Rouault and Raoul Dufy.

The things which seem to have impelled Shahn to rebel against the influence of the School of Paris and become his own man were, first, a friendship with Walker Evans, one of the greatest of American photographers, whom he met in 1929; and, second, a summer spent working at Truro, Cape Cod, in 1930, painting small beach scenes with the painterly technique he had acquired abroad. James Thrall Soby, a longtime supporter of Shahn, quoted the artist's reaction to his own endeavours:

> I had seen all the right pictures, and read all the right books – Voltaire,
> Meier-Graefe, David Hume. But it still didn't add up to anything. 'Here I am,'
> I said to myself, 'Thirty-two years old, the son of a carpenter. I like stories and
> people. The French school is not for me.'[4]

Shahn now evolved an alternative vision that owed something to the art of the Weimar Republic, in particular to the harsh grotesqueries of George Grosz. Other elements are echoes of American folk painting (increasingly popular and collected in America during the 1920s and 1930s; its influence is also visible, as has been said, in some Regionalist work), plus ideas borrowed from the long-established tradition of newspaper caricature.

A further source was photography. However, what interested Shahn was the aberrations of the camera, not its direct access to reality. This point was noted by Clement Greenberg, Shahn's opponent and the chief defender of Abstract Expressionism: 'It was the monocular photograph, with its sudden telescoping of planes, its abrupt leaps from solid foreground to flat distance, that in the early 1930s gave him [Shahn] the formula for the most successful pictures he has painted since then.'[5]

These stylistic elements are all present in the compositions which made Shahn's reputation: a series of twenty-three paintings in gouache devoted to the trial and execution of the Italian-American anarchists Nicola Sacco and Bartolomeo Vanzetti. This was an affair which moved the consciences of many Americans, from the time when Sacco and Vanzetti were convicted of murder on the flimsiest of evidence in 1920 until their execution, after the rejection of all appeals for clemency, in 1927.

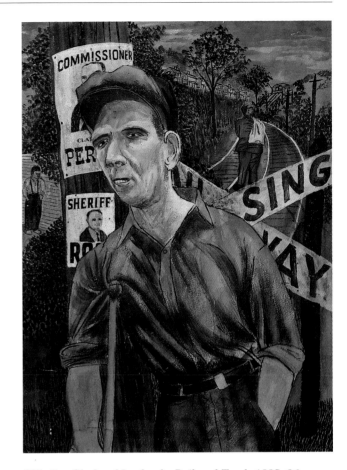

130 **Ben Shahn** *Man by the Railroad Track* 1935–36
Shahn was an accomplished poster-designer and his paintings, as here, often make effective use of type.

131 **Ben Shahn** *Bartolomeo Vanzetti and Nicola Sacco* 1931–32

The Sacco-Vanzetti series points in several different directions. When first shown at the Downtown Gallery in 1932, the paintings were admired by Diego Rivera, then in New York working on his doomed mural at the Rockefeller Center. Rivera immediately asked Shahn to assist him with the project. This is a reminder that Shahn's series can itself be thought of as mural paintings in little. He was later to carry out some mural projects of his own, though these do not occupy a major place in his work.

The Sacco-Vanzetti paintings clearly inspired a number of similar series produced by the African American artist Jacob Lawrence (1917–2000). Lawrence, who studied at various New York art schools, joined the Federal Art Project (FAP, the main New Deal initiative to subsidize individual artists) in the late 1930s, and held his first major one-person exhibition at the Downtown Gallery in 1941 – that is, just nine years after Shahn had exhibited there. It was on that occasion that he showed his *Migration of the Negro* series, which recorded the mass movement of poor Southern blacks to the industrial cities of the North. The series had been preceded by several others, dealing with the stories of Toussaint-Louverture, the liberator of Haiti (1937–38), and of the anti-slavery campaigners Frederick Douglass (1938–39) and Harriet Tubman (1939–40). In all of these, too, the debt to Shahn is apparent. Nevertheless, the ways in which Lawrence differs from Shahn are also interesting. His flat, silhouetted figures owe something to Synthetic Cubism, something to the more abstract townscapes of Sheeler, and something to another leading Mexican muralist, Orozco. Lawrence's realist roots – like Shahn's – did not run deep.

Another parallel can be drawn with the paintings of Jack Levine (1915–). Levine was a precociously brilliant artist who produced what is still perhaps his best-known painting, *The Feast of Pure Reason*, at the age of twenty-two, in 1937. Here Shahn's allegiance to the caricature tradition is pushed even further: the figures are brilliantly imagined grotesques.

As with many paintings by very young artists, the sources of *The Feast of Pure Reason* are complex, and have little to do with direct observation. The composition is derived from a group portrait by the early nineteenth-century Scottish painter Sir Henry Raeburn, a maker of aristocratic likenesses. The title alludes to James Joyce's novel *Ulysses*, and specifically to a scene in which Stephen Dedalus is knocked down by two constables and loses his glasses and his walking-stick. Leopold Bloom helps him to his feet, saying as he does so, 'Your stick, sir.' To which Dedalus replies: 'Stick? What need have I of a stick in this feast of pure reason?' In 'real' terms, the painting alludes to the corrupt regime of the local political boss, Mayor James Curley, in Boston, the city where Levine was brought up. Curley, like many leading Boston politicians, was of Irish descent; hence the appropriateness of an allusion to Joyce.

Like Gropper before him, Levine became a caricaturist in paint. Another, later and less complex example of the satiric impulse in his work is *Reception in Miami* (1948), a reaction to a news item in the *New York Post* describing the way in which rich Florida socialites bowed and scraped to the Duke and Duchess of Windsor. Many of his paintings, however, veer off in completely non-realist directions – there are parodies of the Old Masters, and images of Hebrew prophets which are heartfelt tributes to Judaism.

In a way, the artist who makes the most interesting comparison with Shahn is a contemporary who is not nearly so often mentioned in connection with him as Levine and Gropper. This is Philip Evergood (1901–73). Evergood's father – the family name was originally Blashki – was of Polish Jewish origin, but his background was in other respects quite unlike that of the Jewish artists discussed in this chapter. Meyer Blashki, born in Australia and himself an artist, had already abandoned Jewish belief and practice by the time he met and married Evergood's mother, who came from a prosperous English Gentile family. After the marriage the couple settled in New York, and Evergood was born there. However, when he was eight his mother took him to England to be educated, putting him into various boarding schools. His longest stay in any of

BELOW LEFT
134 Jack Levine *The Feast of Pure Reason* 1937
A satire on the corrupt regime of Mayor James Curley in Boston, inspired by a passage from James Joyce's *Ulysses*.

BELOW RIGHT
135 Jack Levine *Reception in Miami* 1948
Rich Florida socialites bow and scrape to the Duke and Duchess of Windsor.

136 **Philip Evergood** *Dance Marathon* 1934
Evergood here tackles a subject more usually
associated with Reginald Marsh (Ills 121–23).

137 **Philip Evergood** *The Pink Dismissal Slip* 1937
The most 'social realist' of Evergood's paintings.

these was at Eton, from 1915 to 1919. He afterwards spent two years at Trinity
Hall, Cambridge, but abandoned his degree course there because he wanted to
be an artist.

After Trinity Hall, Evergood studied first at the Slade School in London
under Henry Tonks, the most famous (and most feared) professor of drawing of
the time, who had previously numbered Augustus John and Stanley Spencer
among his pupils. He then returned to New York, where his parents were now
settled, and studied at the Art Students' League, where one of his teachers was
George Luks.

The first part of Evergood's professional career, despite these auspices, was
restless and unsettled, spent between the United States and Europe. He was a
long time in finding a direction or a convincing personal style. In fact the earliest
works in which Evergood is truly himself were not painted until the 1930s,
when he settled permanently in the United States. During the previous decade
he had shown little sign of political commitment and equally little interest in
specifically American themes. All this now changed: he worked for the PWAP
and FAP, and was a founder-member of the Artists' Committee of Action and
president of the Artists' Union, which developed out of it. He took part in the so-
called '219 Strike', when 219 artists invaded the offices of the Work Progress
Administration (WPA) to protest against lay-offs, and was injured in a violent
confrontation with the police:

> They beat me insensible, just because I was standing in the front line and
> refused to ungrip my arms with the others around me, and refused to leave
> the building. My nose was broken, blood was pouring out of my eyes, my ear
> was all torn down, my overcoat had been taken, and the collar ripped off. I
> was pushed out by the police at the bottom of the elevator and thrown into a
> Black Maria. Later they took us to a vile jail up on the West Side, and they
> put us in cells where the toilets had overflowed and we were standing, ankle-
> deep, men and women, all night in that filth. We were tried *en masse*, and
> escaped with a warning.[6]

At this period Evergood's subject matter was often close to that favoured by
Marsh. *Dance Marathon* (1934) uses one of the latter's most characteristic
themes, while *Art on the Beach* (*c.* 1936) has much in common with Marsh's
Coney Island compositions, including his tendency to push everything up
against the picture-plane. Other paintings, however, such as *The Pink Dismissal
Slip* (1937), are more propagandist in content and therefore closer to Shahn.

In the paintings where he is most truly himself, such as *Nude by the El*
(1934), Evergood resembles neither of these artists. The act of painting a nude
becomes an excuse for an exuberant domestic conversation piece set in
Evergood's own apartment. In its relish for the bohemian life, the painting is
very like some of the products of the Ashcan School, though different in actual
style. Its idiom owes a good deal to American folk art. It is as if Evergood were
trying to strip away both the stylistic and social conventions which usually
surround the act of making an artwork. Is the result 'realism'? Probably not, in
terms of visual observation; and yet there is a genuine attempt here to get at the
realities of a particular situation. For me, at least, this gives the work a greater
truth than Shahn's customary political rhetoric.

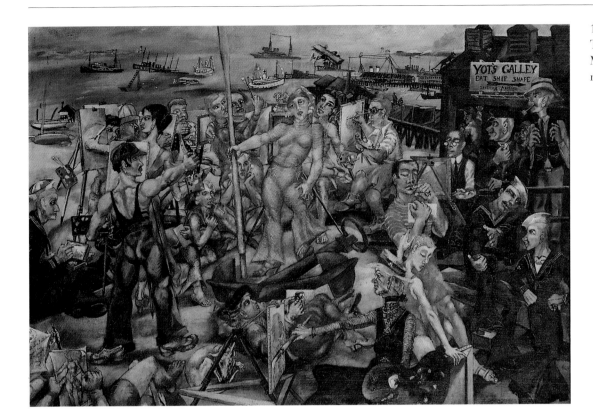

138 **Philip Evergood** *Art on the Beach* c. 1936
This, like *Dance Marathon* (Ill. 136), is similar to
Marsh (Ills 121–23), but with a humorous touch
more typical of Evergood.

139 **Philip Evergood** *Nude by the El* 1934
A celebration of the bohemian life-style in the shape
of a conversation piece set in Evergood's own
apartment, showing the influence on him of
American folk art.

CHAPTER 10

A Revolution in American Art

THE 1940S and 1950s witnessed the most drastic upheaval in the history of American art, and the point at which uses of the term 'realism' tended to change their meaning. Figuration, so long the dominant mode, had been challenged during the interwar period by varieties of abstraction; now, in the minds of many people, it became a marginal means of artistic expression. It was only with the advent of Pop Art in the early 1960s that representation of things seen in the external world returned to prominence. Even then, this representation was generally filtered or refracted through something else: figures and objects were no longer experienced directly by the painter, but through conventions imposed by the photographer, the photographic retoucher and the advertising designer.

The reasons for the fall of realism were complex. Many of the leading painters of the new generation, that of the Abstract Expressionists, did in fact begin their careers with work related to existing realist modes. One of the best-known examples is Jackson Pollock (1912–56), the chief hero of Abstract Expressionism's abolitionist myth. Pollock's close personal relationship with Thomas Hart Benton has already been mentioned. In the mid-1930s he was painting feeble imitations of typical Benton compositions. *Going West* (*c.* 1934–35), once in Benton's own collection, shows how far short he fell of the energetic elasticity of Benton's best work. The typical mannerisms are there, but not the verve. Other Abstract Expressionists whose early work was figurative include Lee Krasner (1908–84), later Pollock's wife, who in the mid-1930s was painting urban architecture in a style reminiscent of Edward Hopper, and who also tried a slightly more surreal mode, complete with plunging perspectives. It has been suggested that this may have derived from the ominously empty piazzas of Giorgio de Chirico. A model nearer home was the work being done in America at about this time by Ralston Crawford.

Some Abstract Expressionists took a long time before making up their minds to abandon figuration. An example is Philip Guston (1913–80), who spent the early part of his career working as a figurative artist. In 1934, for example, he and his friend Reuben Kadish (1913–92) went to Mexico, where they painted a vast mural entitled *The Struggle Against War and Fascism* for Emperor Maximilian's former summer palace in Morelia. The style they employed was pure Siqueiros, which was not surprising, as in fact Siqueiros himself was responsible for getting the two young Americans the commission. Ten years later, Guston – while still working figuratively – espoused a different, more delicate, neo-romantic manner, typified by *If This Be Not I* (1945). This painting, with its use of masks and shrouded faces, typifies a stylistic fashion whose development was aborted by the emergence of the new abstraction.

Realism suddenly lost its central position in American art for many reasons, but the chief of these was the change in the political climate, both domestically and internationally. The isolationist mood which prevailed during the 1930s had found a reflection in Regionalism, just as the sharp social conflicts generated by the Depression were reflected in the highly politicized social realism practised by Shahn and others. In the 1940s the emphasis shifted, and even those who had been emphatic supporters of Marxism managed to reconcile themselves to the new abstract art, with its lack of specific content. Regionalism was eclipsed; the remaining social realists were left fighting a rearguard action.

140 **Paul Cadmus** *Playground* 1948
Cadmus's brother-in-law and long-time champion, Lincoln Kirstein, sees 'the urban disinherited' as the primary subject of this painting. It is also possible to read *Playground* as a work whose theme is the social isolation of the homosexual.

141 Jackson Pollock *Going West* c. 1934–35
A feeble imitation of Pollock's then mentor, Thomas Hart
Benton (Ills 80–85).

One factor in the rise of Abstract Expressionism was that, like Regionalism before it, it soon became an instrument of policy. In particular, it was heavily promoted by American cultural agencies abroad, as a symbol of creative leadership in the fine arts which matched the political supremacy America had achieved as the result of World War II. The fact that the Soviet Union had imposed a rigid doctrine of Socialist Realism on its own painters and sculptors tended to depress the fortunes of realist art still further in the United States. For the first time, realistic depiction, art which reflected the facts of the visible world, could be presented as something alien to American culture.

Supporters of the new non-objective art tried to disable the argument that it was devoid of human concerns. Rather they argued that its perception of these concerns was more refined than anything known to the realists:

> The compulsion behind this art, we can see now, is less that of a physical and
> concrete ideal, in comparison with our more literal past, but in becoming
> abstract is more spiritual, insubstantial, trying to find itself as part of an ordered
> system. For the artist is not like the scientist, who tells us how hot the material
> is; he must accept the ultimate question and say what hot is.[1]

The beleaguered realists tried to defend themselves. In 1950 Raphael Soyer called together a group of artists who included, in addition to himself, Hopper, Shahn, Bishop, Leon Kroll and Yasuo Kuniyoshi. This group, which lobbied museum directors and critics about their championship of non-objective art, continued to meet over the next few years, and in 1953 published the first of three issues of a journal called *Reality*, devoted to the promotion of what were called human qualities in painting. Though it won widespread support among artists, the group and its journal had little effect on the way things were developing in the official art world. By the mid-1950s, abstraction – and Abstract Expressionism in particular – seemed to be everywhere triumphant.

142 Lee Krasner
Fourteenth Street 1934
At this period, Krasner's work showed
affinities with Precisionists such as
Niles Spencer (Ill. 69).

143 Philip Guston *If This Be Not I* 1945
Guston was a neo-Romantic allegorist before becoming an Abstract Expressionist.

144 Philip Guston and Reuben Kadish *The Struggle Against War and Fascism* 1934

There were, however, pockets of resistance. One effect of the defeat of realism was a series of stylistic splits among those who continued to insist on using figurative imagery. The idea of what was 'real' in art became fragmented, and this did not help artists who now thought of themselves as outsiders to make their point. Where the wider audience was concerned, realism increasingly became identified with figuration, and little distinction was made between one kind of figurative work and another.

As we have already seen, the artists classified as social realists – Shahn and Levine in particular – continued to produce paintings in the style they had already established for themselves. Some retained close connections with the official art world, now in theory dominated by the champions of non-figurative painting. One who did so was Shahn, who dropped out of the group founded by Soyer around the time when *Reality* was first published:

> According to Bernada Bryson Shahn [Shahn's wife], he felt that the group was too exclusive and that, while the issues they talked about at the early informal meetings were important, they were not the basis for an official organization. Raphael Soyer felt, however, that Shahn's departure was influenced by a combination of his close relationship with MOMA [The Museum of Modern Art] and the museum's criticism of the group.[2]

At the time, however, the most talked-about opponents of the new abstraction were the Magic Realists, who took their name from an exhibition held at The Museum of Modern Art in 1943, entitled 'American Realists and Magic Realists'. The catalogue noted that the term Magic Realism had begun to be applied 'to the work of painters who by means of an exact realistic technique

145 Peter Blume *The Eternal City* 1934–37
A satire on Mussolini's Italy, heavily influenced by Salvador
Dali.

try to make plausible their improbable, dreamlike or fantastic visions'.[3] This was therefore a realism of style, not of content. Its sources were in part American – the work of William Harnett, for example, now beginning to be better known to the American public after its long eclipse, and that of the Precisionists, notably Sheeler. However, there were also currents of influence from abroad: that of the artists of the German *Neue Sachlichkeit*, such as Christian Schad (to some of these the term Magic Realism had already been applied), that of the Belgian Surrealist Paul Delvaux and, perhaps most of all, that of Salvador Dali. Dali lived in the United States from 1940 to 1948, and garnered enormous publicity through his antics. Meanwhile he earned large sums painting portraits of the American super-rich.

Sharp focus realism combined with hallucinatory vision had already made an appearance in American art, in the work of Peter Blume (1906–92). His painting *The Eternal City* (1934–37), a savage satire on Mussolini's Italy, offered a home-grown equivalent for the kind of work Dali was doing at the same period. It can be compared, for example, with Dali's celebrated *Enigma of William Tell* (1934). Where Blume offers Mussolini as a kind of evil jack-in-the-box, Dali features Lenin seated trouserless at the piano and blessed with one enormously elongated buttock.

There were other important influences in Magic Realism. The art of the Italian Renaissance, which had previously exercised its spell over the practitioners of Precisionism, enthralled the Magic Realists as well: Piero della Francesca and Uccello were among their most obvious sources.

The artists most closely associated with Magic Realism in the public mind were Paul Cadmus (1904–99), Jared French (1905–88) and George Tooker (1920–). They were linked not only by personal association and friendship but by a preference for the demanding tempera technique, which produces a glowing colour and a tight, precise rendering of surface appearances unobtainable in any other, less laborious medium. Their whole technical approach put them at the opposite extreme to Abstract Expressionism.

Cadmus and French started their careers in tandem, though it was Cadmus who excited controversy and who was consequently the better known of the two. However, Cadmus insisted that French was in many respects the initiator: 'He persuaded me that I actually could be an artist and that I needn't be a commercial artist which I had been.'[4] French was also responsible for introducing Cadmus to tempera, though not until the former had made quite a number of paintings in oil. Cadmus, in turn, passed the technique on to Tooker.

Cadmus's beginnings were conventional. His father was an artist, once a student under Robert Henri. He himself attended the National Academy of Design, starting at the age of fifteen, and later studied as a part-timer at the Art Students' League while holding down a job as a commercial illustrator. He and French, who was a fellow student at the ASL, travelled abroad together at the beginning of the 1930s, and spent two years living and working in a Mallorcan fishing village. It was there that the first works Cadmus eventually wished to acknowledge were painted.

One of the peculiarities of Cadmus's position in the Magic Realist movement is that his best-remembered paintings were produced before this term became current, at least in America, and are often closely related to the social realism of the 1930s. His early work often combined a sharp edge of satire with an unmistakable eroticism. The mixture was explosive, and always likely to create a scandal. *The Fleet's In!* (1934) was banned from an exhibition of government-sponsored paintings held at the Corcoran Gallery in Washington. The U.S. Secretary of the Navy of that period, as reported by *Time* magazine, said that the picture 'originated in the sordid, depraved imagination of someone who has no conception of actual conditions in our service'.[5] Cadmus himself commented mildly that he always enjoyed watching sailors when he was young: 'I didn't know them personally, I wasn't going after them or expecting a relationship with them, but they were fun to watch, and I watched them a great deal.'[6]

Coney Island (1935), painted a year later, is a variation on the theme so frequently used by Reginald Marsh, who had a strong influence on Cadmus's work at this period. The tone, however, is openly mocking, in a way foreign to Marsh – so much so that a group of Coney Island realtors actually threatened to sue Cadmus for defamation.

When Edward Bruce's Treasury Section, suppressing well-founded doubts about Cadmus's reliability, commissioned him to produce a mural for the Parcel Post Building in Richmond, Virginia, on the apparently unexceptionable theme of *Pocahontas Saving the Life of Captain John Smith* (1938), the artist managed to generate an uproar with this commission too. It was triggered by a small detail – the fox fur dangling between the legs of one of the brawny Indians who is about to dispatch the victim. This fur hung head downwards, and the animal's mask, in the original version, bore a vivid resemblance to the genitalia the fur was supposed to conceal. Cadmus spent a considerable amount of time teasing Bruce by pretending complete innocence, but was in the end forced to erase the offending detail.

Today the interesting thing about this composition is its balletic mannerism, perhaps inspired by the ballet *Pocahontas* (music by Elliott Carter), which Cadmus's brother-in-law Lincoln Kirstein was busy producing at this time, but also showing an awareness of early sixteenth-century Italian Mannerists such as Jacopo Pontormo and Giovanni Battista Rosso, with their ambiguous attitudes towards both sexuality and violence. In emotional tone, the work is quite unlike any other mural generated by the Treasury Section programme, and its self-conscious sophistication sets it apart from Regionalist art. Its obvious interest in Old Master source material does, however, give it a link with the painting which Jared French produced for the same building, *Stuart's Rebels at the Swollen Ford (Cavalrymen Crossing a River)* (1937–39). This too was censored, but at a preliminary stage, because of its display of male nudity. Like Cadmus's painting, the sketch carries strong art-historical echoes, since the subject is virtually a paraphrase of Michelangelo's *Battle of Cascina*.

In the 1940s Cadmus's work became more esoteric. One project was a series devoted to the *Seven Deadly Sins* – fantastic allegorical figures which have little to do with realism and much with the art of Hieronymus Bosch. Another was a sequence of paintings showing bathers (generally male and nude) at Fire Island, a Long Island beach resort where Cadmus regularly shared a summer cottage with French and the latter's wife Margaret. These paintings are closely related to photographs taken by Cadmus, French and Mrs French at the same epoch.

146 Paul Cadmus *Pocahontas Saving the Life of Captain John Smith* 1938
The first version. The fox fur dangling between the legs of one of the brawny Indians was thought to have too close a resemblance to the genitalia it was supposed to conceal.

147 Paul Cadmus *Coney Island* 1935
Another version of a favourite subject, to which Cadmus has added a characteristic element of grotesquerie.

ABOVE
148 Paul Cadmus *The Fleet's In!* 1934
Cadmus said of this work, which
was banned from an exhibition of
government-sponsored paintings held at
the Corcoran Gallery in Washington, 'I
owe the start of my career really to the
Admiral who tried to suppress it.'

BELOW
149 Jared French *Cavalrymen
Crossing a River* 1938
Patterned after Michelangelo's *Battle
of Cascina*. The Treasury Section
forced the artist to add more clothing
(as seen here) than appeared in an
earlier version.

150 **Jared French** *Evasion* 1947
The figures, who may in fact be different versions of the same person, all avoid one another's gaze, with the figure on the left avoiding even his own reflection.

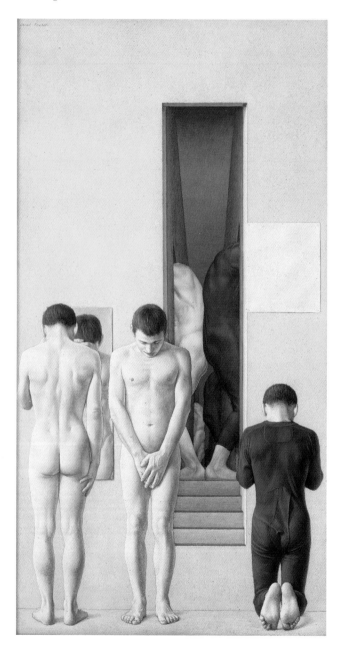

ABOVE RIGHT
151 **Jared French** *The Double* c. 1950
The composition reflects the influence of Carl Jung: the nude youth, the main protagonist, represents the unrepressed self rising from the earth, passing from an unconscious to a conscious state.

When Cadmus returned to contemporary urban subject matter in later years, as he did for example in *Playground* (1948), the social commentary became perfunctory and the erotic element even more pronounced. Cadmus's chief commentator and champion, Lincoln Kirstein, seemingly does not agree with this verdict, but his eloquent description of the painting makes the point none the less:

> The painting is dominated by a gilt-haired earthling, substantially nude, stealing what sun happens to fall on his unblessed ground, appealing to us and the world for some alternate limbo. His bare brawn is marked less by physical hunger than lack of any future. He stands mired in the day's irrelevant news, trashed as garbage. Discrepancy between his beauty and any hope to make use of his potential through thought or skill defines the delinquency that dogs his less pleasing fellows. Rough comradeship, a picked nose, the empty disarray of an unwanted, superfluous generation declare the steady defeat of our urban disinherited.[7]

Of the three chief Magic Realists, Jared French is currently the least well documented: he has only recently been made the subject of a monograph, and there are remarkably few of his paintings in public collections. His name is also missing, except for passing references in entries devoted to other subjects, from standard dictionaries of American art. It is nevertheless clear that both Cadmus and Tooker owe a great deal to him, especially from a technical point of view.

French's best-known painting is *The Rope* (1954), in the Whitney Museum, New York. Ostensibly this depicts a swimming lesson, with older men (perhaps fathers) teaching youths. In fact, like Cadmus's *Playground*, it is a work of extraordinary and deliberate ambiguity. The spectator is given the impression that the six figures are participating in a sadomasochistic ritual, and that the nude youths are in some way enslaved by the mature adults who hold the ropes attached to them.

152 George Tooker
Subway 1950
The artist has said: 'I was thinking of the large modern city as a kind of limbo. The subway seemed a good place to represent a negation of the sense and a denial of life itself.'

French's most typical works, such as *Evasion* (1947) and *The Double* (*c.* 1950), are technical *tours de force*, which offer a play of both visual and psychological ambiguity. In *Evasion*, the figures – which may in fact all be versions of the same figure – sedulously avoid one another's gaze. The male nude to the far left faces a mirror, but nevertheless covers his eyes with his hand so as not to see himself. His companions seem to pray. The exaggeratedly tall doorway approached by a flight of steps reveals more figures, and the space into which it leads concludes with yet another mirror. While all the details are skilfully realistic – note, for example, the bare feet of the kneeling youth – the scene itself takes place out of time. The nearest parallels are with certain kinds of Italian Mannerist painting: *Evasion* is a less elaborate version of Pontormo's *Joseph in Egypt*, now in the National Gallery, London.

The Double reflects the influence of Carl Jung on French's painting. Various physical levels or heights are used to mark stages of physical growth. The protagonist, a nude youth, represents the unrepressed self rising from the earth, passing from an unconscious state to a conscious one. His 'double' is the clothed kneeling figure who seems to urge him upward. The young black man, totally relaxed, symbolizes freedom from repression; the Victorian matron, its opposite.

The mood of anxiety present in both *Evasion* and *The Double* also manifests itself in the work of George Tooker. Tooker's best-known painting, also in the Whitney Museum, is *Subway* (1950), a powerful allegory of urban anxiety. The artist has commented on it as follows: 'I was thinking of the large modern city as a kind of limbo. The subway seemed a good place to represent a denial of the senses and the negation of life itself. Its being underground with a great weight overhead was important.'[8]

Subway is only one of a number of Tooker's paintings dealing with contemporary public themes, but these do not demonstrate the full range of his art. Even more than the other Magic Realists, he is concerned with problems of

153 George Tooker *Window III* 1958
The paintings of the *Windows* series were inspired by
fifteenth-century Italian bas-reliefs, notably those by Agostino
di Duccio in the Tempio Malatestiano at Rimini.

pictorial structure. *Subway* is typical of the way in which he combines figures
with their setting in an intricate visual dance. The setting, with its oblique
angles and its use of complex light sources, is as important as the figures
themselves and their placement. These figures are impersonal, especially when
compared with those depicted by, say, the Soyer brothers when they tackled
similar subject matter. The three protagonists – the woman at the centre and the
two men close behind her – wear identifiable expressions of weariness and fear,
but they are not highly characterized as individuals.

As one might already guess from this single example, some of Tooker's
sources are specifically twentieth-century and American; others come from the
general history of European art. In the mid-1940s Tooker studied at the Art
Students' League under Marsh. At this time, he also came into contact with
Hayes Miller. Their joint influence is visible in an early painting by Tooker of
Coney Island (1948). The subject is drawn from Marsh's repertoire, but it is
Hayes Miller who seems to be paramount stylistically.

In 1949 Tooker made a trip to Italy in the company of Cadmus. *Market*
(1949) was painted immediately after his return. The subject is American – a
small open–air market in Bleecker Street, New York – but the Italian
Renaissance influence, already visible in *Coney Island*, has greatly
strengthened. Tooker says that he was much struck on his Italian trip by the
Cosimo Tura frescoes in the Palazzo Schifanoia, Ferrara.

In many of Tooker's most attractive and typical works, formal pre-
occupations combine with an eroticism that is not without a touch of voyeurism.
This is especially true of the *Window* series, painted after Tooker moved from
Manhattan to Brooklyn Heights in 1953. The series was inspired by the street
life of what was then a very mixed area, where the windows of the brick and
brownstone houses were open and crowded with people all summer long.

In these paintings Tooker often packs the window-aperture with bodies. In
Window III (1958), the man and woman looking out take up almost all the
available space within the window frame. According to the artist, the art-
historical influence here is not fifteenth-century Italian fresco painting but
sculptures from the same period, notably the reliefs by Agostino di Duccio in the
Tempio Malatestiano at Rimini. The artist has said that he thinks of the works
in this series 'in terms of carving, of bas-relief, a solid form supported from
behind. Some artists paint atmosphere, but I want to cut it out, to compress
space, to push it to the front of the painting as much as possible.'[9]

The Magic Realists formed a coherent group, bound together by friendship
as well as by a shared way of working. In addition, there were other realist
artists who pursued a completely independent course. The closest of these to
the Magic Realist ethos was Ivan Albright (1897–1983), who shared with them
a liking for what was undoubtedly 'real' yet at the same time conjured up a
dreamlike or fantastic atmosphere. His work is generally agreed to be technically marvellous; it is also, for many people, something of an acquired taste.

Albright was the son of a successful artist, a pupil of Thomas Eakins, who
also became a successful Midwestern real-estate developer. It seems to have
been assumed from the very start that Ivan and his twin brother Malwin would
become artists. When small, the two boys often modelled for their father, who
specialized in rather sentimental paintings of children. There came a time,

154 **George Tooker** *Coney Island* 1948
The subject matter is indebted to Marsh
(Ills 121–23), although it alludes
stylistically to Hayes Miller (Ills 116–17).

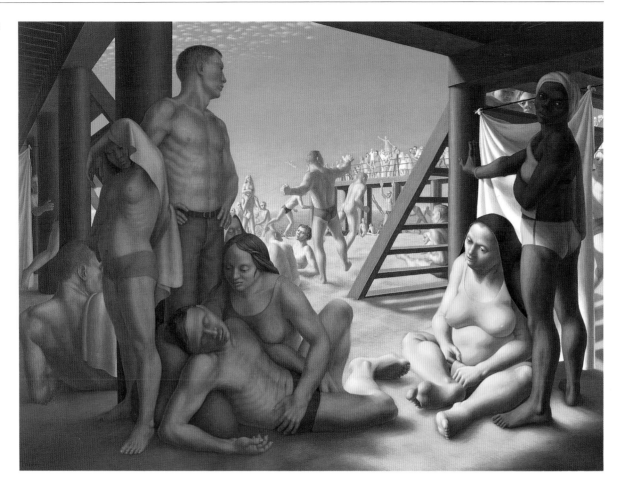

155 **George Tooker**
Market 1949
The market was in Bleecker
Street, New York, but Tooker
treated it in the manner of
Italian fifteenth-century
frescoes.

156 Ivan Albright *That Which I Should Have Done I Did Not Do* 1931–41

however, when Ivan resisted the fate in store for him, repelled by the pretentiousness and vanity of some of his father's artist friends and by the amount of insincere socializing that seemed to be needed if a painter was to sell pictures. However, after trying a couple of related professions, architecture and commercial art, he gave in and entered the Art Institute of Chicago, going on to the Pennsylvania Academy of the Fine Arts and finally (for three months only) to the National Academy of Design. He wanted, at one point, to study under Bellows at the Art Students' League, but never did so, because Bellows was abroad at the crucial time.

Almost from the beginning of his career Albright's work was highly individual. Perhaps the only really comparable artist is the German, Otto Dix. When Albright paints figures, the rendering is obsessively detailed, with great emphasis on details such as folds or creases in skin or clothing, and on body hair, eyebrows and eyelashes. These figures are not portrayed in groups, but are solitary and monumental, isolated against backgrounds which seem to push them forward against the picture-plane. *And God Created Man in His Own Image (Room 203)* (1930–31) is a likeness of a labour leader and ex-bartender from Warrenville, Illinois, where Albright then had his studio. In its insistence on physical ugliness, it makes a striking contrast with the images of heroic workers produced by members of the social realist school. Its meaning is not political but, as the title suggests, religious. At one point Albright insisted that the true title was with the words in a different order: *And Man Created God in His Own Image.* For the artist, the point was not to insist on ugliness but to evoke a sense of pathos, especially in the expression of the sitter's eyes: 'I had to almost put it there myself for people are secretive – they hold it all back.'[10]

Albright came from a prosperous background and eventually, in 1946, married a rich wife; he was therefore able to spend many years elaborating his more important compositions. *That Which I Should Have Done I Did Not Do*, originally entitled simply *The Door*, took him a full ten years (1931–41) to complete to his satisfaction. It is a bizarre variant on Harnett's *trompe-l'oeil* paintings, with a didactic message worthy of the nineteenth century. Where it differs from standard *trompe-l'oeil*, of the kind Harnett practised, is in its use of deliberately twisted perspective and shifting viewpoint. In this it conforms to Albright's highly individual theories about the way in which people actually see. Every blossom in the bouquet, for instance, is painted from a slightly different point of view. Asked to describe his approach, Albright was later to say:

The reason I use an extremely minute technique is to tie down, to freeze, to crystallize various discordant elements so that my painting has a composite feeling. I take well-known objects and handle them so as to make you think this is the old familiar way you have always seen them – but in reality I am forcing you to walk into the picture and see the objects only in my way. I need this meticulous technique to achieve the impact I want, but don't mistake it for a trick. It is not big areas (in either colour or space) that I'm playing up; instead I'm trying to show the interplay of directions, of conflicts and struggles in even the smallest objects and relationships. It's like walking round for one entire day – looking – experiencing – and then crystallizing everything you've felt and seen in one canvas simple enough, familiar enough for anyone to recognize.[11]

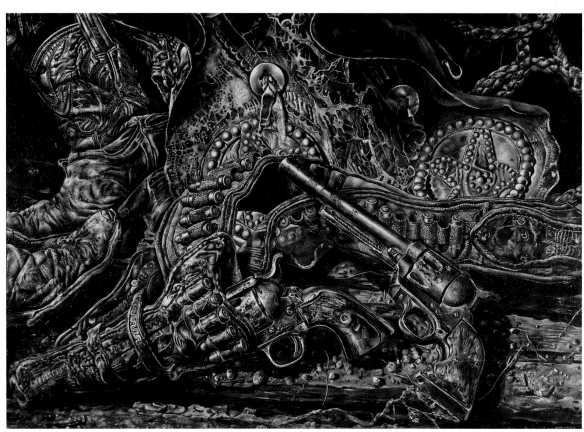

Always moralizing, always pessimistically concerned with the idea of death and decay, Albright's work became increasingly claustrophobic. Some later still-lifes manifest a *horror vacui* of the most extreme kind. A good example is the 'Western' still-life *The Wild Bunch (Hole in the Wall Gang)* (1950–51), the artist's biographer, Michael Croydon, records that

> All but one of the objects chosen for this picture belonged to people who had been in jail, and, much to the artist's delight, it turned out later that even this item had been owned by an employee of the ranch who had been in a reform school.[12]

Perhaps fittingly in the circumstances, the painting itself seems like a prison for the objects Albright has chosen to depict.

The morbid element in Albright's art is obvious to almost everyone, but many people will be surprised to find the same adjective applied to the work of another independent, Andrew Wyeth (1917–). Wyeth's *Christina's World* (1948) has become the best-known image in twentieth-century American art, and many people cling to the idea that his *oeuvre* is one of the few antidotes to the excesses of post-World War II Modernism. Immediately touched by the longing the figure expresses, as she looks up the long grassy slope towards the house in the distance, most spectators seem to remain more or less unaware of the situation the painting depicts. Christina is a cripple, physically unable to climb. Her plight is discreetly indicated by her skeletally thin right arm, while her useless legs are covered by her skirt.

ABOVE LEFT
157 **Ivan Albright** *And God Created Man In His Own Image (Room 203)* 1930–31
The artist insisted that the original title was meant to have been *And Man Created God in his Own Image* and that a museum official reversed it.

ABOVE RIGHT
158 **Ivan Albright** *The Wild Bunch (Hole in the Wall Gang)* 1950–51
This looks back to Harnett (Ills 29–32) and Peto (Ills 28, 33–35) in the way in which it brings objects close to the picture surface.

159 Andrew Wyeth *Christina's World* 1948
Wyeth's most popular work has been widely misunderstood:
the woman in the foreground, Christina Olson, is crippled and
therefore unable to approach the house on the horizon.

In fact, both of Wyeth's main narrative series, one concerned with the lives of
the Kuerners in Chadds Ford, Pennsylvania, the other about the Olsons in
Maine, are focused on enclosed, physically claustrophobic family situations.
While Christina Olson is crippled, Karl Kuerner's wife Anna is mentally ill, as
Wyeth's likenesses of her unflinchingly reveal.

Like Albright, Wyeth is the product of a dominant father who was a
practising artist. N. C. Wyeth was the best-known American illustrator of his
time. Wyeth's love and reverence for his father are amply recorded. So, too, is
the fact that his own art was somehow liberated by N. C. Wyeth's death in an
automobile accident in 1945. Karl Kuerner's farm is close to the unguarded
railroad crossing where N. C. Wyeth died, and Wyeth has admitted that this has
something to do with the fascination he feels for Kuerner and his family.

For all his extreme skill with long-established pictorial techniques, such as
tempera and dry-brush watercolour, Wyeth's work is far less traditional than
the great mass of his admirers assume. Indeed, one reason why they feel at home
with his work may be that he has been much influenced by photography. His
compositions often show the compressed space typical of the camera's
monocular vision – the kind of thing Clement Greenberg noted in the work of
Ben Shahn.

However, Wyeth's links with photography are more specific than this. In his
treatment of isolated fragments of rustic architecture, he sometimes comes close
to the work of Walker Evans, and even closer to that of Charles Sheeler. The
immediate ancestors of much of Wyeth's work are the photographs and
paintings Sheeler made of buildings in rural Pennsylvania. Nevertheless, Wyeth
is also capable of twisting viewpoints in non-photographic ways, in a fashion
which makes another link with the work of Albright.

Though it is Wyeth's portraits and paintings containing figures that have
won him most acclaim – probably because the audience identifies with them

160 Andrew Wyeth *Karl's Room* 1954
A good example of the latent violence often to be found in
Wyeth's imagery.

most easily – these are not always his strongest works. What he is very good at doing is suggesting what people are like, and conjuring up their presence, through carefully selected images of objects associated with them. *Karl's Room* (1954), a sparse watercolour showing a rifle with a telescopic sight hanging on a bare attic wall, with an old chest just visible below it and to the left, is a statement about latent violence in the Kuerner environment. Wyeth later reminisced that Karl had been handling just such a rifle on the day John F. Kennedy was shot:

> 'Karl was showing me a high-powered rifle with a telescopic lens,' said Andy.
> 'I felt like Oswald,' said Karl, smiling briefly, 'It was unbelievable. It really hit me.'[13]

In fact, the interesting thing about Wyeth's work is that, though cherished for its apparent familiarity, it is not at all reassuring. His paintings and watercolours often display extraordinary tension, and constantly deal in contradictions, social as well as psychological. While apparently evoking nostalgia for a vanishing way of life, he often points out how harsh and savage this way of living actually is. Few images, for example, could be crueller or bleaker than the meticulously organized *Tenant Farmer* (1961): snow, a cramped house with few and small windows (so that we surmise how dark it must be inside), and beside it a bare tree with the carcass of a deer hanging from it. The painting challenges the cherished assumption of Wyeth's audience that the rural life is calm, fecund and rewarding – an earthly paradise compared to urban modes of existence.

Because of their realistic style and rural subject matter, Wyeth's paintings have often been condemned by the champions of American Modernism, who are

161 **Andrew Wyeth** *Tenant Farmer* 1961
Wyeth issues a direct challenge to cherished assumptions that rural life is fecund and rewarding, an earthly paradise compared with life in the city.

162 **Norman Rockwell** *Shuffleton's Barbershop* 1950
An interpretation of American small-town and rural life that is
more idealized than anything to be found in Wyeth.

enraged by his mass appeal. It has been customary to compare his work with
that of the hugely popular illustrator Norman Rockwell (1894–1978). Closer
examination suggests that the parallel is illusory. At the core of Wyeth's work
lies sardonic hostility to Rockwell's sentimentality. His own success is the
product of two things – the dissatisfaction felt by many viewers with what
contemporary art offers as an alternative, and the audience's own propensity to
self-deception. Wyeth expresses harsh truths which spectators choose not to see.

Walter Murch (1907–67) was even more isolated stylistically than Albright
or Wyeth. And yet in another sense he is a pivotal figure, since his work forms a
link between Harnett and Peto, on the one hand, and certain aspects of Pop Art
on the other. His artistic range was extremely narrow: he was a painter of still-
life to the exclusion of all other subjects.

Born in Canada (he retained Canadian citizenship to the end of his life),
Murch originally came to New York in the hope of studying with Hayes Miller.
As a very young man, he had admired the work of Marsh, and he knew that
Hayes Miller had been Marsh's teacher. However, when he finally got into Hayes
Miller's class at the Art Students' League in New York, he, like a number of

students before and after him, found the instruction stultifying and the teacher's attitudes discouraging. He left after only a year, and enrolled in a drawing class taught by Arshile Gorky (1904–48) at the Grand Central School of Art. He went on to study privately with Gorky, who became a valued friend, and this friendship in turn proved to be a stepping-off point into the world of the New York avant-garde.

Murch started to visit the Julien Levy Gallery, then the chief showcase for leading European Surrealists in New York. The atmosphere of the gallery seems to have appealed to him more than what it actually showed; one of the artists he liked best was the very minor Pierre Roy, essentially a still-life painter like himself. Through Levy, he came to know Joseph Cornell. Notoriously self-effacing, Cornell nevertheless had a decisive effect on Murch's attention to the special qualities possessed by old photographs, and in particular to the way in which their very defects – fading, scratches and stains – made them expressive by demonstrating how the moment frozen by the camera was, despite all efforts to retain it, inexorably vanishing into the past.

It is a measure of Murch's essential intransigence that he never became a Surrealist, any more than he was tempted to become an Abstract Expressionist, despite his admiration for Mark Rothko and Clyfford Still and his close friendship with Barnett Newman (who actually suggested titles for one or two of Murch's paintings). His still-lifes are not about fantasy but about fact, and also about the way in which time erodes even the things which seem most solid in our experience. His use of machines and machine parts seems to have had roots in his own family background – his father was a jeweller and watchmaker. Solid yet ghostly still-lifes like *The Circle* (*c.* 1948) or *Taking Off* (*c.* 1952) have some of the velvety bloom one associates with a good Peto. Their interest in banal, everyday objects, mass-manufactured, also makes them seem like anticipations of aspects of Warhol. Unlike Warhol, however, Murch was fascinated by the patina imparted by the passage of time. Like Peto, he specialized in objects that were battered and slightly out of date. The subject of *The Circle*, for example, is an old wind-up gramophone, and Murch has suffused his portrayal of it with nostalgic emotion.

163 **Walter Tandy Murch** *The Circle* *c.* 1948
Murch's still-lifes are based on the colour and texture of old, slightly battered photographs; they have many of the qualities associated with the work of John F. Peto (Ills 28, 33–35).

164 **Walter Tandy Murch** *Taking Off* *c.* 1952

CHAPTER 11

The Return to Figuration and the Pop Sensibility

THE BRIDGE for a mainstream return to figuration in American art was provided, not by the Magic Realists, nor by popularly acclaimed 'independents' like Wyeth, but by Fairfield Porter (1907–73). In some ways Porter resembled Murch, since he maintained close friendships with a number of the leading abstractionists of the time, and therefore had some sympathy with the dominant mode, even though he himself did not work within it. He differed from Murch because he had a public voice – in addition to being a painter, he was a well–known critic – and also, towards the end of his career, had a gift for attracting disciples.

In painting, he was a slow starter. After studies at Harvard, he had a period at the Art Students' League, where one of his teachers was Benton. He seems to have disliked both Benton's personality and his teaching methods, which he found too rigid and formulaic. One later comment was that Benton 'liked to pretend, he liked to act as though he were completely uneducated and, you know, just the grandson of a crooked politician'.[1] This gives a glimpse of the rather loftily aristocratic East Coast attitudes which Porter carried with him throughout his life.

These may have checked his development, but there were external factors as well. He married in 1932, and his eldest son, born soon afterwards, was mentally handicapped. Porter later felt that he had given the best part of fifteen years of his life to the search for a cure for his son's problems, beset meanwhile by conflicting specialist advice.

There was also the fact that he felt ill at ease in the cultural climate of his time, which was violently argumentative and highly politicized. He seems to have got his first glimpse of the kind of artist he could become as late as 1938, when he happened to see an exhibition by the two leading French Intimists, Bonnard and Vuillard, at the Art Institute of Chicago. His reaction was positive and immediate: 'It was just a sort of revelation of the obvious and why does one think of doing anything else when it's so natural to do this.'[2]

Nevertheless, he had to wait until after World War II for the revelation to have its full effect. At the beginning of the 1950s Porter settled into a double career, writing reviews and articles for leading periodicals such as *Art News* and *The Nation* and exhibiting regularly at the well-respected Tibor de Nagy Gallery in New York. The paintings were records of his immediate surroundings, and in particular of the domestic life he lived with his large family and equally wide circle of friends in the spacious, comfortably shabby house he owned in Southampton, Long Island – a town just outside New York which was now more and more an artists' colony.

The paintings Porter produced, and his style and manner of approach, varied little during the last two decades of his life – one reviewer called them 'beautiful, well-mannered, WASP-y records of domestic felicity'.[3] These works, though painterly in handling, nevertheless refer the spectator directly to real life: real things, real people, real events. In a sense, they are just as Regionalist as Benton, in their devotion to the light, the landscape and the domestic settings of America's Eastern seaboard. Perhaps inadvertently, they are social realist paintings as well, in the sense that they are very much a reflection of one aspect of the American class-structure: the way of life favoured by reasonably well-off, liberally inclined intellectuals.

166 **Fairfield Porter** *Elaine De Kooning* 1957
Willem De Kooning's wife, who recommended that Porter succeed her in writing reviews for *Art News* in 1951.

OPPOSITE
165 **Fairfield Porter** *Laurence at the Piano* 1953
The artist's musically gifted seventeen-year-old son at the family home in Southampton, Long Island.

167 Fairfield Porter *House, Great Spruce Head Island* c. 1948
The Porter family's vacation home in Penobscot Bay, off the coast of Maine. Porter's father bought the island, then uninhabited, in 1912 and was responsible for building the house.

OPPOSITE
168 Fairfield Porter *Katie and Anne* 1955
Porter's wife and daughter in a conscious homage to Vuillard. Porter wrote later: 'The painting went easily and seemed "finished" almost from the beginning.'

169 **Jane Freilicher** *Early New York Evening* 1954
Freilicher's work of this period clearly shows the
influence of Fairfield Porter (Ills 165–68) on her work.

170 **Jane Freilicher** *Portrait of Arnold
Weinstein* 1955

Porter's gift for friendship attracted a wide circle of disciples and associates. In the work of most of these, one sees the same struggle to reconcile abstract and figurative impulses. In stylistic terms, one of the younger painters who comes closest to Porter is Alex Katz (1927–), but here the impulse towards abstraction is so strong that any realist impulse is almost wholly submerged. Rather than being influenced by Bonnard and Vuillard, Katz has felt the impact of Matisse. He has also, like the Pop painters, learned something from advertising billboards.

More realist, at least at first sight, is the work of Neil Welliver (1929–), a friend of Katz as well as Porter, and a dedicated painter of the Maine wilderness in all weather conditions, winter and summer. At first sight, these wilderness paintings have an almost pedantic literalism and truth to observed fact which make them very different from Porter's work. Welliver agrees that a difference exists, but sets it in a new light : 'Once Fairfield said to me that our work was really antithetical. He came out of the Nabis and French painting and I really come out of American abstract painting. So we approach painting in a very different way.'[4]

In fact, Welliver's wilderness paintings can be thought of as realist elements arranged according to the compositional principles of Abstract Expressionism: the landscape is shown from a point of view which permits the eye no escape. There is no horizon, simply a dense tangle of forms which the eye tries in vain to penetrate, just as it seeks to penetrate the layered brushwork typical of Abstract Expressionism.

Two more of Porter's friendships were of greater significance for the immediate future of American art. Around 1951 he met and formed a bond with Larry Rivers (1923–) and Jane Freilicher (1924–), who had studied together under the leading Abstract Expressionist, Hans Hofmann. They had absorbed Hofmann's advocacy of painterly handling, but had put his commitment to abstraction to one side. Both had been strongly influenced by the Bonnard show held in 1948 at The Museum of Modern Art.

Freilicher's paintings, often cityscapes, were a return to a well-established if currently somewhat neglected aspect of the American tradition. Rivers presented a more complex case. Always restlessly experimental, with an improvisational bent which stemmed from his experience as a professional jazz musician, Rivers was influenced not only by Bonnard but by the great French painters of the mid-nineteenth century. Courbet's *Burial at Ornans* had a profound effect on him when he saw it on a visit to Paris in 1950. One of the things he most liked was its confessional, autobiographical quality: Courbet 'actually put people he knew in it'.[5]

As a freewheeling, bohemian musician, and also as a member of an immigrant Jewish family, Rivers was apt to make his own confessional paintings a good deal less inhibited than Fairfield Porter's decorous images of East Coast family life. One direct result of his enthusiasm for French nineteenth-century art was a series of likenesses of his relations and friends, which were deliberately, indeed provocatively, academic in style, and at the same time almost embarrassingly garrulous about personal relationships. Some of the best-known of these paintings are nude portraits of his then mother-in-law, Berdie Burger.

171 **Alex Katz** *January 1* 1992
Katz's simplifications seem to combine the influence of advertising billboards with that of Matisse.

172 **Neil Welliver** *Suns End and Flurry* 1992
A typical Welliver landscape: the high horizon and densely planted trees contribute to its quasi-abstract quality.

173 **Larry Rivers** *Double Portrait of Berdie* 1955
Berdie Burger was then the artist's mother-in-law. The
painting outraged the art-historian, Leo Steinberg, a
prominent supporter of Jasper Johns (Ills 175, 188), who
described it as a work 'in which genuine nastiness couples
with false charm'.

Rivers's *Double Portrait of Berdie* (1955) is almost as much a manifesto
picture as David's *Marat assassiné*. The Abstract Expressionists were putting
their souls and their psyches on canvas, but their paintings were unspecific. Rivers
would have none of that. The picture shocked the mandarins of the New York
critical establishment, which was undoubtedly Rivers's intention. Leo Steinberg
described it in *Arts* as 'a picture in which genuine nastiness couples with false
charm'.[6] Steinberg was an academic art historian, deeply committed to the avant-
garde, and *Double Portrait* was calculated to offend him on at least three counts:
its lack of personal reticence, its curious formal dislocations, and the way in which
it alluded to the least palatable aspects of nineteenth-century art.

In this connection, Rivers had been examining not only Courbet but
academic studies of the nude made by early nineteenth-century artists such as
Théodore Géricault. One result of this scrutiny, in addition to the nude
likenesses he made of the patient Berdie and of his own two sons, was a nude
portrait of his close friend, the poet and critic Frank O'Hara. O'Hara strikes a
standard academic pose, but the real intimacy and informality of the
relationship between artist and model is signalled by the fact that he is not
completely unclad: he is still wearing a pair of boots. This detail immediately
converts nudity into erotic nakedness.

However, Steinberg was probably most thoroughly alienated, not by the
voyeuristic aspect of *Double Portrait of Berdie*, but by its failure to obey the
standards of the nineteenth-century academicism it seemed to ape.
Anatomically, the two figures of Berdie are distinctly ramshackle. It now seems

obvious, in the light of Rivers's later work, that this apparent carelessness was calculated. Rivers is here a precursor of Eric Fischl and the other practitioners of 'bad painting' who rose to prominence during the 1980s. The painting would not make its effect if there were not something precarious about it, something to suggest that realism was no longer an obvious route to take. There was a centrifugal element in Rivers's work that soon led him away from anything which could be described as truly realistic – his later paintings are deliberately fragmented in composition as well as in drawing.

The appearance of this group of disciples in Fairfield Porter's wake, more especially when it included an artist as provocative as Rivers, helped to make realistic figuration a possible option once again. The change of artistic climate was confirmed by the appearance of an artist very different from those who surrounded Porter: Jasper Johns (1930–), whose first one-person show, held at the Leo Castelli Gallery, New York, in 1957, was one of the most sensational debuts in the history of American art. The Museum of Modern Art alone bought three works, and nearly all the major collectors of the day hastened to follow its lead.

The exhibition featured what are still the artist's best-known images: paintings of the American flag, of targets and of numbers. It is the flag group that raises the question of Johns's connection with the realist impulse in its most acute form. These are, after all, literal representations of an object which has an existence of its own in the world outside the paintings – just as, for example, an apple exists both inside and outside of a still-life by Cézanne. However, Johns himself insists that the literalism with which the flag is shown is only a form of strategy, which sets him free to do other things: 'Using the design of the American flag took care of a great deal for me because I didn't have to design it. So I went on to similar things like the targets – things the mind already knows. That gives me room to work on other levels'.[7]

With their deadpan presentation of an image which is seen absolutely straight on, Johns's flags have sometimes been compared to Harnett's more austere paintings, such as *The Faithful Colt*; but in fact the comparison tends to show that the two artists are working in diametrically opposite ways. Harnett's intention is to deceive the eye; Johns is anxious not to do this. He wants, instead, to make the spectator aware of the fundamental differences between the painted surface and the real object; he is profoundly anti-illusionist. The exquisite modulations of texture and tone he obtains through the use of the wax-encaustic medium become more conspicuous thanks to the banal familiarity of the image.

Johns's flags are rightly regarded as precursors of the Pop Art which appeared in the United States in fully developed form at the beginning of the 1960s. It is often assumed that Pop meant a return to the traditions of American realism, as well as a swing back to figuration. It is true that it did have links both with the popular realism of Harnett and Peto – thanks to its focus on banal objects – and with certain aspects of both the Regionalism and the urban realism of the 1930s. Like Regionalism, it stressed what was generically American, though concentrating on urban and not rural culture. Marsh and other urban realist artists had already shown an interest in phenomena, such as billboard advertising, which were of obsessive interest to Pop.

However, it must be pointed out that the degree of realism to be found in Pop painting varies widely from artist to artist (and also within the work of a single

174 Larry Rivers *Frank O'Hara* 1954
Rivers was bisexual and he and O'Hara were lovers. In this painting, Rivers subverts the conventions of the sexually neutral, academic nude.

175 Jasper Johns *Flag* 1954–55

176 **James Rosenquist** *F–111* 1965
Many details, such as the luscious representation of spaghetti on the right of the composition, are borrowed from the glamorized versions of photographic originals typical of advertising billboards.

177 **Andy Warhol** *Big Campbell's Soup Can, 19c* 1962
Pop Art frequently made use of 'realist' conventions of representation borrowed from advertising.

artist, as in the case of Warhol). Roy Lichtenstein (1923–97), who was somewhat older than his colleagues, possessed an excellent realist pedigree, having been a student of Marsh in 1939–40 and later a commercial artist. Nevertheless his mature style, derived from the graphic conventions used in comic strips, hardly offers a convincing formula for realist representation. In fact – as soon became apparent, when Lichtenstein moved from comic strip material to making deadpan parodies of all the chief Modernist art styles, from Cubism to Abstract Expressionism – what really fascinated him was the formulaic nature of standard conventions of representation. Comic strips, with their reliance on hard outline, plus dots, plus areas of even tone, make this particularly obvious, since there is so little possibility of modulation. An Abstract Expressionist brushstroke translated into the visual coding of the comic strip is still instantly recognizable – the spectator is given the necessary basic information. Yet there is now a gap in perception: being transmuted in this way, the brushstroke has been deprived of the immediacy and spontaneity which are its essential qualities. Lichtenstein makes a sardonic joke out of this.

In general, the issue of realism entered Pop painting not directly, but through a side-door. This door was dependence on and familiarity with advertising. This can be understood most easily by looking at the work of James Rosenquist (1933–), who earned his living, before he became celebrated, as a billboard painter. Rosenquist's gigantic multi-panel *F–111* (1965), probably his best-known work, makes lavish use of techniques which derive from this source, basically a simplification and glamorization of photographic originals. In *F–111*, Rosenquist's strands of spaghetti are – just as they would be in an actual billboard – more lusciously succulent and edible than the real thing, and as much a product of the idealizing impulse as the goddesses of classical art. In addition, the painter fragments and juxtaposes imagery in such a way that the viewer is immediately aware that this is not an objective presentation but a metaphor for contemporary urban life, with its unceasing bombardment of images and information.

Much nearer to traditional still-life are some of the paintings from the soup can series by Andy Warhol (1928–87), particularly those which, like *Big Campbell's Soup Can, 19c* (1962), feature just one can. Though still drawn in the simplified billboard style used by Rosenquist, these do have roots in the work of Harnett and Peto. As in some of their paintings, the spectator is asked to concentrate on a single, intrinsically banal object. There is no suggestion of *trompe-l'oeil*, however – not least because Warhol brutally enlarges the scale.

It is interesting to compare Warhol's paintings in this style with those in the 'Disaster' series which followed only shortly afterwards. These are taken from actual photographs of horrific events, which are not imitated with the brush but silkscreened directly onto the canvas, usually as multiple images, with the same photograph used repeatedly. *Green Disaster Ten Times* (1963), for instance, repeats a documentary shot of an automobile wreck ten times on a canvas washed over with a single hue. There is no argument about the actual reality of the image: we know immediately that what we are being shown happened at such and such an instant, in such and such a place. But this is hardly a 'realist' picture, any more than the pinup-derived paintings of Tom Wesselmann (1931–) or Mel Ramos (1935–) are realist. Warhol seems to want to numb the spectator's feelings, to offer protection from reality. Either this, or he uses the technique as a way of anaesthetizing his own apprehensions about the nature of the world. This is a refusal to experience something: hardly the stuff of realist art. In a more simple-minded way, Wesselmann and Ramos use the established conventions of the pinup to offer the viewer a refuge from the complexities of sexual experience.

Fairfield Porter's aristocratic intimism makes a violent contrast with Pop Art's exploitation of the imagery of mass culture. Nevertheless, both express aspects of the same impulse – the feeling that American art had to renew its connection with the realities of everyday life. Of course, when one compares a Porter interior with a Warhol soup can, one is not comparing like with like. The violent contrast between them represents the existence of fissures in American society, as well as of fissures in the American sensibility.

Warhol, who came from a family of blue-collar Ruthenian immigrants, emphasizes America's brash urbanism, and the rise of a mass-consumer society in which everyone uses the same products. Porter, from upper-middle-class stock long rooted in the United States, stresses a continuing commitment to the reticence, cultivation and quietism typical of important aspects of American life during the nineteenth century. When looking at his paintings, we are still not so far from the universe of Emerson and Thoreau.

In both artists, however, the emphasis is on the symbolic value of the real. Recognition of a shared reality is essentially what they seek to elicit from the viewer. The gap between them is only slightly wider than that between Harnett and Eakins in the late nineteenth century, with Warhol on Harnett's side of the divide and Porter on that of Eakins, an artist with whom he has much in common.

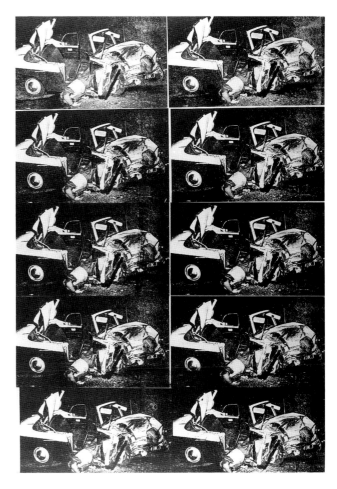

178 **Andy Warhol** *Green Disaster 10 Times* 1963
This is 'realist' only in the sense that it makes use of a borrowed documentary shot of an automobile wreck, which is incorporated into the painting without alteration.

CHAPTER 12

Bay Area Figuration

AT THE beginning of the 1950s a group of artists working in and around San Francisco, who until then had been committed to a version of Abstract Expressionism, made the shift to figuration. What they produced during the following decade and a half offers parallels with the work of Fairfield Porter, but the atmosphere which surrounded this move was polemical, whereas Porter's attitude was one of live-and-let-live.

The polemic hinged on the situation at the California School of Fine Arts (CSFA), then the premier art school in the region. Most of those associated with what came to be called Bay Area Figuration either studied or taught at this school: some were former students taken on to the teaching staff. The faculty also contained one major Abstract Expressionist celebrity, Clyfford Still (1904–80), appointed in the fall of 1946. In the distant past Still had himself worked in a quasi-realist mode. In the 1920s, while still a very young man, he produced paintings which are a little reminiscent of the work of Charles Burchfield. Now, however, he was violently hostile to any form of representation. A powerful and obdurate personality, with a mesmeric influence over many of the students, Still had a catalytic but also a divisive effect. This divisiveness manifested itself soon after his arrival, when Still had a solo show at the California Palace of the Legion of Honor. The abstract painter Hassel Smith, also a member of the faculty, recalled that 'almost immediately a kind of schism developed around that situation, with Elmer Bischoff and David Park and Dick Diebenkorn taking a very adverse attitude towards Clyff's painting'.[1] The three artists whom Smith names were the most important members of the Bay Area figurative group.

David Park (1911–60) was the oldest, and the first to make the break. Born in Boston, the son of a Unitarian minister, he began his career in 1929 as a student at the Otis Art Institute in Los Angeles. He then worked as an assistant to a sculptor who was carving figures for the new San Francisco Stock Exchange, and this brought him into contact with Rivera, concurrently painting a mural in the same building. Later, having joined the FAP, he was close to the group who had painted the murals in the Coit Tower. Many of his early paintings are in a Rivera-influenced social realist mode; the others are provincial variants of Cubism, done under the spell of Picasso. After five years spent in Boston in the late 1930s, Park and his family moved back to Berkeley in 1941. There, for the rest of the war, Park worked night-shifts as a machine operator and painted in his limited spare time. In 1945 he was invited to teach at the CSFA by a new director, Douglas MacAgy (whose first act had been to cover the School's Rivera mural with a sheet).

For the next four years Park worked as an abstract painter, making the large-scale, non-objective works which were becoming *de rigueur* in avant-garde circles. However, he became increasingly dissatisfied with what he was producing. In the late summer or early autumn of 1949 he loaded his car with all the non-objective paintings in his studio and took them to the city dump. In a statement written for an art magazine four years later, he gave some of his reasons for this drastic rejection of the immediate past:

During [that] time I was concerned with the big abstract ideals like vitality, energy, profundity, warmth. They became my gods. They still are. I disciplined

179 Richard Diebenkorn *Interior with Book* 1959
The striking difference between this canvas and the general tendency of American abstract painting, including the abstract works produced by Diebenkorn himself, is the powerful illusion it gives of three-dimensional space.

180 **David Park** *The Market* 1953
Like Porter's work (Ills 165–68), *The Market* shows
the influence of Bonnard and Vuillard.

181 **David Park** *Nude – Green* 1957
From a long series of canvases showing both
male and female nudes.

myself rigidly to work in ways I hoped might symbolize those ideals. I still hold to those ideals today, but I realize that those paintings practically never, even vaguely, approximated any achievement of my aims. Quite the opposite: what the paintings told me was that I was a hardworking guy who was trying to be important.[2]

Park died of lung cancer in 1960, and his second career as a figurative painter was therefore comparatively brief. The pictures he made during the last decade of his life can be divided, with very few exceptions, into groups. Those painted in the first half of the period, such as *The Market* (1953), usually have a certain amount of narrative interest. They are often either street scenes or domestic interiors. Though bolder and more drastically simplified than the work Porter was producing at te same time, they show the same influences: Bonnard, Vuillard and perhaps (though much more remotely) Hopper.

The paintings in the second group are idealizing. They usually show nudes or semi-nudes, often presented as bathing figures. They seem to have roots, not in French Intimism, but in paintings by Edvard Munch, notably his large *Bathing*

Men of 1907–08, a tribute to the vitalism of Henri Bergson (a cult which may also have affected Park more directly, though the immediate source of influence is unknown). Park's work demonstrates the strong pull which realistic impulses continued to have, affecting even artists who seemed well insulated from them.

Much the same can be said of Elmer Bischoff (1916–91). Slightly younger than Park, he had, as a young artist, a rather similar kind of evolution, though he never dabbled in social realism, moving straight from a phase as a Picasso imitator into fully fledged Abstract Expressionism. When he was taken on to teach at the CSFA in 1946, he was still sufficiently young to be awed by its pervading atmosphere. To him it seemed 'like a monastic brotherhood composed of members recently liberated from a world of semi-darkness'.[3] His conversion to figuration was more gradual than that of Park, but the results were comparable, though Bischoff is a painter with a lighter touch. A typical painting from his earliest figurative phase is *Woman with Red Blouse* (1958), a Corot-like study of a woman seated in a garden, holding a parasol. This illuminates the link between Bay Area Figuration and the French realist

182 **Elmer Bischoff** *Woman with Red Blouse* 1958
Despite the wide difference in scale, the inspiration here seems to come from small figure paintings by Corot.

183 **Richard Diebenkorn** *Cityscape 1* 1963
This aerial perspective view of San Francisco is truer to life
than its ordered simplicity might suggest: the city's hilly
terrain often seems to compress space in precisely the same
way. Diebenkorn has, however, reinvented some aspects to
suit the painting – a line of buildings has been removed on
the right.

painting of the mid-nineteenth century – an attraction felt at about the same moment by Larry Rivers, working on the East Coast, though he responded in a very different way. Bischoff continued to make figurative paintings until the early 1970s, and then returned to abstraction.

Though Richard Diebenkorn (1922–93) was younger than either Park or Bischoff, his conversion to figuration in 1956 was seen as much riskier than theirs, since he had already established a major reputation as an abstract artist, not only on the West Coast but in New York as well. It was not the first time Diebenkorn had painted figuratively: in the 1940s, while still a student, he had produced one or two works heavily influenced by Hopper. When he resumed his training, briefly interrupted by the war, it was at the CSFA, and he was soon recognized as an exceptionally gifted student. His work was abstract, though his relationship with Park and Bischoff was much closer and warmer than with Still.

Diebenkorn worked in Albuquerque, New Mexico, as a graduate student, then taught in Urbana, Illinois, before returning to Berkeley, where he was now seen as a rapidly rising star. He had much less difficulty than his elders in breaking out of the West Coast environment and achieving national recognition. In 1954 he was included in the Guggenheim Museum's show of *Young American Painters*, and in 1956 he had a very successful dealer show of his *Berkeley* series of abstractions in New York. He too, however, had begun to feel a certain restlessness. By the time the New York show opened he had already – and against everyone's advice – started to make figurative paintings.

His figurative phase lasted for just over ten years and remains controversial. Diebenkorn painted still–lifes, landscapes, unpeopled interiors, and pictures with figures. The disposition among his committed admirers has been to praise the last of these as the best, because most 'radical'. These pictures are certainly the furthest from realism. Yet one must query this verdict. The figure pictures are awkward, and the awkwardness is not always visually stimulating. Though a good draughtsman, Diebenkorn seems uncomfortable when he has to render a figure on a large scale, in paint. Interior scenes like *Interior with Book* (1960), or still-lifes, or landscapes like *Cityscape 1* (1963), are more successful because spatially more coherent.

One of the incidental fascinations of Diebenkorn's figurative work, and especially the still-lifes and landscapes, is the unexpected link to another Bay Area painter, Wayne Thiebaud (1920–). A little older than Diebenkorn, Thiebaud had to wait longer to achieve celebrity, and his development was erratic and essentially isolated. His figurative work has a density and impact which (to my eye at least) Diebenkorn's lacks. There is also no doubt about his commitment to realism. In a sense he is both the Chardin and the Corot of the West Coast, a man who reinterprets traditional values in purely American terms. How this came about is a curious story, and one littered with misunderstandings, the crassest of which is that Thiebaud is in fact a kind of Pop artist. He owes this to the timing of his first, enormously successful show in New York, which took place in 1962, when he was already over forty.

In his youth and young manhood Thiebaud worked at a large number of marginally artistic jobs: as an animator for Disney, cartoonist, commercial artist, layout man and graphic designer. Then he gradually shifted his focus to

184 **Richard Diebenkorn** *Poppies* 1963
Despite a typically modernist use of tilted and flattened space,
the austere simplicity of this still-life also refers to earlier
aspects of the American tradition.

fine art, though he did not have his first solo show until 1951. At this period,
and for long afterwards, his work was completely eclectic, open to the most
varied influences, from the obligatory Picasso to Byzantine and Persian art. By
1958 he was making paintings which did have a figurative element, but which
were heavily influenced by Abstract Expressionism.

It was at this point that he discovered the work of the Italian mid-nineteenth-
century group I Macchiaioli, characterized by a radically economical way of
rendering light and colour, and also that of the Spanish Impressionist, Joaquín
Sorolla y Bastida, with its equally bold way of handling paint. At this time he
was living in Sacramento, and he owed these discoveries to books found in the
California State Library there, not to direct experience of the pictures

themselves. He also began to look at the work of the Bay Area Figuration group, particularly that of Diebenkorn: he responded to Diebenkorn's still-lifes and landscapes, while ignoring the interiors and paintings with figures.

What made Thiebaud's reputation when he exhibited in New York was his paintings of food. Because of their subject matter, these were erroneously related to what was then being done by Claes Oldenburg and Warhol, who were interested in the way advertising represented objects and not, as Thiebaud was, in the objects themselves – their very essence. He concentrated on the kind of mass-manufactured comestibles found at chain delicatessens and lunch counters, with occasional deviations into objects such as juke boxes. *Four Sundaes* (1963) is a typical example of his still-life painting. The slightly irregular rhythm of the arrangement, the different position of each glacé cherry – all of these give the painting a teasing, slightly syncopated feeling. The creamy density of the paint offers a direct equivalent for the creamy quality of what is being represented. Thiebaud once said: 'The interesting problem with realism [is] that it seem[s] alternately the most magical alchemy on the one hand, and on the other the most abstract construct intellectually.'4 *Four Sundaes* exemplifies this: it is an attempt to offer both a sensual equivalent of the thing seen, and a purely cerebral one – an object in a completely imagined parallel universe.

An almost invariable feature of Thiebaud's still-lifes is the shimmering halation which surrounds the objects. This is part of a process of intensification necessary, in the painter's view, to enable the picture to compete with the distracting movement and dazzle of the real world which surrounds it. 'The problem of the painter,' Thiebaud once declared, 'is to have the painting create its own light – that's the theory of painting.'5

Since he made his breakthrough, Thiebaud has broadened his range. He now paints people, generally single figures represented with a slightly stiff monumentality and a touch and lighting reminiscent of Hopper. In recent years he has also done quite a large number of landscapes. It is in some of these that his debt to the figurative work of Diebenkorn is most apparent. Like the latter, Thiebaud is fascinated by the peculiar topography of San Francisco, with its steep streets which sometimes seem to lead directly into the sky. Views of this type compress space in a way which helps to preserve the integrity of the pictorial surface; here the ultimate source is Cézanne.

Thiebaud's typical landscapes are commonly much smaller than those done by Diebenkorn in his figurative period; perhaps because of this, the design is more tightly controlled. No role is left for chance; these are pictorial mechanisms constructed with the utmost sureness of touch.

In addition to being compared to Chardin and Corot, Thiebaud is sometimes described as the American Morandi. This is a well-deserved compliment. Like Giorgio Morandi, he is able to make the painted surface a unity without compromising the spectator's feeling for the reality – the sheer physical presence – of what is portrayed. What the members of the original Bay Area group invariably have to struggle for – the equivalence of reality and paint – Thiebaud achieves with insolent ease.

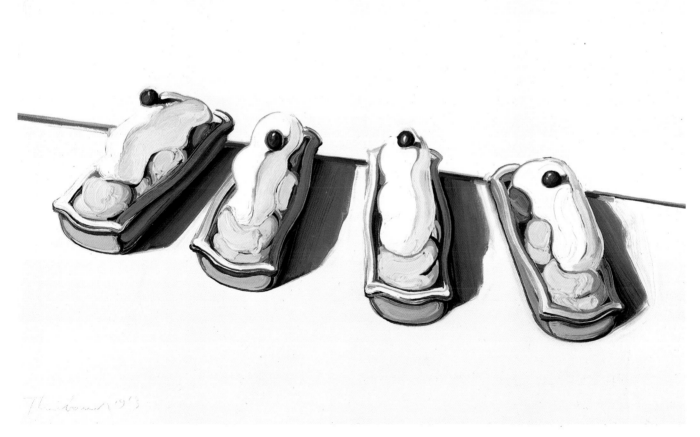

185 Wayne Thiebaud
San Francisco Landscape 1976
The kinship between this and Diebenkorn's *Cityscape 1* (Ill. 183), painted thirteen years before, is clear.

186 Wayne Thiebaud
Four Sundaes 1963
The refined sophistication of Thiebaud's still-lifes evidences their stylistic distance from the Pop Art produced in New York.

CHAPTER 13

The Replicated Object

SINCE THE 1960s, a new category has made its appearance in American art. The objects which belong to this represent the beginning of the breakdown of the traditional frontier between painting and sculpture – something which was to be taken much further in the 1970s by art of all kinds, whether realistic or not. I have called these items 'replicated objects' because in many ways they seem quite different in intention from traditional sculpture. For one thing, they force the spectator to consider what can safely be called 'art' and what is simply 'real life'. In addition, they tend to have an emblematic or narrative function rather than a purely plastic one, despite the fact that they exist in three dimensions. In the majority, formal relationships – the interaction of one form or volume with another – play no part.

These replicated objects have their roots in a number of different traditions. They stem from Duchamp, who did not replicate familiar objects but merely selected them from the surrounding environment and presented them as what he called 'readymades'. They also descend from the objects devised by the Surrealists. These, which involved incongruous juxtapositions of found objects, or unexpected transformations of material (Meret Oppenheim's celebrated *Fur Teacup* is an example of the latter process), had no pretensions to be sculpture, as this is usually defined, but were self-evidently items in the round and not paintings.

The other tradition which gave birth to the replicated object is pre-Modern, but has usually existed very much on the margins of art, so that critics have sometimes debated whether its products counted as objects of art, objects of craft, or as something altogether different. I am speaking here of 'deceptive' objects of various kinds – of platters by Bernard Palissy covered with lifelike lizards, worms and insects, of fairground waxworks, and of funeral effigies of the kind now preserved at Westminster Abbey in London. Though three-dimensional, these have a clear connection with the kind of *trompe-l'oeil* painting practised by Harnett and Peto. Like Harnett and Peto, they have strong links with a 'popular' or demotic tradition of visual representation, as opposed to a sophisticated intellectual approach to artworks and their purposes. In this popular tradition, art has two closely linked purposes: to excite a sense of wonder, and at the same time to provide a clear and accurate mirror in which quotidian things can find themselves reflected.

In the 1950s the reputation of Duchamp, and that of the Dada movement in general, began to revive in the United States. One of the artists most immediately affected by this was Jasper Johns, who made a number of three-dimensional works as more or less direct tributes to Duchamp. However, Johns always preferred to replicate reality rather than take objects directly from the surrounding environment. One of his best-known creations of this type is *Painted Bronze (Savarin)*, of 1960. This is a simulacrum, made of painted metal as the title suggests, of a studio object – a coffee can used as a receptacle for the turpentine in which the artist's brushes were soaked when not in use. To the actual can are added the brushes themselves, or at least that part of them – their handles – which remained visible.

In making this replica, Johns trod a careful line between illusion and the denial of illusion. Cast in bronze, the piece derives from a plaster original which is itself a direct cast of what is shown. The form is thus a perfect replica

188 Jasper Johns
Painted Bronze (Savarin) 1960

OPPOSITE
187 Rigoberto Torres *Shorty Working at the C. & K. Statuary Corporation* 1985

189 **Claes Oldenburg** *Danish Pastry*
1960 (from *The Store* 1961)

190 **Claes Oldenburg**
Dormeyer Mixer 1965

191 **Andy Warhol**
Brillo Box (Soap Pads) 1964

of pre-existing reality; the surface is not. Though it has been painted to correspond with the original, the task has not been performed so meticulously that the spectator cannot, at a glance, tell the difference. The piece is therefore only marginally concerned with illusion. Its real theme, as with many Pop paintings, is the language in which visual information is conveyed.

The Pop artist who, following Johns, seems to have pursued this line most strenuously is Claes Oldenburg (1929–). Oldenburg's earliest replicated objects were actual size – food and artifacts made in coloured plaster for his environmental work *The Store* (1961). These are modelled and painted with a deliberate roughness which signals that they are not intended to be taken for the real thing. Their artificiality is in fact the point. What is 'realist' is the pointed reference to the banality of everyday life.

From these small pieces, Oldenburg progressed to the works for which he is now best known: gigantic enlargements of everyday objects – hamburgers, three-way electrical plugs, egg-beaters. It has often been said that he was influenced by the outsized objects sometimes used as advertising signs. Los Angeles, for example, has many of these; the most celebrated is the Brown Derby restaurant, a small building in the shape of a man's hat, built at 3477 Wilshire Boulevard as long ago as 1926. This can be compared with the gigantic *Stake Hitch* (1984) created by Oldenburg and his wife Coosje van Bruggen (1942-) for the rebuilt Dallas Museum of Art. This is real in one sense, because it is a remarkably faithful representation of the object it portrays; but unreal in another, because it takes something the spectator knows to be small, and blows it up to gigantic size. In Oldenburg's 'middle sized' works – fairly ambitious gallery pieces – the realist element is often subverted even more directly. In his 'soft' egg-beaters made of kapok and vinyl, the drooping shapes become an impudent metaphor for male genitalia. The nearest parallels are perhaps the soft watches in Salvador Dali's paintings of the 1930s.

Warhol's replicas of familiar objects, which form a comparatively minor part of his immense oeuvre, are much closer to what they replicate than anything by Oldenburg. Cartons for Campbell's soup, Kellogg's cornflakes, Heinz tomato ketchup, Del Monte peach halves and Brillo soap pads – all utterly familiar domestic products – are reproduced with such fidelity that it is hard to tell whether or not they are the real thing without touching them: they are made of wood not cardboard. The deceptiveness, in this case, seems to have had a special purpose. An installation photograph of Warhol's exhibition at the Stable Gallery, New York, in 1964,[1] the first occasion on which the boxes were shown, reveals that they were laid out in regular rows on the floor. This indicates that they did not start their lives as things intended to be looked at for their own sake, but as anonymous units in a series, with much the same function as the individual bricks which go to make up some of Carl Andre's Minimalist sculptures.

More traditional in their attitude to replication are a number of sculptures made by contemporary American ceramicists, which are directly in line of descent from Palissy. The work of ceramic sculptors such as Marilyn Levine (1935–) and Richard Shaw (1941–) can be related not only to this but to the whole 'deceptive' or *trompe-l'oeil* tradition mentioned at the beginning of this chapter.

FAR LEFT
192 Marilyn Levine
Rick and Margaret's Suitcase 1976

LEFT
193 Richard Shaw
Stack of Cards on a Brown Book 1977

BELOW
194 The Brown Derby Restaurant, Los Angeles (building now altered) 1926.

BOTTOM
195 Claes Oldenburg and Coosje van Bruggen
Stake Hitch 1984

Levine's speciality is imitating objects made of leather, with such fidelity that it is literally impossible to tell that the object is not what it seems until one attempts to pick it up. One of the attractions of leather, for her, is that fact that – being such a malleable, organic material – it accumulates the traces of human use. The ceramic object thus becomes a statement about the people who have handled and used the thing from which it is replicated. Levine's attitude recalls that of Harnett, with his well-developed feeling for objects which show evidence of long use, and which can therefore be thought of as providing indirect portraits of their owners.

Richard Shaw is a prolific ceramic artist who works in a variety of modes. One involves creating *trompe-l'oeil* objects almost as deceptive as Levine's: elaborate card houses which look as if a breath would make them fall. Here, too, as in Levine's imitations of leather, the element of visual paradox is strong.

Once human beings are introduced into the artistic equation, the whole situation seems to change. Can a human figure plausibly be described as a 'replicated object'? In fact, the characteristic processes used by certain contemporary American artists suggest that this description is not as strained as it might seem.

In the case of George Segal (1924–2000), one has to consider both processes and results. Segal did not begin his career as a maker of three-dimensional objects. His first exhibition, held at the cooperative Hansa Gallery in New York, consisted of paintings. In 1956, he began making expressionist sculptures in the manner of the then fashionable French sculptor Germaine Richier. In 1961 he discovered a new technique – casting from life. From that date until 1971 his work was made of the actual plaster shells which resulted from this process. After that date he shifted to a more refined method, first taking a mould from the living body, then making an inside cast from this in hydrostone.

As William Seitz pointed out in a brief but perceptive study of Segal's early work, this method eliminates 'ancient and fundamental sculptors' problems, among them overall size, figure canon, and the entire repertory of expressive, decorative and perceptual deformation'.[2] Because Segal's figures are moulded from life, they always have the size and proportions of life.

ABOVE
196 **George Segal** *Times Square at Night* 1970
A brilliant evocation of the sleazier aspects of New York.

ABOVE RIGHT
197 **George Segal** *The Gas Station* 1963–64
(see Ill. 114)

Essentially, however, Segal uses this unconventional technique in a relatively conventional way. When he oversteps its boundaries and tackles an 'imaginative' theme, like *Jacob and the Angel* (1984), the result has the slightly bizarre literalism of Eakins's *Crucifixion*. Yet it is not merely that he is fettered, just as Eakins was, by the innate secularism of American society; it is also that the actual nature of his method puts anything transcendental out of reach. Segal's angels, cast from mortal bodies, remain stubbornly earthbound.

His attachment to the quotidian prompts a comparison not only with Eakins but with Hopper. This resemblance was noted, at the very beginning of Segal's career, by none other than the Abstract Expressionist painter Mark Rothko (1903–70), who once said, 'He does walk-in Hoppers.'[3] The accuracy of this observation can be tested by looking at *The Gas Station* (1963–64), one of the most elaborate of Segal's early works, which is Hopper-like in theme as well as style. However, it is worth remarking that the piece achieves its effect through narrative rather than purely plastic means. Though Segal spoke of the need he had felt to strip this piece down to what was 'absolutely necessary and expressive',[4] the actual setting, which plays so large a part in the total effect, is of course completely literal – not sculpture, but the elements of an elaborately literal stage-set.

Like Hopper, Segal had a gift for conveying urban loneliness and isolation. The ghostly whiteness of the two figures in *Times Square at Night* (1970), set against a group of illuminated signs advertising fast food and sleazy entertainment, is an extraordinarily powerful image of the wraithlike existence now led by many city dwellers.

Segal seemed less good at public monuments, of the kind that provided the figurative sculptors of the past with their most cherished opportunities – this, despite the fact that he became the preferred American artist for memorials dedicated to various good causes. Some of these have aroused controversy. Segal's *Memorial of May 4, 1970: Kent State – Abraham and Isaac* (1979) found a site at Princeton University, having been refused by Kent State University itself. His *Gay Liberation Monument* (1980) has yet to find a permanent home. In both cases it is the theme that has made the sculpture contentious, not the style, which remains ponderously literal and therefore rather dull. One has only to think of the emotional charge generated by Auguste Rodin's *Burghers of Calais*, another relatively informal group of figures, to see what Segal's limitations are.

Segal was the precursor of three other artists, all of whom base their work on variations of the same life-casting techniques. Each uses the techniques to slightly different ends.

John De Andrea (1941–) is the most self-conscious. In his work there is a perpetual conflict between realism of the most literal sort and idealization. The conflict is neatly summarized in a version of *The Dying Gaul* (1984), where the life-cast technique, and the fact that the piece has been coloured to resemble life, combine with the familiar classical pose to produce an instructive clash of visions and values. De Andrea's more usual subjects are contemporary young men and women in the nude – the good-looking students who inhabit American campuses. Physically attractive they may be, but they are nevertheless full of the physical quirks and imperfections which traditionally idealizing artists are at pains to remove. The figures are real enough, in most people's terms, yet also curiously lifeless. The spectator is made acutely aware of the fact that this is not something reimagined but something totally literal – a simulacrum.

198 **George Segal** *Memorial of May 4, 1970: Kent State – Abraham and Isaac* 1979

199 **John De Andrea** *The Dying Gaul* 1984
A direct confrontation with a Hellenistic Greek masterpiece which reveals the difference between replication and idealization.

200 **John Ahearn** *Audrey and Janelle* 1983
Segal's technique (Ills 196–98, 201) of casting from life is
given a 'popular' accent by Ahearn, a community artist
working in a deprived urban area – New York's South Bronx.

In the sculptures of John Ahearn (1951–), the main concerns are not
aesthetic but sociological. Ahearn is by deliberate choice a 'neighbourhood'
sculptor who lives and works in a deprived urban area, New York's South
Bronx. Since 1979 he has collaborated with Rigoberto Torres (1961–), a
young resident of the district whom he met at an alternative art space called
Fashion Moda. Ahearn came to sculpture through architecture and film-
making; he learned the moulding process through making masks for films.
Torres had an uncle who owned a factory which made religious statuary, and
he gained his knowledge of casting there.

It was Torres who smoothed Ahearn's way into a tight-knit black and
Hispanic community. By making portraits of neighbours and friends, they
aimed to reveal a heroic dimension in people who lived mundane lives, and
who were regarded by themselves and others as being completely cut off from
art, especially contemporary art. For these artists, working with their sitters is
not a private process. The moulding often takes place in the street; everyone in
the neighbourhood comes to watch. This is one part of the validating process;
the blunt realism of the finished result is another. It is important that the sitters

should be immediately recognizable, and no coding of appearances is involved. Indeed, such coding would probably lead to rejection by the community.

Realism of this same type is what many people would see in the work of Duane Hanson (1925–96). Though only a year younger than Segal, and four years the senior of Oldenburg, Hanson was a slow starter, and belongs to a different generation of artists. His work is often aligned by critics with the Photorealist painting which came to prominence at the same moment, in the late 1960s.

The first works in which Hanson was recognizably himself, made and exhibited in Florida in the second half of the 1960s, aroused violent negative reactions; he continued to be a focus of controversy. What shocked people about the early pieces was the combination of uncoded realism and what they

201 **George Segal** *The Execution* 1967
Unusually violent for Segal, this can be compared with the early work of Duane Hanson (Ills 202–04) of the same period.

202 **Duane Hanson** *Accident* 1969
In a controversial piece, the artist made use of a motorcycle
which had actually been involved in a fatal accident, which
bears comparison to Andy Warhol's use of documentary
photographs of automobile wrecks (Ill. 178).

felt was unacceptable subject matter. The work seemed to cross the boundary
between art and life, and to do so in a threatening way.

Hanson had a precedent for this in some of Segal's work. In 1967, just as
Hanson was beginning to emerge, Segal made a piece called *The Execution*,
which features four corpses, one hung upside down by a rope tied to its ankles.
This is brutal enough, but, because Segal has left the figures uncoloured, it
does not seem to cross over completely into the spectator's realm – there is a
distance between him or her and the actual event.

Realistic colouring and the use of 'real' clothes as well as 'real' props make
Hanson's sculptures much more immediately horrifying. *Accident* (1969),
which features the corpse of a young motorcycle rider and his wrecked
machine (its uncoded aspect is emphasized by the fact that Hanson bought a
motorcycle which had been involved in a fatal accident for use in the piece)
was one of two sculptures by the artist banned from an exhibition at the
Bacardi Museum in Florida because, as the director said, 'People come here to
relax and see some beauty, not to throw up.'[5]

These early pieces have been categorized, not merely by critics but by the sculptor himself, as expressionist simply because of their content. In fact, it could be said that they are outside any form of stylistic categorization, simply because of the life-moulding technique used to make them. They undoubtedly, nevertheless, responded to the mood of the day in the United States. It was a particularly violent moment in American history, with the Vietnam War raging, and race-riots in a number of American cities.

Later, at the beginning of the 1970s, Hanson became a social satirist of memorable skill, concentrating on members of the American and sometimes the German underclass (he lived for a while in West Germany, and his work was popular there), and also, going up the social scale, on the more crassly materialistic aspects of American middle–class life and the consumer culture now integrated with it. A piece like *Tourists* (1970) is a product of intensification, just as much as of simple observation – clothing and accessories are carefully chosen to magnify the intended effect.

Hanson himself insisted that he was a sculptor of a traditional kind, influenced in particular by the Swede Carl Milles, with whom he studied at the Cranbrook Academy of Art, and by Rodin, with whom Milles himself once studied.[6] He rejected the idea that there is any real link between his figures and those to be found in traditional waxwork museums:

> I've looked at them all. I would be glad to see a convincing figure, but they are
> always so stiff; they always look a little dead, and they are never relaxed. And,
> of course, they are supposed to be portraits, yet never come off as portraits.[7]

In addition, Hanson pointed out that his figures were the object of many adjustments after they were cast from life. They seldom bear a strong resemblance to the original model and may in fact be a composite of several models. 'My aim,' he said, 'is to make a sculpture first.'[8]

In fact, if we accept the artist's own description of his aims and attitudes in making these astonishingly realistic works, the replicated object here comes full circle, and becomes, paradoxically, sculpture of a traditional sort, which asks to be judged by criteria which are not merely pre-1960s but in most important respects actually pre-Modernist.

The interesting thing is that Hanson, of all the makers of three-dimensional work here described, is the only one who counts as an acute social critic. In fact, his figures are sharper pieces of observation, with a much tougher satirical edge, than the work of earlier social realists like Ben Shahn and Jack Levine. With them, the spectator is conscious that the verdict is already preempted. With Hanson, there is the feeling – quite false, as it happens – that one has come, inevitably, to one's own conclusions.

TOP
203 **Duane Hanson** *Cowboy* 1991

RIGHT
204 **Duane Hanson** *Tourists* 1970

CHAPTER 14

Photorealism

A RT CRITICISM has not found it easy to deal with the Photorealist episode in American painting, not least because the style itself found so little favour with established critics at the moment when it first emerged. Where it was condemned, it was seen either as a cynical sell-out to popular taste or as a bizarre, rather naive continuation of Pop Art. Where it was welcomed, which happened much more rarely, this was because it was seen as a disguised extension of the kind of thinking which also went to create Minimalism and Conceptualism. The conceptual element, according to enthusiasts, was to be found in the fact that this style 'raises questions about the way we see and reminds us of the many physical and psychological factors that alter, compensate, or diminish the things we look at'.[1]

In fact, the motivating forces behind Photorealism seem to be more complex than either its detractors or its enthusiasts admit. The real message is neither a simple (or cynical) dependency on photographic imagery, nor an intellectual analysis of ways of seeing things dictated by the camera lens, but a hunger for figurative images that contain a strong emotional and subjective element. Despite critical and curatorial opposition, this affected a whole generation of American artists. These artists, in addition to looking at what the camera had to give them, looked back at much earlier American art. Their historical perspective included the work of Eakins, Harnett and Peto, and also that of the Precisionists (Sheeler's *Rolling Power* bears a particularly close relationship to typical Photorealist work). Yet another ancestor was Edward Hopper; some of the Photorealists shared his fascination with the melancholy ordinariness of American daily life.

Enthusiasts for a conceptual interpretation of Photorealism tend to concentrate on the work of Chuck Close (1941–), and sometimes on the early paintings of Malcolm Morley. In Close's case the reasons are obvious: he makes paintings which are enormously enlarged versions of snapshot photographs of friends – the head only, usually seen absolutely frontally. In creating these he deliberately reproduces some of the aberrations peculiar to the camera – such as the way in which, when a wide aperture is used, the volume of the head may be divided into zones of focus, with the tip of the nose blurred, the cheekbones sharp, and the ears once again blurred. These characteristics have led some commentators to suggest that Close is 'much more involved with the systematization and codification of information than he is with the actual image'. He rejects this: 'That's not accurate, because the way you choose to make something influences the way it looks and therefore what it means.'[2]

What Close says he wants to do, in painting his giant portraits, is 'to rip the imagery loose from the context in ways in which we would normally view an image of a person'[3] – in other words, to challenge and refresh the spectator's vision of reality in a way that is typical of all the more ambitious and intellectual types of realist art. The same can be said of Parmigianino's youthful *Self-Portrait in a Convex Mirror*, Caravaggio's *Boy Bitten by a Lizard*, or Goya's portrait of the blind beggar *Tío Paquete*, now in the Thyssen Collection.

Yet there are aspects of Close's work which suggest that the eager theoreticians do after all have something on their side. Looking at the full range of his production, one sees that, over the years, he has allowed himself a considerable variety of approach. It is not only that, at a certain stage, he

205 **Chuck Close** *Stanley (Large Version)* 1980–81
Close often builds up an apparently faithful representation through near-mechanical repetition of small, simple, predetermined abstract units.

206 **Chuck Close**
John 1992

OPPOSITE
207 **Chuck Close**
Self-Portrait 1968
Based on a casual snapshot taken by
Close in his studio, this is the first in
his sequence of large paintings of
heads. Close was attracted to the
photograph partly because of its
technical imperfections: 'They did
interesting spatial things to the
image ... they added another range
of information to deal with,
something to paint.'

abandoned the austere black-and-white with which he had begun, and started
to use full colour. It is also that the standard image of the head is presented in
very different ways. In later paintings, from the end of the 1970s onwards, the
images are built up from separate touches of pure colour, in the manner of
Georges Seurat, and there is no attempt at photographic illusionism.

Close seems to have arrived at this method, not through direct imitation of
Seurat's divisionist technique, but through restless experimentation with
different ways of creating an image on a surface. He has made paper-pulp
collages, fingerprint and rubber stamp drawings and also finger-paintings, both
with and without an overriding grid. His experiments seem to have two sources,
above and beyond a simple desire for change and variety. One is a fascination
with the idea of recognizability. How much or how little information do we need
in order to be able to recognize a particular face? The other is an interest in the
logic of printing processes, not dissimilar to Lichtenstein's obsession with this
area of technology as applied to comic strips. In Close's case, however, the
interest is turned towards the techniques used to reproduce photographs.

When Close first began to paint his heads in colour, he looked for a method
which would be true to his intentions. Since photographs were his basic source,
it was natural to look at colour printing. 'I looked,' Close said, 'for a way of
working where all the paint would physically mix on the canvas, *in situ*, where I
would see what I was doing.'[4] Essentially this is what modern print technology
does, superimposing one colour on another to produce the desired hue. Close set
out to replicate this situation by hand. He selected a transparency, had three
continuous-tone colour separations made from it, and used them as a guide in
overlaying three basic hues in sequence so as to produce a full colour result: 'It is
rather like magic. When I get to the last colour, yellow, you can't see the pigment
come out of the airbrush – it's like waving a magic wand in front of the picture
and the purple becomes brown. It's really quite wonderful.'[5]

Despite the fact that he is sometimes paired with Close, the attitudes of Malcolm Morley towards photographic source material seem in fact to have been very different. The difference is symbolized by the fact that his photographic source was 'found' rather than made. What Morley did, at a certain stage in his career, was to take banal picture postcards, initially of ships, and reproduce them as literally as possible. His declared intention was 'to find an iconography which was untarnished by art'.[6] He was thus following in the footsteps of Duchamp and Johns. Close had a personal stake in the subject matter he chose; for Morley, it was irrelevant – it became 'a by-product of surface'.[7] In these circumstances, the completed painting was indeed a disguised abstraction, which revealed its significance (as a record of process, painted according to a rigid grid system) only to cognoscenti. The fact that others, not in the know, sometimes took pleasure in finding recognizable imagery in Morley's work was not his concern.

He did not persist in this direction for long. Soon the images borrowed from photographs began to be deliberately disrupted and torn; then Morley's work abandoned all connection with the camera. In his Photorealist phase he forms a bridge between the deliberate banalities of some of the Pop artists, especially

208 **Malcolm Morley**
United States with NY Skyline 1965

Warhol, and those of Jeff Koons. His aim, like theirs, was to produce an imagery without affect, so familiar that all possible responses were already preempted.

Though they have tended to occupy so much space in discussions of Photorealism, neither Close nor Morley seems to me typical of the movement. Basically, this was a response to needs in American society which were despised or disregarded by the prophets and bureaucrats of the avant-garde.

One of the analogies which most immediately spring to mind when one looks at a range of typical Photorealist paintings by different hands is that of the Dutch still-life and genre painting of the seventeenth century. There is the same high degree of finish (a guarantee of both effort and skill). There is the concentration on making recognizable images of contemporary life. Finally, there is the fact that these are all clearly goods made for sale, addressed, as nearly all Dutch art was, to a bourgeois public of private collectors. Like the Dutch 'little masters' of the seventeenth century, American Photorealist painters are often highly specialized. Each confines himself or herself to a particular range of subject matter: motorcycles for one, glittering arrays of glassware for another, horses and riders for a third.

Some Photorealists dazzle chiefly by their extremely high degree of technical skill. One such is Charles Bell (1935–), a specialist in gumball machines, groups of glass marbles, and enlarged images of children's toys. Bell's work does make one important point. As he himself points out, Photorealist painting often depends, not merely on the photographic vision, but on the way in which

209 **Charles Bell** *Sixteen Candles* 1992
The artist notes that it would be impossible to paint a subject of this type without the aid of a camera because of the intensity of the illumination required.

photography opens the door to things which otherwise would be impossible for the painter on purely practical grounds. The extreme luminosity of Bell's paintings of marbles requires an intensity of lighting which probably could not be achieved in a traditional still-life set-up. Even if it were achieved, it would be dangerous, with so much light, and the accompanying heat, focused on the motif for hour after hour.

Since Photorealist artists are now so numerous, and often so nearly identical in style, it seems best to concentrate on a handful who offer features of special interest, and who at the same time seem to transcend the evident limitations of the mode in which they work.

One of the most eloquent of the main Photorealist group is Ralph Goings (1928–). Goings was born and raised in northern California and trained as an artist at the College of Arts and Crafts in Oakland, courtesy of the GI Bill of Rights. The effect of this piece of legislation on the American art scene of the postwar period was comparable to that of the New Deal before the war. Goings recalled:

> Most of the males at the college were ex-GIs, and we were a few years older than students normally are, so there was a high degree of seriousness and intensity about going to school. A lot of the guys were like me, from poor families. Without the GI Bill we would never have been able to go to this very expensive school, and in a way we were in awe of where we were and what we could do. Even though we often didn't like the assignments, we did them, sometimes three- and four-fold, simply because we wanted to be professionals. On the other hand there were these few faculty members who were interested in abstraction, and they were the ones who encouraged us to go home at night and try things that were not related at all to what we were doing in the academic classes.[8]

This quotation highlights the difficulties faced by students of Goings's generation, who went to college in the early to mid-1950s. Two imperatives confronted them. One was to conform to a system of training which was old-fashioned and academic, but which promoted a respect for craftsmanship that was already bred into many of those who came from working-class backgrounds. The other was to obey the shibboleths of the new abstraction, which taught that care for craft inhibited the all-important thing, which was self-expression. Goings, like many others, was torn by this contradiction and found his development blocked. Even Pop Art, when it emerged, did not offer a way out, especially when he saw the work itself, as opposed to reproductions in magazines:

> When I saw the actual paintings I was disappointed. The paintings were so tacky. They were so crudely done, with little strings hanging off the corners. And I thought, hell, these guys are not any better craftsmen than the Abstract Expressionists. They've got a terrific idea but they're just not painting it right.[9]

The impulse to do something different, 'to step back and let the thing stand for itself',[10] came when Goings, living and working in Sacramento, was asked to participate in a group show. The stipulation was that every painting must be a view of Sacramento. Seeing a pickup truck on a parking lot led him to think that this, after all, was something which perfectly reflected the locality and its

210 **Ralph Goings** *Still-Life with Creamer* 1982
A modernized version of one of John F. Peto's (Ills 28, 33–35) still-lifes of humble, everyday objects.

lifestyle. The painting which resulted (in 1969) was done directly from a 35 mm colour slide, and became the first in a series featuring trucks. From these, Goings went on to make pictures showing the insides and outsides of fast food places. Later, when he moved to upstate New York in 1974, Goings started to paint diner interiors, where figures for the first time played an important role. He also produced still-lifes featuring typical items one might see on a diner table or counter – sauce bottles, paper-napkin dispensers, or salt, pepper and sugar shakers with chrome or plastic tops.

Goings now protests that social implications 'were not an important part of what the pictures were about to begin with',[11] and says that he cannot object to the term Photorealism because what he wants is 'a painting style based partly on the language of photography – the visual effects of photography and how that can be translated into a painting language'.[12] Interestingly enough, it is this apparently modern and technological aspect of his work which brings

211 Ralph Goings *Burger Chef* 1970
Discussing Californian culture of the late 1960s, Goings remarked that pickup trucks 'weren't really work vehicles any more, they were something people bought when they became affluent, because pickups were sort of the last vestige of Western man ...'

212 Ralph Goings *Country Girl Diner* 1985
In many respects closely comparable to interiors painted by Vermeer.

him closest to Dutch seventeenth-century painting, and in particular to the art of Jan Vermeer, an artist whom he admires enormously. It is now generally accepted that Vermeer made extensive use of the seventeenth-century equivalent of the modern reflex camera, the *camera obscura*, an optical instrument that could produce the same sort of image but could not fix it permanently.

In addition, and despite the artist's denials, Goings's work is indeed full of sociological content. He himself has commented on the significance of the pickup truck in the Californian culture of the late 1960s: 'They weren't really work vehicles anymore, they were something people bought when they became affluent, because pickups were sort of the last vestige of the Western man, but they weren't really used to do anything but show off.'[13] Most of Goings's work, in fact nearly all of it, can be read as a nostalgic lament for the kind of blue-collar American culture which was gradually passing away at the time when the pictures were painted. Far from being neutral, his work is suffused with feeling, much of it melancholy.

The same loyalties surface in the work of another California artist associated with the Photorealist movement, Robert Bechtle (1932–   ). In a statement written in 1973, Bechtle had this to say:

> I try for a kind of neutrality or transparency of style that minimizes the artfulness that might prevent the viewer from responding directly to the subject matter …
> My subject matter comes from my own background and surroundings. I paint them because they are part of what I know and as such I have affection for them.
> I see them as particular embodiments of a general American experience.[14]

As the years have passed, Bechtle has become less interested in the informality of the snapshot, which a number of Photorealist artists turned into a convention. While seeking to retain the photographic transparency which has always attracted him, and while still using photographs for reference, he has

213 **Robert Bechtle** *Oakland Intersection – 59th and Stanford* 1990
This Oakland townscape is closely comparable to Childe Hassam's *Rainy Day, Boston* (Ill. 45), painted over a hundred years before.

214 Robert Bechtle *Broome Street Still-Life* 1991
A double portrait of the artist and his wife.

become a painter with a finely tuned sense of space and with an eye for monumentality of form. One proof of this is the recent fine double portrait of the artist with his wife, *Broome Street Still-Life* (1991).

Even those who decried Photorealism from the first tended to make an exception for the work of Richard Estes (1932–). The flawless elegance of his New York townscapes seduced many who were otherwise resistant on principle to all realist art. Estes's early paintings were generally close-up, straight-on views of storefronts, such as *The Candy Store* (1969), which derived much of their effect from the artist's skill in combining reflection and transparency produced by large sheets of glass. Later, he began to tackle more complex views, where the windows are at an angle to the spectator and the pattern of reflections

is more complex. These developed into urban panoramas, mostly of New York, which make use of deep perspective rarely found in Photorealist painting.

Estes has never made any secret of his use of photographs as a basis for his paintings. It is also no secret that he alters the source material:

> One evolves ways of doing this. A photograph is just values. It doesn't have line. When you use the photograph, you are using the values, but you are adding line and space and movement, coming from your experience. That's why, although I work from photographs, I like the subjects to be things I'm really familiar with. I don't think I could use someone else's photograph of some place I've never been to and make a painting. Although I could copy the photograph, I wouldn't really have a feeling for the place. You're always remembering, and the photograph is like a reference you use, a sketch.[15]

The photographic material for *Downtown* shows how much Estes modifies the original *donnée*.[16] The painting is a composite of many photographs, not a straightforward reproduction of a single image, and many details have been changed, among them the perspective of the street behind the subway entrance

215 **Richard Estes** *The Candy Store* 1969
Estes's early paintings tend to be close-up views of storefronts.

216 **Richard Estes** *Downtown* 1978
Published photographic documentation for this work shows how radically the artist modified the original source material.

217 **Richard Estes** *Accademia* 1980
Estes makes a fascinating comparison with Canaletto's views of the Grand Canal in Venice, some made from a nearly identical viewpoint.

and the height of the building in the centre, in relation to the other buildings surrounding it. The finished painting does not have the single vanishing point which would have been imposed by the camera's fixed monocular view of such a scene. Estes explains these deviations as typical of the fashion in which people actually see: 'You don't see everything at once. When you look at a room, an object or a person, you look at different parts and the brain puts it all together as a picture.'[17]

Far from having a rigid attitude to the camera, Estes is very much a pragmatist. The purely traditional aspect of his work can be understood by looking at a group of paintings which have remained little known because they are all in private collections. These are views not of New York, Estes's usual subject, nor of other American cities, but of Paris, Florence and Venice. The Venetian views are particularly instructive because they enable one to make a direct comparison with Canaletto.

Accademia (1980) is certainly not based directly on Canaletto, quite apart from the fact that it features the Accademia bridge, which did not exist in the eighteenth century. It does, however, show a stretch of the Grand Canal which Canaletto painted frequently. It is the differences that spring to the eye first: there are no gondolas or other boats to animate the scene; the church of La Salute is smaller and further away than Canaletto would have allowed it to be; and the glass enclosure of the *vaporetto* landing stage offers typical Estes effects of combined reflection and transparency. The fundamental likeness is nevertheless close enough for it to be seen that Estes is an artist of the same sort as Canaletto, who absorbs and moulds together various bits of topographical information to produce a unified view which is not an absolutely direct mirror of nature, but which can be accepted as such by most viewers. There is no great chasm of assumed 'modernity' between Estes and his predecessor. Instead there is a quiet absorption of a still-usable part of the Old Master tradition.

Another artist associated with Photorealism who has clearly learned something from a study of the Old Masters is Audrey Flack (1931–). Prolific and enterprising, Flack has spent only part of her career making photo-based paintings. During the 1950s she did some probing expressionist self-portraits, and more recently she has been working as a sculptor, making figures which owe something to the sixteenth-century Mannerism of Benvenuto Cellini' Perseus, but more to the so-called New Sculpture of later nineteenth- and early twentieth-century England – as exemplified by the work of Sir Alfred Gilbert, sculptor of *Eros* in Piccadilly Circus, London.

Flack's most striking Photorealist canvases are still-lifes. These feature jewels, cosmetics and/or luscious arrays of fruit, plus a diversity of other objects. As in traditional still-life painting, there is almost always an allegorical subtext, generally a *Vanitas* theme, sometimes actually symbolized by the presence of a skull.

The paintings have untraditional features as well. For instance, the fruits, though greatly enlarged (following the practice of Pop artists, who routinely made objects much larger than life, as in billboard imagery), are always luscious and free of blemish. 'In this sense,' as Lawrence Alloway remarked in an essay on Flack's work, 'the artist's meditation on the emblems of death becomes a victory over mortality as she exemplifies the objects of the world as

218 Audrey Flack *Fruits of the Earth* 1983
The fruits in the foreground seem suspended in the air, which
intensifies the visionary quality of the painting.

whole, lustrous and full'.[18] A second, equally untraditional feature is the
instability of the objects shown, which often seem to be magically suspended in
the air, so that they acquire a visionary quality.

One influence, especially apparent in the later paintings in the series, is
the work of the American landscape and still-life painter Martin Johnson Heade
(1819–1904). Closest in style to Flack's paintings of fruit are Heade's
depictions of huge magnolias, made at the end of his life when he was living and
working in isolation in Florida. These have been felicitously described
by a modern critic as being 'arrayed in sumptuous velvet like odalisques
on a couch'.[19] Flack's fruits have something of the same quality. Their sensual
presence makes them very different from Georgia O'Keeffe's enlarged paintings of flowers, which often have a curiously flat quality – heraldic and
emblematic rather than realized in all their sensual richness.

What the four artists I have just discussed have most in common is the fact
that they all provoke comparisons with traditional Old Master painting –
Goings and Bechtle with Vermeer, Estes with Canaletto, Flack with Dutch still-
life as well as with Heade. This means that each tends to break out of a narrowly
Photorealist mould and become a more complex and therefore more interesting
kind of artist. The trouble with those all-too-numerous Photorealist painters
who fail to do this is that the dependence on the camera, originally perceived as
a way of freeing figurative painting from traditional rules, itself becomes
a straitjacket. In terms of the whole American art scene, Photorealist painting
has become a narrow specialism, which targets a particular market with great
success but shows little possibility of further development. Photorealist
painters continue to appear – there are now perhaps three generations of them
working in the United States – but they remain apart from the mainstream of
contemporary American realist art.

219 Philip Pearlstein *Mr and Mrs Edmund Pillsbury* 1973
Pearlstein's portraits are more conventionally composed than his familiar paintings of
nudes. Here there is the directness of Copley's *Boy with a Squirrel* (Ill. 7), although
the woman's profile, seen in a mirror, is an allusion to Ingres's portrait of *Mme
Moitessier* in the National Gallery, London.

CHAPTER 15

Looking to the Past

THE MOVE back to figuration which took place in American art at the beginning of the 1960s, and which continued into the 1970s and 1980s, embraced a plurality of trends. Photorealism was only one of these, and in the long run it was not the most fruitful. Some of the most original and creative realists tried to learn from the immediate past, from the gestural abstraction of the 1940s and 1950s. Others started to look again at the Old Masters. In particular, they re-examined the intensified early Baroque realism of Caravaggio and the classicism of Poussin and David.

The best known of those realists who tried to assimilate the lessons of abstraction was Philip Pearlstein (1924–). What interested him was not the loose Abstract Expressionist handling but the 'all-over' quality typical of Abstract Expressionist compositions.

The paintings Pearlstein made in New York in the 1950s – after studies at the Carnegie Institute in Pittsburgh, where Warhol was a friend and fellow student – already had a figurative element. They were primarily landscapes, much influenced by expressionists such as Chaim Soutine. During this decade, Pearlstein was searching in several different and apparently contradictory directions. Like many artists at that time, he was caught up in the resurgence of interest in Dada, and he wrote a master's thesis on Francis Picabia which led him to some unexpected conclusions. The first of these was that appearance in art is more important than any underlying programme: 'The only thing that matters in the long run is what the work of art looks like.'[1] The second was just as far-reaching: 'The effort to try to understand the recent past was so great that at its conclusion I asked myself why need I … feel bound to continue the traditions of modern art. I didn't, and with that rejection I felt liberated.'[2]

Despite this, he continued to produce paintings where the handling of paint was basically Abstract Expressionist. His drawings, however, began to signal a change. In the mid-1950s Pearlstein went to Maine, where he made a series of realistic drawings of rocks which he intended to use as the basis of freer painted compositions. This was followed, in 1958, by a year in Italy on a Fulbright grant. There he made some elaborate and increasingly specific drawings of Roman ruins and of the dramatic cliffs along the Amalfi coast. These, and still more so the paintings he based on them when he returned to the United States, could definitely be described as realist. However, the real breakthrough did not take place until 1961, when Pearlstein started to make paintings directly from nude models posed in the studio. He wrote a year later:

The naked human body is the most familiar of mental images, but we only think we know it. Our everyday factual view is of the clothed body, and on those occasions when our dirty mind will strip a person, it will see something idealized. Only the mature artist who works from a model is capable of seeing the body for itself, only he has the opportunity for prolonged viewing. If he brings along his remembered anatomy lessons, his vision will be confused. What he actually sees is a fascinating kaleidoscope of forms; these forms arranged in a particular position in space constantly assume other dimensions, other contours, and reveal other surfaces with the breathing, twitching, muscular tensing and relaxing of the model, and with the slightest change in viewing position of the observer's eyes. Each movement changes the way the form is revealed by light;

220 **Philip Pearlstein** *Palatine No. 14* 1959
One of the drawings of Roman ruins which marked the artist's conversion to realism.

221 **Philip Pearlstein** *Temple of Hatshepsut* 1979

OPPOSITE
222 Philip Pearlstein
Two Models on a Kilim Rug with Mirror 1983

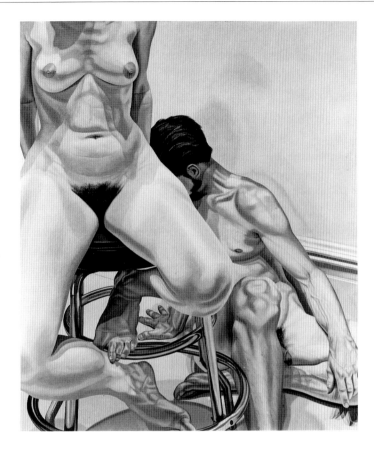

223 Philip Pearlstein
Female Model on Chrome Stool, Male Model on Floor 1979
The radical cropping of the figures is typical of the artist. The forms shoot out towards the edges of the canvas, as they tend to do in Abstract Expressionist paintings.

> the shadows, reflections and local colours are in constant flux. The relationship
> of the forms and colours of the figure to those of the background becomes mobile
> and tenuous. New sets of relationships continuously reveal themselves.[3]

Pearlstein does not seem to have been aware of Larry Rivers's paintings of the nude, made some six years earlier. At any rate, he never alludes to them in his own discussions of this subject. The aims pursued by the two artists were in any case very different. Rivers wanted to re-examine the nineteenth-century realist tradition; Pearlstein, on the other hand, wanted to find a way of applying the compositional principles of mid-twentieth-century abstraction to close-focus realism. Though both paint nude figures in a studio setting, the atmosphere each conjures up is very different. Rivers's nudes, even those of the plump and elderly Berdie, tend to have a perversely erotic overtone; Pearlstein's use of the theme is strictly, and indeed rather puritanically, non-erotic.

His aims can be judged by looking at a fully developed example from his long series of paintings of the nude. *Female Model on Chrome Stool, Male Model on Floor* (1979) shows precisely what the title states. Yet the title alone could not prepare the uninstructed spectator for the actual appearance of the work. Both figures are radically cropped. The female nude is bereft of head and shoulders; the male, placed somewhat behind her, is partly hidden by her left thigh, which conceals his face, one arm, and half his torso. Pearlstein has explained that his method is to start by rendering a single anatomical detail as accurately as possible:

> I draw the entire hand finger by finger, wrinkle by wrinkle, and then go on to the
> next form. But the first form drawn provides a module for the rest of the

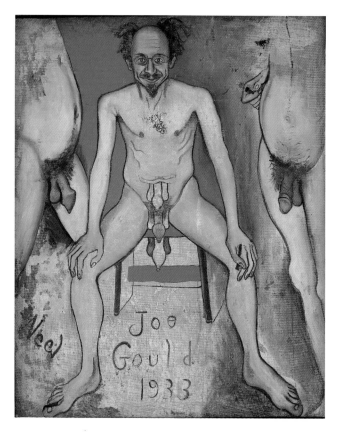

224 Alice Neel *Joe Gould* 1933
Gould was a Greenwich Village character of the time.
According to the artist, he came from 'an old, intellectual
Boston family' and was 'compiling an aural history of the
universe'. The literary critic, Malcolm Cowley, commented:
'The trouble with you, Alice, is you're not romantic.'

drawing … It doesn't matter where they [arms, legs and torso] stop … Finding the scale [of the forms within the rectangle] is the essential problem.[4]

The result of this procedure is paintings whose underlying structure remains close to Abstract Expressionist work – a complex design shooting out towards the edges of the canvas, and usually with the forms pressed closely against the surface. To achieve the latter, Pearlstein often places himself so that he is higher than the models, looking down at them as they sit or recline on the floor. He also uses patterned fabrics to help compress the space or, as in *Female Model on a Chrome Stool*, positions the models close to a wall whose presence is emphasized by a skirting or baseboard.

Pearlstein's nudes, in addition to being non-erotic, are essentially impersonal. This is also true, in a rather paradoxical way, of his portraits. These are obviously good, closely observed likenesses, yet at the same time the artist seems to be saying that human character is essentially impenetrable – and also that it is in any case no affair of his, since his business is with surfaces only.

As a portrait painter, and indeed as a practitioner of realism, he makes a striking contrast with another leading American artist of the same epoch, the veteran Alice Neel (1900–85). Neel's personal circumstances – which were difficult, and made still more so by the fact that she was a woman – meant that she achieved recognition late. Not surprisingly, given the generation she belonged to, her work has an expressionist tone reminiscent of some of the American social realism of the 1930s. Nevertheless, her most striking and characteristic work does in fact come from the final decades of her long career. Most of her output consisted of portraits. The sitters she painted often came from the same social group as Pearlstein's – the New York intelligentsia – and on two occasions at least they both portrayed the same person: Andy Warhol and the critic John Perreault. The intensity of Neel's likeness of Warhol (1970), shown with his shirt off to reveal the terrible wounds inflicted by an assassination attempt in 1968, is totally contrary to Pearlstein's approach. The contrast serves to emphasize the latitude offered by contemporary definitions of realism, since both Pearlstein and Neel are commonly categorized as realists by commentators on their work. The difference is that Neel imposes a much more emphatic conception, that is to say characterization, of her sitters than Pearlstein does in his occasional ventures into portraiture.

The most important direction taken by recent American realist art is neither the attempt to reconcile it with abstraction, as exemplified by Pearlstein, nor the Photorealist accommodation with the camera, but the re-exploration of aspects of Old Master painting. The central figure is Alfred Leslie (1927–). Like Pearlstein, Leslie had the beginnings of a reputation as an abstract artist before he committed himself to figuration. As he later said: 'We were all in our twenties and the new abstract painting still astonished us, so we kept dragging our feet back and forth between what we did and what we should do.'[5]

During this period of vacillation, Leslie was also a narrative film-maker. His best-known film was *Pull My Daisy* (1956), based on the third act of Jack Kerouac's play *The Beat Generation* and featuring the voice of Anita O'Day. The early figure paintings have little in common with the insouciance of this piece – they are large-scale single figures, such as the *Self-Portrait* of 1966–67.

225 **Alice Neel** *Andy Warhol* 1970
The terrible wounds Warhol sustained in
the assassination attempt by Valerie
Solanis. Neel's comment on her subject was
typically tart: 'As an art world personality,
he represents a certain pollution of this era.'

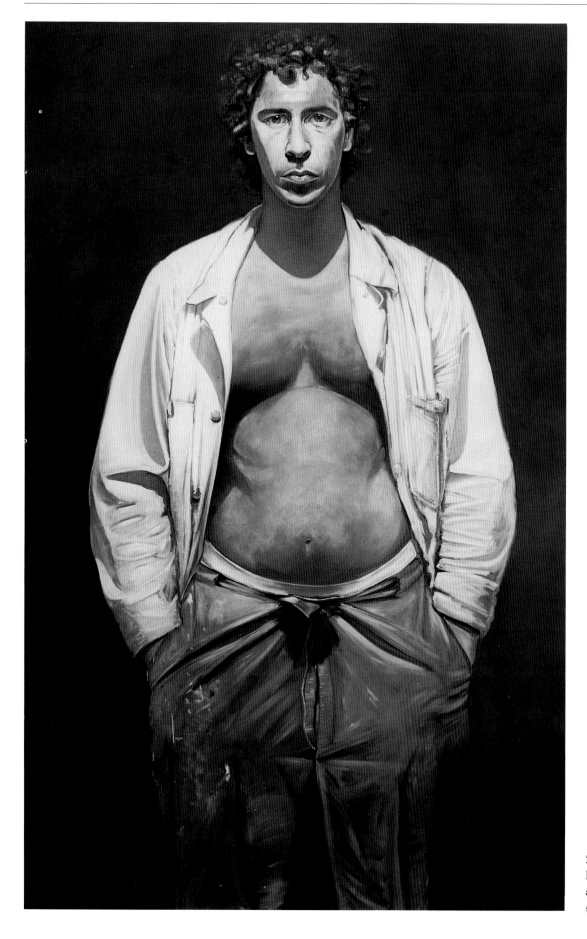

226 Alfred Leslie *Self-Portrait* 1966–67
From Leslie's earliest series of realist paintings,
all in monochrome. Most were destroyed in a
studio fire.

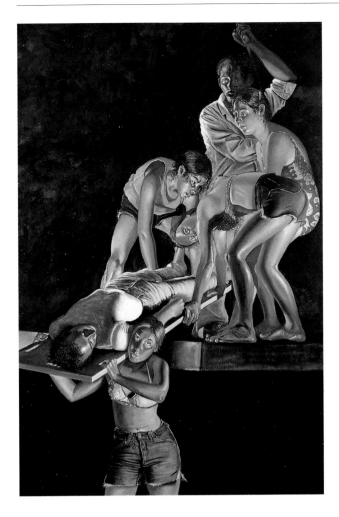

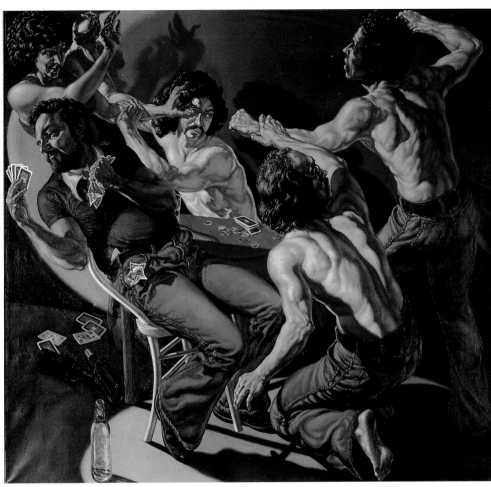

This is monumental in scale, but also deliberately brutish with its open shirt and bulging abdomen; it seems designed as an explicit statement that modern painting can reject the stylistic precedents offered by the pre-Modern era, while remaining unquestionably realist. Gradually Leslie became less self-conscious about Old Master influence and began to paint narrative cycles. The most ambitious of these is devoted to the untimely death of Frank O'Hara, run down by a Fire Island taxi on the beach at night. Leslie spent a period on the island in order to catch its authentic light and atmosphere, but also made direct use of precedents taken from the art of the past. *The Killing Cycle No. 6 – The Loading Pier* (1975) shows the victim's body being removed from the island. The composition is a close paraphrase of Caravaggio's *Entombment* (sometimes wrongly called a *Deposition*), painted in 1603–04. Leslie's choice of Caravaggio as a model is clearly not a matter of caprice, since Caravaggio is the origin of the dramatically realist strain in seventeenth-century art.

Leslie's work offers a point of vantage from which to examine the work of a number of other contemporary American realists with Old Master links. For example, Jack Beal (1931–) is, like Leslie, a painter of ambitious narrative and allegorical compositions. *Prudence, Avarice, Lust, Justice, Anger* (1977–78), from a series devoted to the Virtues and the Vices, is at least as elaborate as the most complex of Leslie's *Killing Cycle* paintings. Yet there are important

ABOVE LEFT
227 **Alfred Leslie** *The Killing Cycle No. 6 – The Loading Pier* 1975
From a series devoted to the death of Frank O'Hara (see Ill. 174). In this, his body is shown being removed from Fire Island, a composition paraphrasing Caravaggio's *Entombment* in the Vatican.

ABOVE RIGHT
228 **Jack Beal** *Prudence, Avarice, Lust, Justice, Anger* 1977–78

229 James Valerio *Paul's Magic* 1977
Inspired by the artist's son, then aged six or seven, who
wanted to learn conjuring tricks, but who couldn't believe that
they were only tricks.

differences between the two artists. Beal has never been an abstract painter and
has always been a conscious anti-Modernist. His indifference to contemporary
American abstraction, with its almost obsessive pursuit of surface continuity,
sets him free to exploit Baroque spatial effects. As he puts it,

> One of the big excitements about painting representationally is trying to
> represent the illusion of the third dimension on a two–dimensional surface.
> As I said in my diatribe against the sanctity of the picture plane, I think
> that illusion is magical, and that artists should use any tool necessary to achieve
> that sense of magic.[6]

Some works by James Valerio (1938–) underline this message by representing
what is literally a magical scene. *Paul's Magic* (1977) was inspired by the
artist's son, then aged six or seven and very interested in learning conjuring
tricks:

> When Paul tried to learn magic tricks, he thought the magic was in the words he
> said. He would try to do the tricks after I had explained them – go through the
> procedure and expect the magic to happen because he was so naive. That's why I
> wanted him to be the focal point of the picture because the whole thing was
> really about that.[7]

One subject of the painting is therefore the gap between realistic description as
such (description codified in words) and the alchemy of art, which can
momentarily make us believe things we know to be untrue. Since *Paul's Magic*

was painted, Valerio has reverted to a more literal mode, preferring the painting to be a mirror of what exists in real life, though one which enables us to see more because it freezes the moment for leisurely examination. The result is sometimes rather crowded and claustrophobic.

Leslie's *Self-Portrait*, already described, can be regarded as a key work in relation not only to his own development but to that of other, younger artists. One of the more ambitious of recent ventures into self-portraiture is *Double Nude* (1978) by William Beckman (1942–). Beckman met and was influenced by Leslie during the early period of his career, and this painting, a nude self-portrait of the artist with his wife, Diana, reveals the fact.

The picture offers comments on a number of topics of pressing interest to contemporary American realists. There is the issue of honesty: nudes are here presented as likenesses of named individuals, and, in the most literal sense, the painter exposes himself and his private life to the spectator. There is the relationship to tradition: *Double Nude* can be construed as a paraphrase of a work even more famous than Caravaggio's *Entombment*, namely Dürer's *Adam and Eve*. This is a Jean-Jacques Rousseau-like retort to the doctrine of original sin, and a bold suggestion that the 'ideal', with all its many resonances, is embodied in the persons of the handsome painter and his equally good-looking wife.

Dürer was the foundation of a tradition of boastful yet candid self-portraiture in European art. It is natural that this should have found followers in the present-day United States, where so much emphasis is placed upon self-examination and self-realization. The artist who explored the tradition most determinedly was Gregory Gillespie (1936–2000), who once thought of painting self-portraits to the exclusion of all other subjects. His long series of these has been aptly described as offering a collective image of 'self-perception and independence'.[8] Despite Gillespie's own assertion that the portraits were inspired largely by his own desire to look at things 'without having art in the way',[9] their link with the Old Master tradition – and especially in this case with German Renaissance art – seems plain. What is modern about them is the way in which Dürer's anxiety about personal salvation (inspired by the rise of Protestantism) has been transformed into anxiety about artistic salvation. Gillespie held tightly to traditional techniques in a situation where the whole established tradition of making art seems to be in the process of dissolving.

Yet another artist who has tended to specialize in self-portraiture is the California-born Richard Shaffer (1947–). In Shaffer's case there is a metaphysical underpinning to the exercise, a courting of alienation rather than a desire for self-recognition, which is reminiscent of certain aspects of Italian Mannerism. On one occasion, the artist said:

> Art bears relation to phenomenology in that it takes one's natural attitude about our common shared world, and changes it into a private vision of a transcendentalized world … The transformation comes about by taking this common natural world that you become familiar with, that you have a pre-acquaintance with, and undermining it. You know, taking the legs out from underneath it and flipping it over, so it's this private world but you have to start from the beginning.[10]

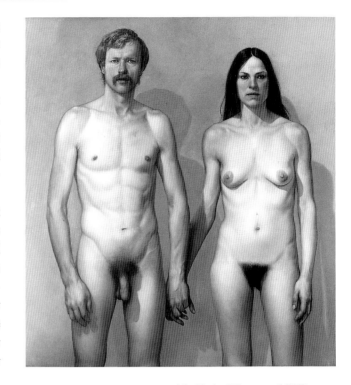

230 **William Beckman** *Double Nude (Diana and William Beckman)* 1978
A double portrait of the artist and his wife, which is also a modern version of Dürer's *Adam and Eve*.

231 **Gregory Gillespie** *Self-Portrait (at 54)* 1991
Gillespie once thought of painting self-portraits to the exclusion of all other subjects.

232 Richard Shaffer *Tondo (Self-Portrait)* 1991
Like Gillespie (Ill. 231), Shaffer has painted a long series of
self-portraits; this features *trompe l'oeil* effects reminiscent of
William M. Harnett (Ills 29–32).

What Shaffer means by this is well exemplified by a recent image, his *Tondo (Self-Portrait)* (1991), in which the likeness is distanced by appearing within the depths of a dark circular mirror, with flowers standing in front of it and *trompe-l'oeil* 'collage' elements apparently pasted to the surface. This, though the image is not distorted, has qualities reminiscent of Parmigianino's youthful self-portrait, painted as if seen in a circular convex mirror. At the same time, because of its use of *trompe-l'oeil*, this *Tondo* can be regarded as yet another manifestation of the tenacious Harnett tradition.

American painting influenced by Old Master practice often uses traditional elements in a deliberately dissonant way, thus signalling the artist's intention to endow the familiar forms and concepts with new meanings. For example, in *Fate Comes* (1991), by Martha Mayer Erlebacher (1937–), the subject is a female nude, half rising from a Regency-style chair over which is thrown a crimson satin drape. An oriental rug lies on the floor. The props are specific; the nude is deliberately generalized and timeless, though with a strong flavour of the Venetian paintings of the early sixteenth century. Erlebacher's source seems to be the work of Palma Vecchio; but Palma's sumptuous harmonies have been subverted to create the ominous mood suggested by the title.

The clash between style and expectation is even more acute in a superb *Descent from the Cross* (1988–90) by Steve Hawley (1950–). Here the analogy is with some aspects of fifteenth-century Flemish painting, and especially with Rogier van der Weyden's *Deposition* in the Prado. As in Rogier's painting, the participants in the sacred event appear in modern dress. However, Hawley goes a good deal further than his fifteenth-century exemplar in the use of deliberately anomalous elements. The scene is set indoors; there is a flood-lamp wrapped in paper, plus a modern stepladder. A couple of Polaroids are pinned to the ladder. The implication is that this is a studio-based photographic shoot – a fictional reconstruction of an essentially mythic event. Yet there is one thing which is real in the fullest sense: the dead body of Christ, forehead deeply marked by the crown of thorns (now removed), his side and feet still bleeding from their wounds. At the same time, however, the victim, beardless and grey-haired, does not have the traditional physiognomy of Christ, though the traditional image appears in one of the Polaroids mentioned above. The picture questions the spectator's reactions in a very contemporary way. The riddle it poses, in a deliberately literal fashion, is whether seeing is in fact believing: the theme of Valerio's *Paul's Magic* is restated in a much more sombre key.

233 **Martha Mayer Erlebacher** *Fate Comes* 1991
A paraphrase of sixteenth-century Venetian painting, which incorporates visibly 'modern' elements.

235 **David Ligare** *Landscape with Eros and Endymion* 1989–91
Ligare's work takes ideas from Claude, Poussin and the mythological paintings of Jacques-Louis David and blends them into a contemporary synthesis.

As will be seen, contemporary American realists feel free to draw on all aspects of the Old Master tradition. embracing Caravaggio, Dürer, the great Venetians and the sixteenth-century Mannerists. Those artists who have had most impact are perhaps those who express some aspect of classicism, in particular Poussin and David. One artist whose roots are obviously in the work of Poussin is the California-based painter David Ligare (1945–). Ligare is especially fond of Arcadian scenes – an example is his *Landscape with Eros and Endymion* (1989–91). His mythological personages, nevertheless, are an irregular combination of ideal and non-ideal elements, and thus differ from Poussin's, where both landscape and figures are rigorously unified in style. It is evident that the models for Ligare's figures are the same healthy California students as are represented in the sculptures of John De Andrea.

A perhaps more surprising connection with Poussin can be found in many of the still-lifes of William Bailey (1930–). Superficially, Bailey's art may seem like that of Peto, in the sense that he paints clear-cut compositions featuring everyday objects. Like Peto, Bailey accepts his subject matter chiefly because it is *there*:

> The reason I select these objects [he says] is because they are the kinds of things I've always had around me, the kinds of objects I like. They are the things I look at out of the corner of my eye, whether in the kitchen or some other place in the house, so they have been convenient in that way.[11]

On the other hand, the use he makes of such objects is much more sophisticated that anything attempted by Peto. The nature of the context he provides is suggested by the titles given to some recent still–life paintings. These are often

OPPOSITE
234 **Steve Hawley** *Descent from the Cross* 1988–90
Based on Rogier van der Weyden's painting of the same subject in the Prado, in which the participants are also wearing contemporary dress.

simply place-names; even if they are not, they nevertheless hint that the painting, in addition to being a still-life, can also be read as a kind of landscape (*Strada Bianca*, 1990). Despite the difference in subject matter, Bailey's paintings have reminded commentators of the eerily deserted piazzas depicted by Giorgio de Chirico. An even better analogy, to my mind, is with some of Poussin's bleaker and less peopled landscapes, such as the *Diogenes Throwing Down His Bowl* in the Louvre. They give the same sense that a concentrated underlying order is to be found just beneath the quotidian surfaces that we see.

The usually tiny still-lifes of Nick Boskovich (1949–) are equally disciplined in effect. *Homage to the Serenity of Charlotte Corday* (1992) offers just three objects: an arum lily, the plain green vase that contains it, and an abalone shell. These are placed on a table covered by a white cloth. The allusion to Corday, the young woman who murdered Jean-Paul Marat in 1793, is probably twofold. First, there is the lily itself, a traditional symbol of purity. Second, and more subtly, there is the cloth, which is reminiscent not only of an altar covering but of the white cloth that envelops the bath of the dying Marat in David's famous *Marat assassiné*. This, like the *Marat*, is a picture from which the active protagonist has just departed, leaving her tokens behind.

David's attraction for American artists seems to indicate the beginnings of a revolt against the whole Modernist tradition. In *Rinaldo and Armida* (1991), Vincent Arcilesi (1932–) offers a reshaping of a once-popular subject taken from Torquato Tasso's *Gerusalemme Liberata*, a frequent source for artists from the sixteenth century to the nineteenth. The two figures – Rinaldo lying in a bewitched sleep, Armida bent on revenge, but just about to fall in love with him – are painted in a variant of classical style with distinctly Davidian overtones. Like David's own *Cupid and Psyche*, a late mythological composition painted during the artist's final years of exile in Brussels, the figures are a combination of the scrupulously real with the imagined: real, convincing bodies, imagined settings and gestures.

It might well be argued that, because of its mythological subject, Arcilesi's *Rinaldo and Armida* cannot rank as a fully realist work. Despite the title, one cannot raise the same objection to his *Venus and Adonis in Rome* (1993), where the goddess and her mortal lover are shown in modern dress, against a meticulously rendered Roman panorama – the classical world in ruin, the guise in which it is now most familiar to us.

Equally contemporary, but subtler in its approach to the notion of classicism, is *2nd of May, Los Angeles* (1992), by John Nava (1947–). In a broad sense, this shows resemblances to the work of Alfred Leslie. Like Leslie in *The Killing Cycle No. 6*, Nava depicts a contemporary event, using Old Master models. There are even religious overtones in this painting, just as there are in Leslie's paraphrase of Caravaggio. The model, once again (and despite the title, with its implied allusion to Goya), is David's *Marat assassiné*. Many features apart from the obvious political content – the painting is about the Los Angeles race riots of 1992 – refer the viewer to David's work, not only *Marat* but other paintings such as *The Oath of the Horatii*. These features include the geometric angularity of the underlying compositional schema, the way in which the figures, including that of the victim, are placed strictly parallel to the picture plane, and the solidity with which these figures are realized.

236 **William Bailey**
Strada Bianca 1990
Bailey's austere still-lifes can
often be read as metaphorical
transformations of cityscapes.

237 **Nick Boskovich**
*Homage to the Serenity of
Charlotte Corday* 1992
Like seventeenth-century Dutch
Vanitas still-lifes, this has a
hidden allegorical programme.

238 Vincent Arcilesi
Venus and Adonis in Rome 1993
The artist puts his mythological lovers in modern dress and shows them against the ruins of the Palatine.

239 Vincent Arcilesi
Rinaldo and Armida 1991

What is contemporary, nevertheless – and here one finds a reminder of mid-century Magic Realists such as Jared French – is the ambiguity of the final effect. This is a realist painting which raises more questions than it answers. *Marat* was a direct cry of indignation about a contemporary crime, with strong political and social implications. Though Nava's painting seems to allude to the police beating of Rodney King, it is not a representation of it. Nor is it an attempt to portray a riot. The protagonist, the figure lying on the ground, may or may not be dead. Essentially the work embodies not only the troubled atmosphere of contemporary Los Angeles, but the loss of bearings, social as well as moral, which the riots brought with them. Despite the stylistic debt to the past, it remains very much a creation of its own epoch. At the same time, like Arcilesi's work, it suggests a deliberate turning away from the accepted idea of the Modern.

240 **John Nava** *2nd of May, Los Angeles* 1992
Like Alfred Leslie's *The Loading Pier* (Ill. 227), this depicts a contemporary event with the help of Old Master models: here Jacques-Louis David, rather than Caravaggio, is the main source.

CHAPTER 16

Polemical Realism

Q<small>UESTIONS ABOUT</small> the true nature of contemporary American realism are raised in acute form by some aspects of the art of the 1980s and 1990s. In addition to the two forms of realist activity just described – art dependent on the camera and to some extent on the Dutch tradition of genre painting; and art dependent on a broader version of the Old Master tradition – there are artists who use realist tropes for largely polemical ends. That is, they are not interested in realist representation for its own sake but as an efficient means of making an ideological point.

These 'ideological' works are sometimes closely linked to the new currents in American art which have made the artist a spokesperson for those increasingly vocal minorities who use the museum as their platform. For example, John Valadez (1951–), who is perhaps the best-known product of the militant Chicano art movement in Los Angeles, paints in a style which owes little to Modernism and a good deal to old-fashioned realist magazine illustration. Valadez's purpose is that of the magazine illustrator: he wants to communicate in a direct, unequivocal way with a public which is not very sophisticated visually, and which would be bewildered by unfamiliar stylistic tricks. He is in much the same situation as the community sculptors Ahearn and Torres, discussed in an earlier chapter.

In other instances, the polemical message is put across in works of greater complexity and ambiguity. *The Persecution of an Esthete: Sebastian and Diocletian* (1990), by Delmas Howe (1935–), belongs to a group of multi-figure compositions which the artist has christened the Rodeo Pantheon series. These paintings bring together three different types or systems of imagery. The first is that of the rodeo, the popular American equivalent of the Roman circus, which pitted man against beast as well as man against man. Secondly, as with Nava and Alfred Leslie, there are allusions to pre-Modern painting, including in this case the nude, bound figure of St Sebastian in the centre of the composition. Finally, the Rodeo Pantheon paintings are openly homoerotic. The real subjects of *The Persecution of an Esthete* are the feeling of vulnerability the homosexual feels in a world where his sexuality is often condemned, his longing to conform to what is 'normal', and at the same time his eroticization of specifically masculine imagery, such as that of the rodeo and the cowboy. Given Thomas Hart Benton's notorious homophobia (which may indeed have concealed something very different), it is amusing to note that Howe's picture deliberately transposes a typically Regionalist theme into a different and dissonant key. It is the dissonance that makes the painting memorable.

Inevitably, because of its subject matter and imagery, *The Persecution of an Esthete* has sadomasochistic overtones. These recur, in much more powerful and frightening form, in the work of Leon Golub (1922–), whose progression to realism (of a sort) has been an unconventional one. Born and trained in Chicago, he lists among his important early influences Picasso's *Guernica*, which he first saw in 1939, when the painting was on tour in the United States, and Orozco's mural *The Triumph of Prometheus* at Pomona College, Claremont, California, which he saw in 1956.

Golub's own early work was strongly expressionist, with elements borrowed from the European *Art brut* of Jean Dubuffet, though his chosen themes were sometimes classical – a *Sphinx* series, followed in the 1960s by a group of

241 **Eric Fischl** *Sisters* 1984
The raunchiness is typical of Fischl's work in general. A preliminary drawing exists where the figure straddling the bidet is shown in precisely the same attitude, under a shower. The alteration is symptomatic of Fischl's wish to disturb.

242 Delmas Howe *The Persecution of an Esthese: Sebastian and Diocletian* 1990
Many of Howe's 'Rodeo Pantheon' paintings play on the common fantasy of being forced to appear nude in public. The rodeo boss – Diocletian – covers Sebastian's genitals with a hand holding a coiled rope in a symbolic gesture of castration.

ambitious *Gigantomachies* influenced by the rhythms and imagery of the Hellenistic Great Altar of Pergamon. In the early 1970s, his art became much more specific, and he produced a series of protest paintings about the war in Vietnam. These remained, however, expressionist rather than realist in style.

Golub's current reputation, as America's most important political painter of the closing decades of the century, rests on the enormous paintings he has made since the mid-1970s. These are grouped into several series – the *Mercenaries*, the *White Squad* paintings (specifically about events in El Salvador), the *Riots*, the *Interrogations* and the *Horsing Around* paintings, showing mercenary soldiers nastily at play. The pictures are an extremely graphic presentation of 'man's inhumanity to man'.

From a stylistic point of view, Golub's later work is extremely individual and interesting. Like much realist-inclined art of the past two decades, both polemical and non-polemical, it shows the influence of Greek and Roman classicism. Here, however, the influence is specific. Golub has progressed from the Pergamon Altar to the Roman Imperial paintings and mosaics of the mid-third century AD onwards – those with gladiatorial subjects in particular. His compositions show the staccato, disrupted rhythms and flattened volumes which are typical of later Imperial art.

At the same time Golub makes use of photographic source material, though he seldom uses one single photographic image as the source for a whole composition: the camera supplies not the compositional framework but the details. His adroitness in adapting this kind of material can be judged from a series of statesmen and world leaders – likenesses of General Franco, Fidel Castro, Nelson Rockefeller, Henry Kissinger, Ho Chi Minh, General Pinochet, and others, adapted from news photographs – which are used in a very different spirit from that which animated Warhol when he made use of similar material (for example, in his portraits of Chairman Mao). Golub chooses the instant when the photograph betrays the character of his subject; Warhol smoothes out the photographic particularity to make an impassive mask.

In the big compositions, however, Golub's technique is different: the literal reality of the event depicted is in some paradoxical sense guaranteed by the rhetorically heightened, phantasmagoric quality of the depiction. Warhol once again supplies a direct contrast: in his *Race Riots*, which use news photographs unaltered, the reality of the scene is deliberately distanced by a whole series of devices – the mechanical repetition of the image, a deliberately blotchy and imperfect use of silkscreen printing, and overall washes of sweet colour.

243 **Leon Golub** *Interrogation I* 1980–81
In his book on Golub, Donald Kuspit comments that the artist sees torture as a kind of Dionysiac mystery, implying that it has a sexual meaning for him, and intentionally or unintentionally, the image has a strong sexual charge.

ABOVE
244 Leon Golub *Mercenaries IV* 1980
The paintings in this series seem based
on reports of the activities of white
mercenaries in Africa. Other paintings
comment on similar situations in
Pinochet's Chile and in El Salvador.

245 Leon Golub *Mercenaries V* 1984

Yet the rhetorical heightening in Golub's work seems to go beyond simple matters of stylistic choice. A painting like *Interrogation I* (1980–81) has an emotional charge which is not strictly the product either of stylistic affiliation or of political and social beliefs: like the charge in Howe's *Persecution of an Esthete*, it is sexual. Golub's recent paintings contain a confessional element which sets them miles apart from the work done by social realists of Shahn's generation.

The confessional element seems to link Golub not only to Howe but to Eric Fischl (1948–), perhaps the most controversial realist artist of the 1980s until the appearance of Jeff Koons. Yet there is an important difference between Golub and Fischl. The ambiguity and unease in Golub's recent work, though ever-present, often seem extraneous to the artist's declared intentions. These same qualities, by contrast, are absolutely integral to what Fischl does. His paintings, drawings and prints exactly catch one aspect of 1980s American society: its slightly shamefaced reaction to the stresses of the new prosperity.

Fischl's most typical paintings – as Calvin Tomkins noted, in a review of the artist's retrospective at the Whitney Museum, New York, in 1986 – are the work of a committed moralist: 'In his late thirties, Fischl has it in for contemporary, affluent, middle-class American society. He likes to take the viewer by the scruff of the neck, direct his gaze toward some fairly disagreeable goings on, and say, in effect, "This is your life."'[1]

Fischl himself offered a somewhat similar, though more complex, interpretation in a statement issued in connection with his third solo exhibition, held at the Edward Thorp Gallery, New York, in 1982:

> I would like to say that central to my work is the feeling of awkwardness
> and self-consciousness that one experiences in the face of profound emotional
> events in one's life. These experiences, such as death or loss or sexuality,
> cannot be supported by a life-style that has sought so arduously to deny their
> meaningfulness, and a culture whose fabric is so worn out that its public rituals
> and attendant symbols do not make for adequate clothing. One, truly, does not
> know how to act! Each new event is a crisis, and each crisis is a confrontation
> that fills us with much the same anxiety we feel when, in a dream, we discover
> ourselves naked in public.[2]

The moralizing, the ambiguity and the sense of otherness which are central to Fischl's work are summed up in the painting which has become his best-known image, *Bad Boy* (1981). This shows a woman on a bed in a darkened room. She may be dozing, but is certainly not fully asleep because she is playing with her big toe. Her pose is open and vulnerable: she lies on her back, completely uncovered, legs bent, vulva exposed. At the foot of the bed stands an adolescent boy, contemplating her avidly. He is leaning back against a table or chest of drawers, and, while he looks, he has one hand behind him, rifling through the woman's handbag. The blatancy of the sexual symbolism does not diminish the impact of the picture. Rather, it establishes a kind of complicity between the spectator and the thief, as does the indication that the victim is not fully asleep and thus remains aware of what is happening. Like her, and also through her, the viewer becomes an accomplice to adolescent voyeurism and petty crime.

246 **Eric Fischl** *Bad Boy* 1981
Fischl's sly use of sexual symbolism is apparent: the handbag
the boy rifles is a Freudian metaphor for the vagina he is so
avidly contemplating.

OPPOSITE ABOVE
247 **Jeff Koons** *Jeff in the Position of Adam* 1990

OPPOSITE BELOW
248 **Jeff Koons** *Rabbit* 1986

Much has been made of Fischl's position as an exponent of 'bad painting',
and he himself has sometimes implied that his technical means are barely
adequate to the ends he has in view. In fact, the air of technical strain in the
paintings tends to reinforce the things they say: the spectator reads this aspect
of them as a confession of the artist's own shame and difficulty in dealing with
subject matter of this type, and also of his compulsion to do so.

Fischl offers one example of the rapidity with which major artistic
reputations could be established in the United States during the art boom of
the 1980s. Another, even more striking, was the rise of Jeff Koons (1955–). In
art-historical terms, Koons's lineage is clear. He is a child or grandchild of
Marcel Duchamp. Basically he works with found objects; and recently these
objects have been himself and his wife, the Hungarian-Italian porn-star Ilona
Staller (La Cicciolina – 'the little pinchable one'). The two have been
photographed together in various erotic poses, to create large-scale dye-
transfer prints which are offered as artworks.

The dye-transfer prints have the same subject matter as some of Koons's recent woodcarvings and glass sculptures, produced with the help of craft woodcarvers in Bavaria and of the expert glass workers of Murano. These are the result of traditional artistic processes, though in each case the designated author has no hands-on involvement. Koons conceives the piece and initiates the making process by contacting and instructing specialists; from then on, he has a purely supervisory role. The result is a realistic artwork of a traditional sort, though critics may differ over its aesthetic merits, just as they do with any artwork.

The image produced by a camera is realistic in a slightly different way. In Koons's case, the photographic image guarantees the fact that the lens was confronted with two live human bodies which, for its benefit, and ultimately for that of the viewer, proceeded to engage in complicated sexual acrobatics. Everything about the resultant pictures, however, from the blatantly artificial settings to the few scraps of fantasy clothing the participants choose to wear,

249 Mark Tansey *The Innocent Eye Test* 1981
A live cow is brought into an art gallery for a confrontation
with Paulus Potter's painting, *The Young Bull* (1647). A group
of scientists, one carrying a mop, waits to see what her
reaction will be.

encourages us to feel that what we are seeing cannot in fact be described as 'real
life'. Though realistic in one sense, the work undermines the notion of realism at
every turn. Koons confirms all this by boldly claiming a degree of transcendence
for his erotic images: 'when the viewer sees it, they [*sic*] are in the realm of the
Sacred Heart of Jesus'.[3]

Some of Koons's early work is different. His rabbit party balloon (*Rabbit*,
1986), rendered in stainless steel, has a great deal in common with Johns's
Savarin or with a Warhol Brillo box. It is a replica, but one subjected to a
change of material which makes it clear that it is not the real thing.

Koons raises problems about both realism and representation without
offering answers to them. Another artist, who also made a large reputation in
the 1980s, examines these problems in a more intellectual and detached way.
This is Mark Tansey (1949–). Tansey's signature painting – it occupies the
same position in his career as *Bad Boy* does in Fischl's – is *The Innocent Eye
Test* (1981). This shows an improbable scene. A cow has been led into an art
gallery and confronted with Paulus Potter's life-size canvas *The Young Bull*
(1647). A group of scientists waits to see what her reaction will be. The painting
is not in full colour, but in a rather dingy monochrome. As Tansey's admirer, the
philosopher Arthur C. Danto, remarks, it has 'that serviceable realism, flatly
illustrational, that guarantees the veracity of what is being shown'.[4]

Tansey himself, on the other hand, categorically denies that he is a realist at
all, saying:

I am not a realist painter. In my work, I'm searching for pictorial functions that
are based on the idea that the painted picture knows itself to be metaphorical,
rhetorical, transformational, fictional. I'm not doing pictures of things that
actually exist in the world. I think of the painted picture as an embodiment of
the very problem that we face with the notion 'reality'. The problem or
question is, which reality? In a painted picture, is it the depicted reality, or the

reality of the picture plane, or the multidimensional reality the artist and viewer exist in? That all three are involved points to the fact that pictures are inherently problematic.[5]

It so happens that Tansey has produced another painting which might well serve as an emblem of the difficulty of the task undertaken in this book. *Key* (1984) is one of the artist's simpler images. A woman in evening dress, arms akimbo, is rather impatiently surveying the efforts of her escort to open a large and elaborate wrought-iron garden gate. The painting, like *The Innocent Eye Test*, is in monochrome, but the lighting tells us that the incident is taking place late at night. The image looks like a still from a 1940s movie, and the implication, unmistakably, is that the couple want to enter the locked garden in order to make love. Despite the clarity with which the basic situation is presented, there are significant details which it is easy to miss at first glance. On top of one gate pier stands a statue of an angel, brandishing a sword. On top of the other is a tree-trunk, with a serpent wound around it. The couple, so these adornments tell us, are vainly attempting to make their way back into the Garden of Eden.

The primary meaning is sexual, but *Key* can also, if one insists, be read as an allegory of the situation of the contemporary artist working in realist modes. Works of this kind are still being made – more and more of them, it seems, as confidence in Modernism wanes. Yet our belief in the reality of realism – in its closeness to the world as we perceive it – has been for ever undermined by the ways of thinking and feeling which Modernism itself has now made second nature.

250 **Mark Tansey** *Key* 1984
The main clues to the meaning of the painting are the two carvings on top of the gate-piers – one shows an angel with a sword, the other a serpent, the implication being that the couple in evening dress are vainly trying to make their way back into a state of primal innocence.

NOTES

INTRODUCTION (pp. 8–17)

1 Anderson, p. 105.
2 [Paul Cadmus, Margaret Cadmus and Jared French,] *Collaboration*. Twelvetrees Press, Santa Fe, 1992.
3 Kozloff, p. 44.
4 S. J. Freedberg, *Circa 1600: A Revolution of Style in Italian Painting*. The Bellknop Press of Harvard University Press, Cambridge, Mass., and London 1983, p. 2.

CHAPTER 1 (pp. 18–27)
From the American Revolution to the Civil War

1 Quoted in Stebbins et al., p. 34.
2 Ralph Waldo Emerson, *The Basic Writings of America's Sage*, ed. Edward C. Lindeman, New York 1947, p. 114.
3 Novak, p. 61.
4 Novak, pp. 116-17.
5 Quoted in Stebbins et al., p. 249.
6 Hills, *Genre Paintings*, p. 152.

CHAPTER 2 (pp. 28–39)
Thomas Eakins and Winslow Homer

1 Wilmerding, *Homer*, p. 42.
2 Adams, 'The Identity'.
3 Wilmerding, *Homer*, pp. 132-33.
4 Goodrich, *Eakins*, vol. 1, p. 27.
5 Goodrich, *Eakins*, vol. 1, pp. 82-83.
6 Goodrich, *Eakins*, vol. 1, pp. 285.
7 Goodrich, *Eakins*, vol. 2, p. 84.
8 Goodrich, *Eakins*, vol. 2, p. 84.
9 Goodrich, *Eakins*, vol. 2, pp. 84-85.
10 Goodrich, *Eakins*, vol. 1, pp. 185-186.
11 Goodrich, *Eakins*, vol. 1, pp. 197-198

CHAPTER 3 (pp. 40–49)
Still-Life and Populist Trompe-l'Oeil

1 Charles Sterling, *Still Life Painting from Antiquity to the Present Time*, New York and Paris, 1959, pl. 34.
2 Bolger, p. 309.
3 Frankenstein, p. 54.
4 Frankenstein, p. 55.
5 Frankenstein, pp. 79-80.
6 Frankenstein, p. 79.
7 Frankenstein, p. 50.
8 Frankenstein, p. 23.

9 Wilmerding, *Important Information*, p. 134.
10 Wilmerding, *Important Information*, p. 17.
11 Frankenstein, p. 82.

CHAPTER 4 (pp. 50–59)
Realism and the American Impressionists

1 *Cassatt*, p. 11.
2 *L'Art et les artistes*, 12 (Nov. 1910), p. 72.
3 Gordon and Forge, p. 35.
4 Weitzenhofer, p. 136.
5 Weitzenhofer, p. 103.
6 Lomax and Ormond, p. 19.
7 Lomax and Ormond, p. 29.
8 Lomax and Ormond, p. 11.
9 Pisano, p. 25.
10 Pisano, pp. 57, 60.
11 Hoopes, p. 11.

CHAPTER 5 (pp. 60–71)
The Ashcan School

1 Perlman, p. 196 n.
2 Perlman, p. 178.
3 Quoted by Homer, p. 177.
4 Quoted by Homer, p. 32.
5 Quoted by Homer, p. 76.
6 Perlman, p. 71.
7 Michael Quick in Quick et al., p. 12.
8 Marianne Doezema in Quick et al., p. 119.

CHAPTER 6 (pp. 72–91)
Precisionism: the Realist Impulse and the New Avant-Garde

1 Tsujimoto, *Images of America*, pp. 23-24, citing Martin Friedman's 1960 exhibition, *The Precisionist View of American Art*.
2 Tsujimoto, *Images of America*, p. 24.
3 Troyen and Hirshler, p. 4.
4 Troyen and Hirshler, p. 44 n. 15.
5 Troyen and Hirshler, p. 44 n. 25.
6 Quoted Troyen and Hirshler, p. 10.
7 Quoted Troyen and Hirshler, p. 11.
8 Quoted Troyen and Hirshler, p. 16.
9 Troyen and Hirshler, p. 20.
10 Troyen and Hirshler, p. 170.
11 Henry McBride, New York *Sun*, 21 November 1941, quoted by Troyen and Hirshler, p. 25.
12 Haskell, *Crawford*, p. 70.
13 Quoted Robinson, p. 282.

14 Quoted Robinson, p. 282.
15 Quoted Robinson, p. 278.
16 Beaumont Newhall, *The History of Photography*, 2nd, revised edition, Secker and Warburg, London 1964, quoted p. 114.
17 Robinson, p. 352.
18 Robinson, p. 353.
19 Robinson, p. 481.

CHAPTER 7 (pp. 92–115)
Regionalism

1 Corn, *Wood*, p. 131.
2 Quoted Dennis, p. 120.
3 Quoted Martin Seymour-Smith, *Guide to Modern World Literature*, Funk & Wagnall, New York 1973, p. 100.
4 Adams, *Benton*, p. 97.
5 Adams, *Benton*, p. 97.
6 Quoted Adams, *Benton*, p. 185.
7 Quoted Adams, *Benton*, p. 189.
8 Quoted Adams, *Benton*, p. 190.
9 Quoted Adams, *Benton*, p. 217.
10 Quoted Adams, *Benton*, p. 221.
11 Quoted Adams, *Benton*, p. 221.
12 Quoted Adams, *Benton*, p. 227.
13 Quoted Adams, *Benton*, p. 239.
14 Quoted Adams, *Benton*, p. 241.
15 Quoted Adams, *Benton*, p. 270.
16 Quoted Adams, *Benton*, p. 273.
17 Quoted Kendall, p. 22.
18 Quoted Kendall, p. 22.
19 Quoted Kendall, p. 26.
20 Quoted Kendall, p. 131.
21 John Dewey, 'Americanism and Location', *The Dial*, 68 (June 1920), pp. 678–87.
22 Quoted Stewart, p. 21.
23 Quoted Stewart, p. 43.
24 Quoted Stewart, p. 109.
25 Marling, p. 48.
26 Marling, p. 48.
27 Marling, p. 211.
28 Marling, p. 85.
29 Marling, p. 177.

CHAPTER 8 (pp. 116–127)
Charles Burchfield and Edward Hopper

1 Burchfield, p. 173 (entry for 15 August 1922).
2 Burchfield, p. 549 (letter dated 8 December 1922).
3 Levin, p. 24.
4 Levin, p. 27.

CHAPTER 9
Urban and Social Realism

1 Quoted Hills and Tarbell, p. 82.
2 *Bishop*, p. 25.
3 *Social Art in America*, p. 32.
4 Shapiro, p. 301.
5 Reprinted Shapiro, p. 296.
6 Quoted Baur, p. 35.

CHAPTER 10 (pp. 142–159)
A Revolution in American Art

1 Carol Seeley, 'On the Nature of Abstract Painting in America', *Magazine of Art*, 43 (May 1950), p. 168.
2 Pohl, p. 107.
3 Matthew Baigell, *Dictionary of American Art*, John Murray, London 1979, p. 220.
4 Kirstein, p. 22.
5 Kirstein, p. 25.
6 Kirstein, p. 25.
7 Kirstein, p. 74.
8 Quoted Garver, p. 30.
9 Quoted Garver, p. 56.
10 Quoted Croydon, p. 55.
11 Quoted Croydon, pp. 273-74.
12 Croydon, pp. 127-28.
13 Corn, p. 24.

CHAPTER 11 (pp. 160–169)
The Return to Figuration and the Pop Sensibility

1 Quoted Spike, p. 20.
2 Spike, p. 62.
3 Grace Glueck in *New York Times*, 1968, quoted Spike, p. 226.
4 Interview with John Arthur in Arthur, *Realists at Work*, p. 148.
5 Hunter, *Rivers*, p. 15.

6 Quoted Hunter, *Rivers*, p. 23.
7 Quoted Francis, p. 10.

CHAPTER 12 (pp. 170–177)
Bay Area Figuration

1 Quoted Jones, p. 8.
2 Quoted Armstrong, p. 30.
3 Quoted Jones, p. 20.
4 Quoted Tsujimoto, *Thiebaud*, p. 39.
5 Quoted Tsujimoto, *Thiebaud*, p. 47.

CHAPTER 13 (pp. 178–187)
The Replicated Object

1 McShine, p. 198, fig. 182.
2 Seitz, p. 9.
3 Seitz, p. 16.
4 Seitz, p. 15.
5 Barr, p. 26.
6 Varnedoe, p. 31.
7 Barr, p. 49.
8 Varnedoe, p. 30.

CHAPTER 14 (pp. 188–201)
Photorealism

1 William Dyckes, 'The Photo as Subject', in Battcock, p. 152. Essay reprinted from *Arts Magazine*, vol. 48, no. 5 (February 1974).
2 Interview with Chuck Close in Arthur, *Realists at Work*, p. 41.
3 Arthur, *Realists at Work*, p. 43.
4 Lyons and Storr, p. 31.
5 Lyons and Storr, pp. 31-32.
6 Kim Levin, 'Malcolm Morley: Post-Style Illusionism', in Battcock, p. 174. Essay reprinted from *Arts Magazine*, vol. 47, no. 4 (February 1973).
7 Ibid., p. 177.

8 Chase, p. 18.
9 Chase, p. 19.
10 Chase, p. 20.
11 Chase, p. 29.
12 Chase, p. 67.
13 Chase, p. 22.
14 Meisel, *Photorealism*, p. 27.
15 Meisel, *Estes*, p. 19.
16 Photographs published in *Estes*, pp. 36 and 37.
17 *Estes*, p. 39 (interview with the artist conducted by John Arthur).
18 Lawrence Alloway in Gouma-Peterson, p. 83.
19 Quoted in Stebbins et al., p. 282.

CHAPTER 15 (pp. 202–219)
Looking to the Past

1 Bowman, p. xvii.
2 Bowman, p. xvii.
3 Quoted Perreault, pp. 77-78.
4 Bowman, p. 19.
5 Quoted by Goodyear, *Contemporary American Realism*, p. 95.
6 Interview with John Arthur, in Arthur, *Realists at Work*, p. 23.
7 Arthur, *Realists at Work*, p. 136.
8 Goodyear, *Contemporary American Realism*, p. 58.
9 Quoted Goodyear, *Contemporary American Realism*, p. 58.
10 Interview with the artist in *Richard Shaffer*, p. 13.
11 Quoted Strand, *Bailey*, p. 26.

CHAPTER 16 (pp. 220–229)
Polemical Realism

1 Tomkins, pp. 218-19.
2 Quoted Schjeldahl, p. 21.
3 Koons, p. 130.
4 Danto, p. 17.
5 Mark Tansey in Danto, p. 132.

BIBLIOGRAPHY

Adams, Henry. *Thomas Hart Benton: An American Original*. Alfred A. Knopf, New York 1989.

Adams, Henry. `The Identity of Winslow Homer's "Mystery Woman"', *Burlington Magazine*, vol. 132, no. 1045 (April 1990).

[Ahearn, John, and Rigoberto Torres.] *The South Bronx Hall of Fame. Sculpture by John Ahearn and Rigoberto Torres*. Catalogue of exhibition at Contemporary Arts Museum, Houston 1991.

American Viewpoint, An: Realism in Twentieth-Century American Painting. Catalogue of exhibition at Contemporary Arts Center, Cincinnati 1957.

Anderson, Nancy K. *Albert Bierstadt: Art and Enterprise*. The Brooklyn Museum in Association with Hudson Hills Press, New York 1990.

Armstrong, Richard. *David Park*. Whitney Museum of American Art, New York, in association with University of California Press, Berkeley, Los Angeles and London 1989.

Arthur, John. *Realist Drawings and Paintings: Contemporary American Works on Paper*. New York Graphic Society, Boston 1980.

Arthur, John. *Realists at Work*. Watson-Guptill Publications, New York 1983.

Baigell, Matthew. *Thomas Benton*. Harry N. Abrams, New York 1973.

Barr, Martin H. *Duane Hanson*. Wichita State University, Wichita 1976.

Battcock, Gregory, ed. *Super Realism: A Critical Anthology*. Dutton, New York 1975.

Baur, John I. H. *Philip Evergood*. Harry N. Abrams, New York 1975.

Beckham, Sue Bridwell. *Depression Post Office Murals and Southern Culture*. Louisiana State University Press, Baton Rouge and London 1989.

Bishop, Isabel. Catalogue of exhibition at University of Arizona Museum of Art, Tucson 1974.

Bolger, Doreen, ed. *William M. Harnett*. Catalogue of exhibition at Amon Carter Museum, Fort Worth, and Metropolitan Museum of Art, New York 1992.

Bowman, Russell. *Philip Pearlstein: The Complete Paintings*. Alpine Fine Arts Collection, New York and London 1983.

Burchfield, Charles. *Charles Burchfield's Journals*, ed. J. Benjamin Townsend, State University of New York Press, Albany 1993.

Burroughs, Alan. *Kenneth Hayes Miller*. Whitney Museum of American Art, New York [1933].

Cassatt, Mary (1844-1926). Catalogue of exhibition at National Gallery of Art, Washington D.C. 1970.

Celant, Germano. *A Bottle of Notes and Some Voyages: Claes Oldenburg and Coosje van Bruggen*. Northern Centre for Contemporary Art, Sunderland 1988.

Chase, Linda. *Ralph Goings*. Harry N. Abrams, New York 1988.

Clark, Garth. *American Ceramics, 1876 to the Present*. Booth-Clibborn Editions, London 1987.

Cohen, Marilyn. *Reginald Marsh's New York*. Whitney Museum of American Art and Dover Publications, New York 1983.

Conningham, Frederic Arthur. *Currier & Ives Prints*. Crown Publishers, New York 1949.

Corn, Wanda M. *The Art of Andrew Wyeth*. Fine Art Museums of San Francisco and New York Graphic Society, San Francisco and Boston 1973.

Corn, Wanda M. *Grant Wood: The Regionalist Vision*. Minneapolis Institute of Arts and Yale University Press, New Haven 1983.

Cowert, Jack, and Juan Hamilton. *Georgia O'Keeffe: Art and Letters*. National Gallery of Art, Washington D.C., and New York Graphic Society, Boston 1987.

Croydon, Michael. *Ivan Albright*. Abbeville Press, New York 1978.

Danto, Arthur C. *Mark Tansey: Visions and Revisions*. Harry N. Abrams, New York 1992.

Dennis, James M. *Grant Wood*. University of Missouri Press, Columbia 1986.

D'Harnoncourt, Anne, and Kynaston McShine, eds. *Marcel Duchamp*. The Museum of Modern Art, New York 1983.

Doss, Erika. *Benton, Pollock and the Politics of Modernism: From Regionalism to Abstract Expressionism*. The University of Chicago Press, Chicago and London 1991.

Downes, William Howe. *The Life and Works of Winslow Homer*. Dover Publications, New York 1989.

Drucke, Johanna. `Harnett, Haberle and Peto: Visuality and Artifice among the Proto-Modern Americans', *The Art Bulletin*, vol. 74, no. 1 (March 1992).

Estes, Richard. The Urban Landscape. Catalogue of exhibition at Museum of Fine Arts, Boston 1978.

Flynn, Barbara. *Alfred Leslie: The Grisaille Paintings 1962-1967*. Barbara Flynn and Richard Bellamy, New York 1991.

Francis, Richard. *Johns*. Abbeville Press, New York 1984.

Frankenstein, Alfred. *After the Hunt: William Harnett and Other American Still Life Painters 1870-1900*. University of California Press, Berkeley, Los Angeles and London, revised edition 1969, 2nd revised edition 1975.

Garver, Thomas H. *George Tooker*. A Pomegranate Artbook, San Francisco, 2nd revised edition 1992.

Goodrich, Lloyd. *Winslow Homer*. New York 1959.

Goodrich, Lloyd. *Raphael Soyer*. Whitney Museum of American Art, New York 1972.

Goodrich, Lloyd. *Thomas Eakins*. National Gallery of Art, Washington D.C., and Harvard University Press, Cambridge, Mass., and London 1982.

Goodyear, Frank H., Jr. *Contemporary American Realism since 1960*. New York Graphic Society, in association with the Pennsylvania Academy of the Fine Arts, Boston 1982.

Goodyear, Frank H., Jr. *Welliver*. Rizzoli, New York 1985.

Gordon, Robert, and Andrew Forge. *Degas*. Thames and Hudson, London 1988.

Gouna-Petersen, Thalia, ed. *Breaking the Rules: Audrey Flack, Retrospective 1950-1990*. Harry N. Abrams, New York 1992.

Grimes, Nancy. *Jared French's Myths*. Pomegranate Art Books, San Francisco 1993.

Haskell, Barbara. *Ralston Crawford*. Whitney Museum of American Art, New York 1986.

Haskell, Barbara. *Charles Demuth*. Whitney Museum of American Art, New York, and Harry N. Abrams, New York 1987.

Heiman, Jim, and Rip Georges. *California Crazy: Roadside Vernacular Architecture*. Chronicle Books, San Francisco 1980.

Hills, Patricia. *Eastman Johnson*. Clarkson D. Potter, in association with the Whitney Museum of American Art, New York 1972.

Hills, Patricia. *The Genre Painting of Eastman Johnson: The Sources and Development of His Style and Themes*. Garland Publishing, New York and London 1977.

Hills, Patricia, and Roberta K. Tarbell. *The Figurative Tradition and the Whitney Museum of American Art, New York*. Associated University Presses, Cranbury, N.J., Toronto and London 1980.

Hills, Patricia, *Alice Neel*. Harry N. Abrams, New York 1983.

Hills, Patricia. *Social Criticism and Urban Realism: American Painting of the 1930s*. Boston University Art Gallery, Boston 1983.

Hobbs, Robert Carleton, and Gail Levin. *Abstract Expressionism: The Formative Years*. Cornell University Press, Ithaca and London 1978.

Homer, William Innes. *Robert Henri and His Circle*. Hacker Art Books, New York, 2nd revised edition 1988.

Hoopes, Donelson F. *Childe Hassam*. Watson-Guptill Publications, New York 1972.

Howe, Delmas. *Rodeo Pantheon*. Editions Aubrey Walter, London 1993.

Hunter, Sam. *Larry Rivers*. Rizzoli, New York 1989.

Hunter, Sam. *George Segal*. Rizzoli, New York 1989.

Jewett, Masha Zarkheim. *The Coit Tower: Its History and Art*. Volcano Press, San Francisco 1983.

Jones, Caroline A. *Bay Area Figurative Art, 1950-1965*. San Francisco Museum of Modern Art and University of California Press, Berkeley, Los Angeles and Oxford 1989.

Kendall, M. Sue. *Rethinking Regionalism: John Steuart Curry and the Kansas Mural Controversy*. Smithsonian Institution Press, Washington and London 1986.

Kirstein, Lincoln. *Paul Cadmus*. Imago Imprint, New York 1984.

Koons, Jeff. *The Jeff Koons Handbook*. Thames and Hudson and Anthony D'Offay Gallery. London 1992.

Kozloff, Max. `American Painting During the Cold War', *Artforum*, vol. 11, no. 9 (May 1973).

Kuspit, Donald. *Leon Golub: Existential Activist Painter*. Rutgers University Press, New Brunswick, N.J. 1985.

Levin, Gail. *Edward Hopper: The Art and the Artist*. W. W. Norton Company, New York and London 1980.

Levine, Jack, and Milton W. Brown, eds. *Stephen Robert Frankel - Jack Levine*. Rizzoli, New York 1989.

Lomax, James, and Richard Ormond. *John Singer Sargent and the Edwardian Age*. Leeds Art Galleries and National Portrait Gallery, London 1989.

Lyons, Lisa, and Robert Storr. *Chuck Close*. Rizzoli, New York 1987.

Marling, Karal Ann. *Wall-to-Wall America: A Cultural History of Post-Office Murals in the Great Depression*. University of Minnesota Press, Minneapolis 1982.

Martin, Alvin. *American Realism: Twentieth-Century Drawings and Watercolors from the Glenn C. Janss Collection*. San Francisco Museum of Modern Art and Harry N. Abrams, New York 1985.

Mathews, Nancy Mowll, ed. *Cassatt and Her Circle: Selected Letters*. Abbeville Press, New York 1984.

Mayer, Musa. *Night Studio: A Memoir of Philip Guston*. Alfred A. Knopf, New York 1988.

McShine, Kynaston, ed. *Andy Warhol: A Retrospective*. The Museum of Modern Art, New York 1989.

Miller, Dorothy C., and Alfred H. Barr, Jr, eds. *American Realists and Magic Realists*. The Museum of Modern Art, New York 1943.

Meisel, Louis K. *Photorealism*. Harry N. Abrams, New York 1980.

Meisel, Louis K. *Richard Estes: The Complete Paintings 1966–1985*. Harry N. Abrams, New York 1986.

Monte, James K. *22 Realists*. Catalogue of exhibition at Whitney Museum of American Art, New York 1970.

Murch, Walter. Catalogue of retrospective exhibition at Rhode Island School of Design, Providence 1966.

Neglected Generation of American Realist Painters, The. Catalogue of exhibition at Wichita Art Museum, Wichita, Kansas 1981.

Stebbins, Theodore, Jr. Carol Troyen and Trevor J. Fairbrother. *A New World: Masterpieces of American Painting 1769–1910*. Catalogue of exhibition at Museum of Fine Arts, Boston 1983.

Nordland, Gerald. *Richard Diebenkorn*. Rizzoli, New York 1987.

Novak, Barbara. *American Painting of the Nineteenth Century: Realism, Idealism and the American Experience*. Icon Editions, Harper and Row, New York 1979.

O'Keeffe, Georgia. A Studio Book, The Viking Press, New York 1973.

Perlman, Bernard B. *Painters of the Ashcan School: The Immortal Eight*. Dover Publications, New York 1988.

Perreault, John. *Philip Pearlstein: Drawings and Watercolors*. Harry N. Abrams, New York, 1988.

Peters, Harry Twyford. *Currier & Ives*. Garden City, New York, 1942.

Pisano, Ronald G. *William Merritt Chase: A Leading Spirit in American Art*. Henry Art Gallery, University of Washington, Seattle 1983.

Pohl, Frances K. *Ben Shahn: New Deal Artist in a Cold War Climate, 1947-1958*. The University of Texas Press, Austin 1989.

Quick, Michael, Jane Myers, Marianne Doezema and Franklin Kelly. *The Paintings of George Bellows*. Amon Carter Museum, Fort Worth, Los Angeles County Museum of Art and Harry N. Abrams, New York 1992.

Robinson, Roxana. *Georgia O'Keeffe: A Life*. Bloomsbury Publishing, London 1990.

Schjeldahl, Peter. *Eric Fischl*. Art in America. Stewart, Tabori and Chang, New York 1988.

Seitz, William C. *George Segal*. Thames and Hudson, London 1972.

Shaffer, Richard. Selected Work 1979-83. Catalogue of exhibition at L.A. Louver, Venice, California 1984.

Shapiro, David, ed. *Social Realism: Art as a Weapon*. Frederick Ungar Publishing, New York 1973.

Social Art in America, 1930-1945. Catalogue of exhibition at ACA Galleries, New York 1981.

Soyer, Raphael. *A Painter's Pilgrimage*. Crown Publishers, New York 1962.

Spike, John T. *Fairfield Porter: An American Classic*. Harry N. Abrams, New York 1992.

Stewart, Rick. *Lone Star Regionalism: The Dallas Nine and Their Circle*. Dallas Museum of Art and Texas Monthly Press, Austin 1985.

Strand, Mark, ed. *Art of the Real: Nine Contemporary Figurative Painters*. Clarkson N. Potter, New York 1983.

Strand, Mark. *William Bailey*. Harry N. Abrams, New York 1987.

Tomkins, Calvin. *Post- to Neo-: The Art World of the 1980s*. Penguin Books, New York and London 1988.

Trapp, Frank Anderson. *Peter Blume*. Rizzoli, New York, 1987.

Troyen, Carol, and Eric E. Hirshler. *Charles Sheeler: Paintings and Drawings*. Museum of Fine Arts, Boston 1987.

Tsujimoto, Karen. *Images of America: Precisionist Painting and Modern Photography*. San Francisco Museum of Modern Art and University of Washington Press, Seattle and London 1982.

Tsujimoto, Karen. *Wayne Thiebaud*. San Francisco Museum of Modern Art and University of Washington Press, Seattle and London 1985.

Varnedoe, Kirk. *Duane Hanson*. Harry N. Abrams, New York 1985.

Weinberg, H. Barbara. *The American Pupils of Jean-Léon Gérôme*. Amon Carter Museum, Fort Worth, Texas 1984.

Weitzenhofer, Frances. *The Havemeyers: Impressionism Comes to America*. Harry N. Abrams, New York 1986.

Wheat, Ellen Hawkins. *Jacob Lawrence*. University of Washington Press, Seattle and London 1986.

Wilmerding, John. *Winslow Homer*. Praeger Publishers, New York, Washington and London 1972.

Wilmerding, John. *American Art*. Penguin Books, Harmondsworth and New York 1976.

Wilmerding, John. *Important Information Inside: The Art of John Peto and the Idea of Still-Life Painting in Nineteenth-Century America*. National Gallery of Art, Washington D.C. 1983.

Wilmerding, John. *Fitz Hugh Lane*. National Gallery of Art, Washington D.C. 1988.

[Wyeth, Andrew.] *Two Worlds of Andrew Wyeth: Kuerners and Olson*. The Metropolitan Museum of Art, New York 1976.

Yglesias, Helen. *Isabel Bishop*. Rizzoli, New York 1989.

Young, Mahonri Sharp. *The Eight: The Realist Revolt in American Painting*. Watson-Guptill Publications, New York 1973.

LIST OF ILLUSTRATIONS

Measurements are in inches before centimetres, height before width before depth